O Congress

O Congress

DONALD RIEGLE
with Trevor Armbrister

1972

Doubleday & Company, Inc., Garden City, New York

Library of Congress Catalog Card Number 71-182842
Copyright © 1972 by Donald W. Riegle, Jr. and Trevor Armbrister
All Rights Reserved
Printed in the United States of America

For Cathy, Laurie and Donny

FOREWORD

Most books by members of Congress are sanctimonious puff jobs contrived to inflate the author's reputation and get votes. Because these books don't *say* anything, they have little effect and fade quickly away.

Reading these vacuous books, one is struck by the pity that no one writes intimately about Capitol Hill, from the inside, for Congress is a fascinating institution much in need of greater understanding. But which member would be willing to portray the human side of Congress honestly and to reveal its inner workings? A politician's first instinct, after all, is self-preservation. Could a congressman name names and speak frankly not only about his job but about his private life—and still hope for re-election? I began to search among the 100 senators and 431 representatives for one man who would accept the risks that accompany candor and would let me help him produce such a book.

That rare person was discovered when my wife, DuBos, suggested that I speak to Donald Riegle, a liberal Republican congressman from the seventh district of Michigan. Before running for Congress, Riegle had worked for IBM and studied at Harvard Business School, both citadels of the organization man; and Richard Nixon himself had made Riegle something of a protégé. But by the time I approached him a year ago, thirty-three-year-old Don Riegle was going through a profound change of attitude. He had been only twenty-eight when he first came to Congress, just young enough to be affected by the changes affecting American youth generally;

still young enough to suspect the hypocrisies that older congressmen accept as operating principles. By 1971 Riegle had developed a habit of independent voting and, engaged in a David-and-Goliath battle with his former patron, was feeling the sting of presidential vengeance. Altogether, Riegle seemed an interesting man in an interesting situation—and the right man for this book.

Riegle liked the idea almost immediately. He felt no obligation to preserve the myths of his colleagues in the House. Rather, he worried about citizens' lack of faith in their government. As a very first step in making Congress worthy of faith, he thought, people should see what really happens there. And so, at the end of the Easter recess, he began keeping a diary.

Riegle turned out to be a particularly fortunate choice—because he can write well. His daily record, which he wrote by hand on yellow legal pads, was full of finely observed detail and showed a flair for dialogue and anecdote. Twice a week he and I would meet and go over what he had written. I would ask for explanations and amplifications. He would answer into a tape recorder or go home and write out additional text. The final book, which is no longer literally a diary but a narrative in diary form, was distilled from some 4000 pages of material. I found myself in agreement with most of Riegle's opinions and disagreed with him on some. Still, every word is Riegle's own.

The reader will find little speechifying here. On the other hand, this is not a sensational, "tell-all" kind of book, full of backstairs gossip. Nor does this book pretend to record all that Congress accomplished or neglected between April 19, 1971, and March 7, 1972. This is simply a highly personal account of one year in a congressman's life, a year in which he observed his colleagues during moments of tension, tedium and horseplay, as they behaved courageously or gutlessly, treating each other viciously or with affection and respect. It was a year in which Riegle agonized over how he would vote on crucial bills; helped allocate some $200 billion in the federal budget; and performed countless chores for his Michigan constituents—while he felt more and more alone in an increasingly conservative Republican Party; helped his friend Representative Pete McCloskey challenge Richard Nixon in the New Hampshire

primary; worried about the shrinking of his circle of financial contributors and about paying his own personal bills; didn't spend the
time that he wanted to spend with his three children; endured the
pain of a divorce and got married again. The aim of the book is
to help readers to a better understanding of Congress by showing
how its members live and work.

Riegle's office staff is very close to him and thus were of great
help to him as he wrote this book. Dave Brunell and Carl Blake
provided extremely valuable advice. Kathleen Sadler was enormously helpful in many ways, and she, along with Lisa Finkelstein
and Angie Hogan, devoted evenings and weekends to typing the
final manuscript. Riegle and I are also indebted to our literary
agent, Don Gold, for guidance and support, and to our editor, Tom
Congdon, who helped us develop the concept of the book and
labored at the infinite tasks involved in publishing a book well.
And we are especially grateful to our families and close friends for
their patience and encouragement.

TREVOR ARMBRISTER

Chevy Chase, Maryland
March 8, 1972

CONTENTS

O Congress

I. APRIL

Monday, April 19, 1971. The House reconvened today after the Easter recess and two of my first visitors were from my congressional district, Jim and Margo Frazier, of Davison, Michigan. Several months ago their six-year-old daughter Cathy was selected as this year's cystic fibrosis poster child. The usual procedure in such cases is for the child to come to Washington and be photographed with the President. The Fraziers worked hard for Richard Nixon and for me in 1968. So when they asked me to arrange a date for their visit I didn't anticipate any problems.

Clark MacGregor, the congressional liaison man in the White House, said I'd have to submit a letter. I did. Nothing happened. Weeks went by. My staff began to make follow-up telephone calls. Each time the answers seemed more and more vague. When it became obvious that we were getting the run-around I asked David Laro, a county Republican chairman from my district, to make some inquiries through the office of Michigan Senator Robert Griffin. Laro reported back that as long as I was associated with the request the Fraziers would not receive an audience with the President. If I withdrew my name Griffin would make a new request and the White House would set a date.

I agreed, and that's why the Fraziers were here today. I didn't see any point in telling them why their visit had been delayed so long.

Tuesday, April 20. There was a breakfast this morning for the National Alliance of Postal Workers, and Hubert Humphrey was the main speaker. He was brief, which was refreshing. He's wearing a hairpiece now and looks much younger than he did in 1968. That's partly because of the hairpiece and partly because he's rested. Being away from here for two years, teaching in Minnesota, has let his metabolism readjust itself to normal.

As I looked at him, I couldn't help thinking that politics takes a physical toll. I commented on that to a young couple from Flint at breakfast. The girl nodded and remarked that I looked so much older to her than I did when I first came here, a little over four years ago. People are often struck by what they perceive as a "difference" in my manner and expression. There must be something to it. I thought to myself that many of the experiences that have made me feel old have taken place at Arlington National Cemetery.

I recall one young man from my district whom I'd helped with a minor problem. In November 1967 he was killed in Vietnam. His parents came here for the funeral, and I met them in the stark basement of the chapel at Arlington. The mother walked up to me and just collapsed, crying in my arms. The father wrapped his arms around her and began to sob too. Both parents were the same age as my own parents. I was not much older than their son.

I wanted to find the words to justify what had happened, but there weren't any. There was no way I could say that what had happened was in their interest or in the national interest or in anyone's interest; I could only weep with them. I felt anger and bitterness toward President Johnson. If there was one man who could change the situation, he was that man and his unwillingness to do so was producing such unjustified and intolerable results.

We walked upstairs into that cold, forbidding chapel. It was springtime, but snow was still on the ground. There was a caisson with horses outside and I can remember seeing wisps of breath coming from their nostrils. I remember, too, that there was a twenty-one-gun salute. What I remember most, though, was that the mother wouldn't let go of my hand.

This was a mass-production operation. We were commemorating thirty-five men who had been killed in action, but all the bodies were not there. Most of them had been buried earlier. We had only one anonymous, symbolic coffin in the chapel with us. The chaplain had a standard speech which he delivered four or five times every day. In an hour and a half we'd leave; another group would file in and he'd repeat the message for them.

The chaplain began to read the names of the dead: Donald Jones III, of Florida, and Marvin Anderson, Jr., of Tennessee, and Willie Page, Jr., of New York. They came from every state. I was struck by the number of times I heard the words "Junior" and "Third." The war was slicing through families, truncating the lines. Going to Arlington Cemetery and attending those services, seeing the hills full of crosses, is almost more than I can bear.

Late this afternoon there was a vote on the House floor to authorize spending $508 million to help beef up the merchant marine. Waiting for the roll to be called, I observed Wendell Wyatt, a Republican from Oregon, take off his wedding ring and hold it in his right hand. He noticed my puzzled expression and walked over to explain. He always removes his wedding ring when a roll call starts, he said, and puts it back on when he votes. That way he doesn't forget and fail to vote before leaving the floor.

As I was walking through the Speaker's lobby on my way out of the Capitol, I bumped into Tom Steed, a Democrat from Oklahoma, who is chairman of my Post Office and Treasury Subcommittee. Although he's nearing seventy, he keeps in shape and doesn't appear older than fifty-five. He's a noted storyteller and he likes to use what he calls "sugar-coating stastistics" (sic) to illustrate the intricacies of the federal government. The U. S. Treasury, he said today, mails out 660 million checks each year. At the end of the year all the canceled checks are recycled into toilet tissue for government use—some 56 million rolls of it—which saves the American taxpayer $1.08 per carton. I knew there had to be some wondrous double meaning here, some reason why he was telling me this, but I couldn't figure out what it was.

When I got to my office, some communications workers from Flint were waiting for me, and I talked to them for almost an hour. Their contract expires May 1, and they seemed to think a strike is inevitable. They want a twenty-five per cent pay hike. One

reason they're so deeply troubled is they realize that the problem
they face is more serious and that extra money in their pay envelopes, while helpful, won't solve it. Their industry is fully auto-
mated. What they're really concerned about, I think, is their im-
portance as people, their increasing loss of leverage. I'm beginning
to run into more and more situations like that.

Wednesday, April 21. On the floor this afternoon I spotted a group
of young colleagues. One had just returned from a government-
financed trip to Italy and, when someone asked how he'd enjoyed
the junket, he replied by forming a circle with his thumb and
index finger—the A-O.K. sign. Another member laughed and
flashed the same sign—only with a tighter circle—and asked,
"Wasn't it more like this?"

"No," a third member said. "That was Japan. Rome was that
other size."

Last week two Republican leaders from my district asked me if
either Jerry Ford, the House minority leader, or Senator Bob
Griffin, the minority whip, had approached Nixon yet to say that a
continuation of his policies would hurt the GOP's chances in the
state next year. I put the question to Ford this afternoon.

Jerry's a tall, good-looking former All-America football player
from the University of Michigan. He's stubborn and very partisan,
so much so that Lyndon Johnson once lashed out at him bitterly,
claiming that Jerry's trouble was that he'd played too much football
with his helmet off. Jerry and I don't always agree on the issues,
but I respect him and we've maintained a direct, friendly relationship. Our conversation today was cordial.

He said he feels the situation in Vietnam is improving steadily.
So is the economic outlook. Nixon is right in continuing his present
policies. It's just a question of people staying steady during a rocky
time. If people would have faith in the Administration, everything
would be all right. Nixon's popularity has decreased, Jerry admitted, but the worst is past. Even now, his polls suggest, Nixon
would defeat Muskie, Humphrey or Kennedy.

I countered, citing a Gallup Poll showing that only eighteen per cent of young people identify with the Republican Party. Twenty-five million new voters are about to cast their first ballots for President next year and we have to make an effort to earn their support. I want to see Jerry replace Carl Albert as Speaker of the House; I want Republicans to organize Congress, but I feel if we just continue on the same course we'll suffer a defeat next year worse than the one in 1964.

Jerry said it was important that I refrain from criticizing the President by name. The White House is troubled about me, concerned that California Congressman Pete McCloskey and I might do to the Republican Party what Gene McCarthy did to the Democrats in 1968. We ought to tone down our remarks, he said, and consider what we're doing very carefully before we get so far down the road that we can't turn back.

I took that as an opportunity to tell him how estranged I feel from the Nixon Administration. I said I haven't talked to Nixon except as a member of a large group for almost three years and that my name has been taken off the White House invitation list even for such routine events as bill-signing ceremonies and prayer services. Jerry said he'd try to bridge that gap, act as peacemaker.

I wish he could find a way, but I'm not sure it's possible. My disagreements with the White House extend far beyond the war. They include the lack of moral leadership, the economy, civil rights, the Haynesworth and Carswell nominations to the Supreme Court, the seeming contempt for young people. The White House is running this party like a social club. There aren't enough of us that we can afford to purge independent men like former Senator Charles Goodell and former Interior Secretary Wally Hickel. We've controlled the Congress only *four* of the last forty years and the party is still losing ground, willfully destroying itself. Richard Nixon is the most political man I know, even more political than LBJ. Liberal Republicans feel that he's the one who's systematically liquidating the GOP—and now many conservative Republicans are saying the same thing.

I first met Nixon in Cambridge, Massachusetts, in 1965, when I was at the Harvard Business School. I was delighted to meet him. I had supported and worked for him in 1960 and again in 1964 when

I thought he might emerge as a compromise candidate from a dead-locked convention. He had come to Harvard to recruit lawyers for his New York City firm. He hosted an open house in his hotel suite to which he invited young Republicans from the business and law schools. Out of that session came an invitation, in February 1966, to join him for dinner in his New York City apartment. The other guests left his apartment about eleven, but I stayed on to ask his advice about running for Congress. He pointed to certain parallels in our personal situations. He urged me to run, said he'd campaign for me and offered me staff advice on television commercials.

We sat by the fireplace in his study and talked until one or two o'clock in the morning. I missed the last plane back to Boston, so I called home to say I was spending the night in New York. Nixon got on the phone and said that he was looking forward to meeting my family and that he hoped I could be persuaded to enter the race. It was a nice gesture for him to make, and I appreciated it. Furthermore, he delivered on all his promises to me. I remember specifically his appearance at a fund-raiser in Flint. I was so in-experienced that I thought once he was introduced I should leave the room on the pretext of having to appear somewhere else. I thought it would be easier for him to say nice things about me if I were not present. So I left—and found out later that he had been greatly disturbed. He had *wanted* me to stay and hear what he had to say.

Early in 1968 Bob Ellsworth, one of Nixon's campaign directors, came to my office and said that Nixon wanted me to serve on his nine-member congressional campaign advisory staff. The invitation apparently stemmed from a detailed study my staff and I had done on the Vietnam war for an Appropriations subcommittee; Nixon had read the report and had written me about it. But George Romney, then governor of Michigan, wanted the Michigan House members to stay out of the presidential thing and give Romney a free hand. I explained the situation to Ellsworth and told him I was pleased to be asked but felt I had to decline. I said I would be willing to make available all of our staff work on the Vietnam war. That seemed agreeable enough and, on June 22,

Nixon invited me to his New York apartment to make an in-depth presentation.

My administrative assistant, Carl Blake, and I talked with him for about two hours. We recommended a policy of "de-Americanization"—systematically turning over full responsibility to the South Vietnamese. He seemed to agree that there wasn't a military solution to the war and said he was interested in the idea of a phased withdrawal of U.S. troops. At one point he looked me in the eye and said matter-of-factly, "Well, you know, Don, if we're elected we'll end this war in six months."

He asked if he could send his staff people to Washington the next day to review the information in much greater detail. In the morning Pat Buchanan, Ray Price and Dick Whalen arrived at my Washington office. Whalen was in charge of composing Nixon's Vietnam position for the Republican convention. His statement to the platform committee was relatively dovish; it called for "de-Americanization" and urged new efforts toward a negotiated settlement. Carl and I were jubilant when we read that statement. Nixon had approved Whalen's position. Then, as the convention got under way in Miami Beach, Nelson Rockefeller slipped in the national polls and Ronald Reagan suddenly appeared to be Nixon's main challenger. Nixon decided that the threat to him came not from the left but from the right. He asked Ray Price to draw up another, less conciliatory statement on Vietnam and this was the one Nixon used on the convention floor.

Nixon's selection of Spiro Agnew as his running mate was a great disappointment to me. It touched off immediate fireworks in the Michigan delegation. In a stormy caucus meeting I said I thought Agnew represented everything we didn't, that we ought to find another candidate and make a fight of it on the convention floor.

The obvious first choice was New York City Mayor John Lindsay, but he refused to do it. Finally, at the last moment, Romney said he'd run. We tried frantically to round up some delegates on the floor. We were much too late; it was a hopeless cause. The delegates were in Nixon's pocket and Lindsay wound up seconding Agnew's nomination. In the midst of that effort to find delegates, I was buttonholed by John Chancellor of NBC. Apparently Agnew saw the interview and that's probably one reason why there's bad feeling between us today.

I saw Nixon once or twice during the '68 campaign, but my next real insight into him occurred at a White House congressional breakfast in November 1969. He talked about the issues for thirty or thirty-five minutes, nothing controversial. The first few comments and questions from my colleagues were laudatory. I raised my hand and he called on me. I stood up and remarked, "I heard you say in your inaugural address that it was time to lower voices and bring people together. I was inspired by that statement. But the Vice President is behaving in exactly the opposite way. He's dividing people, turning them away. He's hurting the country, and that's not consistent with your theme."

Nixon seemed flustered by the comment. He responded by saying that the Vice President's way wasn't always *his* way. Then he added, smiling, "With respect to Agnew and the press, well, you know, they've been giving it to us for years." He clenched his fist and leaned forward. "Now they're getting a taste of it themselves and they just aren't liking it very much."

There were about sixty congressmen at the breakfast and at least a dozen of them started to applaud. I was disturbed by Nixon's apparent delight in getting back at the press, using Agnew to even an old score. That, for me, was a turning point. Since that time Nixon and I have spoken only at formal occasions. Last year there was a picture-taking session at the White House for all Republican candidates. I went through the receiving line and mentioned to Nixon that I'd received an endorsement from the United Auto Workers in Flint. I said I thought that was a breakthrough for Republicans. "Yeah," he said, and stuck out his hand to the person behind me.

During my first two terms in Congress I was asked to do, and did, as much party work as any new Republican member. I appeared at several fund-raisers, and usually I was introduced as "Exhibit A," a young candidate who had won an impossible victory, defeating an incumbent Democrat in a Democratic district. I'm not receiving that kind of invitation any more. This year, for the first time, I was not invited to address the Young Republican Leadership Training School. Pete McCloskey was asked, then disinvited. He went anyway and spoke in the parking lot.

Thursday, April 22. This morning, as I was walking to the floor for a quorum call, I heard some people running behind me. I turned to see Sam Gibbons, a Democrat from Florida, and Jim Corman, a Democrat from California, jogging toward the steps of the Capitol. Since their names come early in the roll call, they often end up going over for the vote together. Gibbons was beginning to puff a little when he pulled abreast of me.

"How come you're not jogging?" he gasped. "You're supposed to be representing the young people."

I smiled as they trotted by and ran up the stairs to answer their names.

Friday, April 23. The Bilderberg meetings are designed to get about a hundred top people in business, government and education together privately for two or three days every spring to discuss the political and economic challenges facing the Western world. This year's meeting, the twentieth in a series, began this morning at the Woodstock Inn in Woodstock, Vermont. I felt flattered to be on hand, but I found myself wondering why I'd been invited and thinking that it was like being initiated into a secret society.

The other participants represent a cross section of the international power structure: Baron Edmond Rothschild, Robert Anderson of Atlantic Richfield, former Ambassador to Brazil John Tuthill, and Chase Manhattan Bank Board Chairman David Rockefeller. Most are in their fifties or sixties; their reference points seem to be rooted in the facts and circumstances of the cold war.

The first topic on the agenda was the role of business in encouraging social change; the second, the changing directions of American foreign policy. David Rockefeller gave an assessment of the U.S. economy. Earlier I had watched him write his speech in longhand without making a single correction.

At the end of the session there was a cocktail party; then we moved on to dinner. The appetizer consisted of steamed clams the size of a silver dollar, thick and very tough. I pried one loose from its shell and began chewing on it. Nothing happened. This went on for a minute or two until it became obvious that I had two choices: swallow the thing whole or spit it out somewhere. Neither seemed very attractive.

Finally I decided to spit it into my cupped hand. Then the problem became what to do with it. This was a beautiful table with elegant silver and china. I couldn't just set it down on the mahogany. I reached under the table, placed the clam inside the cuff of my right trouser leg and tried to rejoin the conversation. But I could still feel the thing. It was wet and sort of disgusting. I excused myself, went to the men's room and flushed it down the toilet.

Saturday, April 24. One of the first speakers at the conference this morning was an Air Force general named John Vogt who identified himself as an architect of our bombing policy in Southeast Asia. He was very intense. As he spoke his face became livid; you could see the veins in his neck. He said we use elaborate safeguards to make sure we don't kill innocent civilians. As an example, he cited the fact that he had been denied permission to bomb 350 freight cars on the tracks at Haiphong because of the civilian population. Clearly, he believed what he was saying, yet there was no willingness on his part to admit that when you're dropping bombs from an altitude of 30,000 feet you're going to hit civilians, whether intentionally or not. The hundreds of thousands of refugees who've had to flee their homes in Vietnam, Laos and Cambodia provide evidence of this.

When the general had finished, Representative Henry Reuss of Wisconsin turned to me and whispered, "That's as close to Dr. Strangelove as I ever want to get." I was dismayed by Vogt's statement too, and as the discussion continued, I felt compelled to offer another view.

"The physical reality of what's happening to the people of Southeast Asia," I said, "should not happen to any human beings on the globe. We must not close our eyes, our ears, our human instincts to an American war policy that in its practical effects has become as savage and inhumane as anything the Communists have ever produced."

When I finished there was no applause, no way to judge the impact of my words. But having made the statement, I felt an enormous emotional release.

At noon I skipped the formal luncheon and wandered in and out of some small antique shops close to the Woodstock Inn. I ended up buying an antique bottle and a brass milkcan lamp. Walking back to the inn, I bumped into Peter Frelinghuysen, a Republican from New Jersey. He's a quiet, sensitive man whose family dates back to the founding of this country. He doesn't have much stomach for controversy. I said I hoped my Vietnam statement hadn't bothered or embarrassed him too much.

"Well," he replied, "I'm not sure it helps to talk about these things any more. It would almost be better if we could stop talking about them."

At dinner this evening Henry Kissinger sat across the table from me and we talked at length about the Administration's foreign policy. He said that, "as a practical and moral issue," the war in Vietnam is over. The Laos and Cambodian operations were designed "to thwart a Tet offensive next year." He saw a ten per cent chance of a real breakthrough in the Paris peace talks, probably coming in the fall. The odds aren't any better than that because the protests in this country have prompted Hanoi to decide there's no need to negotiate; all they have to do is wait until this mounting pressure breaks the back of the Administration's policy.

If forced to choose between the ultimate failure of Vietnamization and acceptance of a negotiated settlement on the National Liberation Front's terms, Kissinger said, he isn't sure which alternative he'd pick. He did say, however, that the Administration had probably made a mistake in not trying to make a deal with the "sincere" doves in 1969, asking them for a three-year moratorium on public comment about the war. That's his one major regret.

Hearing Henry's comments on the moratorium brought back memories. He has obviously forgotten—or chosen to forget—the session Pete McCloskey and I had with him in the spring of 1969. We'd urged the Administration to keep its campaign promise to "end the war." Kissinger had replied that a breakthrough might be imminent. "Be patient," he said. "Give us another sixty to ninety days. Please, stay silent for the time being." Pete and I agreed.

We waited until September. With the war continuing and American losses mounting, we went to Kissinger again. We stressed that public disillusionment was increasing and that we would have to withdraw our support unless the war were ended soon. He conceded the Administration's initial plan had not worked and said they were devising another plan.

Tonight, Henry went out of his way to be courteous and pleasant to me. He said he knew I was on the black list at the White House. Nonetheless, I still had "one friend" there. At the end of our dinner he stood on the stairs leading up to his room and said, "I hope we'll have the opportunity to work together someday—beyond this time."

As I was walking through the lobby, Joe Johnson, the U.S. co-ordinator for the Bilderberg meetings, intercepted me and suggested we have a drink together. He's about sixty-five and one of the grayest of the gray eagles who dominate these conferences. I was happy to accept. He echoed what seemed to be a fairly unanimous view among the participants here: Kissinger and HEW Secretary Elliot Richardson are the only men of quality on Nixon's entire team. As for Nixon himself and his advisers, there is a low regard.

Sunday, April 25. As I was packing my suitcase this morning, I couldn't help thinking how very old and beat-up it was, how different from all the other suitcases that guests bring to an elegant inn like this. I closed it with some difficulty, placed the rest of my gear in one of those $3.98 hang-up travel bags and headed toward the lobby.

Outside, about a hundred anti-war demonstrators were milling in front of a TV camera. As I left the building a large blond girl saw me and shouted, "Welcome to Vermont, rich man." I stopped. My impulse was to say, "Wait a minute. You're protesting an indiscriminate war, yet you're making indiscriminate charges." But I thought better of it because of the TV camera. I continued down the driveway and heard her shout again, "Don't worry, rich man, you'll have your Mercedes, too."

Checking in at the Boston airport for my flight to Washington, I spotted Henry Cabot Lodge sitting by himself in a corner reading a newspaper. The other passengers didn't seem to recognize him. I reflected that power comes and attaches itself to someone; then it leaves and the person is alone again.

Monday, April 26. Just before noon I passed Chuck Teague, a Republican from California, on the floor of the House. He's a tall, baldish, distinguished-looking man who is serving his ninth term here. His office is just down the hall from mine in the Longworth Building, so we see quite a bit of each other.

Ever since Richard Lyons wrote an article in the Washington *Post* last year about my interest in running for President someday, Teague has referred to me as "Mr. President." He'll bow deferentially and ask, "How are you today, Mr. President?" or "Any news today, Mr. President?" That's what he did this morning. Frankly, I wish he'd stop.

At lunch today Bill McLaughlin, our Republican state chairman, asked me if I intended to oppose Senator Griffin in a primary next year. I told him I'd decided against it. I said, however, that I was becoming increasingly distressed with Griffin. If he continued to defend Nixon's policies, I might have to reconsider and at least challenge some of those positions.

Some of the Republicans in the state apparatus are suspicious of me, McLaughlin said. If I were to take off my coat, lay it across a puddle, pick up an old lady and carry her to the other side, he added, these people would question my motives. Basically, they don't respect my political judgment. They feel I'm too stupid to realize that my activities are probably destroying my future within the Republican Party. I recognize that better than most.

Tuesday, April 27. Today the House took up a handful of minor bills affecting the District of Columbia. At one point, I was standing at the food counter in the Republican cloakroom between Bill Steiger from Wisconsin and Phil Crane, a handsome, conservative member from Illinois. Crane was gulping down bites of hard-boiled egg and seemed preoccupied.

"Remember," I asked, "when you were able to enjoy eating an egg like that?"

"Yeah," he replied, "and I can remember, too, when they weren't a substitute for lunch." He rubbed a napkin across his mouth and hurried off to vote.

On the floor this afternoon, H. R. Gross, a conservative Republican from Iowa, blasted a statement by Secretary of State Rogers offering to contribute U.S. forces to an international group which would guarantee the neutrality of a re-opened Suez Canal.

Wayne Hays of Ohio chimed in to support Gross, panning the idea. Speaking with obvious sarcasm, he said: "It seems to me that the Secretary of State and Senator Fulbright must be the two most gullible men, where the Egyptians are concerned, since Marc Antony believed Cleopatra when she said, 'Marc, you are the first one.'" As he walked slowly from the well of the House, Hays flashed a tight smile at the chuckles this brought from around the chamber.

Moments later, Ben Blackburn of Georgia made a point of order that a quorum was not present, and a call of the House was ordered. As I stood by the brass railing on the Republican side of the House floor, I saw Jerry Pettis from California and George Goodling from Pennsylvania enter the chamber together and stand just inside the door waiting for their names to be called. They were dressed in suits and ties—but both were wearing tennis shoes. The quorum bells had obviously interrupted their game of paddleball in the House gym. Jerry noticed me eying his sneakers—and said with a self-conscious smile, "We're the little old men in tennis shoes that you read about."

Wednesday, April 28. My phone was acting up again today. From time to time I've heard strange noises on the line. Or I've picked up the phone and haven't been able to get a dial tone. When I was a private citizen I didn't have the same trouble that I have now. It wouldn't surprise me at all to learn that the FBI or the Defense Intelligence people had selected me for a tap. I don't have any real evidence that my phone is bugged; I'd figure the odds are fifty-fifty.

This is a cold, overcast day. I have to fly to Minneapolis this evening to participate in a planning session for the voter registration rally that will take place there next month. That's the last thing I want to do. There are days when I dread having to get on an airplane—I feel like a piece of meat being hauled here and there—and this is one of those days. But in this business you've got to meet the schedule. If the schedule says "Minneapolis," you pack up. You go.

For most of my life I've been caught up in a cycle of endless activity, driven both by other people's expectations of me and by my own desire to excel. I was obsessed with doing the jobs that I felt were my "responsibility." It got to the point where my private, personal life was a secondary concern. I could listen to beautiful music and never really hear it, sit down to a wonderful meal and go through the motions of eating but never really taste it. I didn't really care what I ate or even if I ate at all. I was all action. All I cared about was accomplishing things that really mattered. And I made no secret of it. In Congress, I would brashly admit, "I'm here to try to do an outstanding job," and "Yes, I want to move up the ladder." I talked openly about trying to move from the House to the Senate, from the Senate to a Cabinet position, and perhaps, someday, to the presidency. That just seemed a logical progression and most of the people around me expected me to follow that route.

I'm not sure that my colleagues used the word "naïve" when referring to me. They properly could have. Certainly some said I was "arrogant," "superambitious," "a young man in a hurry." Traditionally, those who want to be President the most have to go to the greatest lengths to disguise their hopes. Stated ambition casts a shadow over you. It calls into question everything you do and it blunts your effectiveness. It took me a long time to realize that.

I'm still candid, but I don't say these things any more. Not because I'm hiding them. I just don't think or feel the same any more. It's almost a paradox. While my commitment to the things I believe in has deepened, the future—in personal political terms—has lost its former meaning. I'm not sure there is a political future for me— and that's no longer the issue.

One day in 1969 I was rummaging through a box of assorted old papers, faded clippings, the kinds of things that accumulate in desk drawers. I came across some short stories I'd written several years before and began reading one entitled "The Joy of One More Day." In a rambling, philosophical way, it talked about life's endless promise and about death as well.

"Perhaps we shall never die," one of my characters said. "Perhaps we shall never live. Perhaps we will walk unknowing past life on our way to the cemetery." The more I thought about those lines, the more they got to me. That was *me* the character was talking about: that's exactly what *I* was doing. It was one of those insights that made a difference in my life. It jarred me into a realization that things weren't right and had to be changed. Changing them has had an enormous effect on my personal life. Of the eighteen Michigan members of the House who have been married, seven have been divorced. I never thought I'd be one of them, but I am.

Nancy and I eloped in 1957. She was seventeen; I was nineteen. We had been high school sweethearts. But as we grew older our essential differences became more sharply etched, and we grew further apart. My hyperactivity didn't help matters. But I wasn't thinking in terms of ending the marriage. Marriages are forever— that message had been drummed into me as a kid. My mother has an almost pathological fear of divorce; to her it's almost worse than murder. For me, the most painful thought of all was being away from my three children. Yet when I finally began to face the realities, it was clear that our differences were not reconcilable. We were beyond the point when simple solutions could work. In March 1970, after months of soul-searching and difficult discussion, I moved from McLean, Virginia, into a small basement apartment near the Capitol.

Thursday, April 29. This was scheduled to be a busy day on the Hill. The House was due to vote on an amendment to increase funding for the Committee on Internal Security from $450,000 to

$570,000; a floor fight was likely. I didn't want to miss the debate and took an early morning flight back from Minneapolis.

In the men's room off the House floor, I saw Bill Scherle, an extremely conservative Republican from Iowa, and was reminded of the fact that we don't speak to each other. We look at each other but never exchange a word. During the 1970 campaign he and his henchmen gave false information about me to a national columnist. The story alleged that a member of my family had held a part-time government job because of my influence as a member of the Appropriations Committee. When the column appeared in the Flint *Journal*, right before the primary, it was quite embarrassing. Factual denials never seem to catch up with the original smear.

The debate on the Internal Security Committee authorization was brief but acrimonious. I have never seen evidence that the committee any longer serves a useful purpose, so I voted against the amendment. One hundred twenty-eight other members apparently agreed with me, but we were defeated by a lopsided margin.

On the floor this afternoon I talked with Garner Shriver from Kansas. He's the ranking Republican on the Foreign Operations Subcommittee, a thoughtful and hard-working guy. Wichita is in his district; cutbacks in defense spending and the declining economy have had a disastrous effect there. The city's unemployment rate is almost fifteen per cent.

In the course of our conversation I mentioned the Republican insurgency that Pete McCloskey is leading and said I had no idea what it would mean in terms of my own political future, whether or not I could even be re-elected. Garner said I ought to continue to say and do what I thought was right. I respect him for that, and if I can help him by speaking at some colleges in his district next year, I will.

Friday, April 30. I flew to Detroit from Washington on the noon plane and went directly from the airport to a state-wide meeting of high school student council members. Then I drove to Flint for a press conference on the Model Cities program. I taped an interview for a black-oriented radio station and then met with a Chamber of Commerce committee. My last stop this afternoon was a "think session" at Al Blackmon's house. Al was my finance chairman in 1966, and in 1968 he headed the Genesee County Nixon campaign. He's a stalwart Republican worker and fund raiser. He's also a successful businessman, a pragmatic problem-solver. Although he feels Nixon is in real trouble today, he's even more worried about the GOP insurgency. He said he feared that I might be destroying my own political future. He may well be right.

The Seventh District of Michigan is full of paradoxes. Flint was the first city in America to pass an open housing law in a public referendum, and it was the first major city to have a black mayor (elected by the City Council). It has elected and re-elected a congressman with a progressive voting record. Yet in many other respects the district is conservative. Its people have a distrust of government spending and bureaucracy, an aversion to "restrictive" gun laws and an outright hostility toward "welfare free-loaders." For a while, some older auto workers actually refused to work alongside young men with long hair. At the same time, there is a tremendous eagerness for education. We have two colleges, and more than 80,000 adults take part in some 1200 different evening programs at schools in the area. More adults study high school algebra at night in my district than students do during the day.

Few congressional districts have so enormous a concentration of industrial production, so large a weekly payroll or so many blue-collar workers. General Motors started in Flint in 1908 and remains there today. Some 80,000 men and women—ten per cent of GM's world-wide work force—are employed at Buick and Chevrolet plants and other facilities in the district. The United Auto Workers also began in Flint and, in the bloody sit-down strikes of the 1930s, won the right to bargain for the workers at GM. The roughly 200,000 residents of Flint—and the additional 300,000 in its surrounding surburbs and towns—represent most of the ethnic groups and subgroups in America. They express their cultural heritage in clubs, dances, picnics and other activities. The district is the nation in microcosm.

The district's patriarch, grand old man and most respected citizen is philanthropist Charles Stewart Mott. At ninety-six, he's the senior member of the board of the General Motors Corporation and the largest single shareholder of corporation stock. He founded and heads the Mott Foundation, which has pioneered in the field of community education. He is also one of the most incisive, unostentatious men I've ever met. Behind his shaggy white eyebrows is a unique combination of quickness, common sense, humor, toughness—and compassion for those in need.

I remember our first meeting in his office in 1966. As I explained somewhat nervously why I was running for Congress and why I thought I could win, Mr. Mott sat back behind his desk and shut his eyes. I feared he had fallen asleep. Later I learned that he had heard and weighed every word—and had decided to help. He has continued to help ever since. In the last year, things may have changed. Mr. Mott is a strong Nixon supporter and I know he feels that I should support the President more than I have been able to do. I hope Mr. Mott decides he can support both of us.

II. MAY

Sunday, May 2. The telephone rang at my apartment about seven o'clock this morning. My son Donny was on the other end. He had been thinking about me and wanted me to come see him. Except for the sound of his voice, you'd never guess he was three years old. He uses big words and talks in complete sentences. He's as far along as any three-year-old I've ever met and that's a little disarming.

I drove to McLean about eleven and picked up Donny and my girls, eight-year-old Laurie and Cathy, who's twelve. I had hoped we could play in a park somewhere, but it was rainy. We drove to Tysons Corner shopping center, examined a jet trainer in the parking lot and looked in the windows of all the stores. For a while we pitched pennies into a water fountain.

We bought some fried chicken, took it back to McLean and had lunch together. After another forty-five minutes or so I drove back to my apartment. I started to work on my thesis proposal for my doctorate in business-government relations at the Harvard Business School, but I had trouble concentrating. It's always depressing to be with the children and then not to be with them and know that they are sad.

I've noticed that I really treasure the times when I'm with the kids now. Even though I don't see them nearly as much as I want to and need to, my sense of involvement with them, the love that flows back and forth, is so much deeper than ever before. While I'm not physically present at the house in McLean, available daily for them to see and use as a reference point, the quality of our relationship has improved enormously. I'm really with my kids now—seeing, touching, kissing them—in a much deeper way. They feel that way about me, too, and that by itself is a plus. To have gotten from where we were—physically together but missing each other in the deepest sense—to where we are now—really touching each other—seems a very important gain.

Monday, May 3. On the House floor this afternoon I stopped and talked to Bill Stuckey, a Democrat from Georgia. Bill and I arrived here together in January 1967; we shared offices on the same fourth-floor wing of the Longworth Building and became good friends. During a congressional recess that summer I flew down to his district to spend a few days relaxing. Bill was scheduled to speak one night at a Democratic dinner in Waycross. He asked me to come along with him. As he was greeting the dinner guests, then-Governor Lester Maddox entered the large banquet room with considerable fanfare. Bill introduced us, saying, "Don and I have been voting together up in Washington against all that federal spending." Maddox was extremely gracious in welcoming me to Georgia.

After he'd moved away I said to Bill that Maddox probably didn't know that I was a Republican with a liberal voting record. Bill grinned and nodded his head. The payoff was still to come. During his speech after dinner Maddox digressed from his prepared remarks and told the large audience, "And what we need up there in Congress is more representatives like Bill Stuckey and Don Riegle."

I nearly fell off my chair. The last thing I wanted or needed was praise from Maddox. A few days later an enterprising reporter from the Atlanta *Constitution* dug up the story and published it. Fortunately, Maddox's offhand remark was never quoted back in Michigan.

Today's session was mercifully brief. The House convened at noon and adjourned at two. There was one quorum call and one roll call —just to establish the fact that, despite 7400 arrests at the May Day protest in Washington today, the House of Representatives met and cast a vote on an issue which didn't really require a vote but which served as proof positive that those answering the roll call were present and accounted for. The Republic still stands.

Tuesday, May 4. I was on the House floor during the one-minute speeches today and several members started by condemning the May Day demonstrators and praising the police. Then their rhetoric escalated. They began teeing off on anti-war people generally.

Bella Abzug, a Democrat from New York, tried to stem the tide. She was wearing dark stockings, a long dress and a wide-brimmed hat that looked to me as if it came from the LBJ Ranch. She grabbed the lectern with both hands and spoke forcefully about the fact that the war had dragged on for ten years, that it violated the Constitution, that Congress hadn't done anything about it. We ought to recognize, she said, that there was a relationship between the war and the turmoil loose in our country today.

When she sat down Wayne Hays, a Democrat from Ohio, declared that if the war were over tomorrow the protests would still continue; the demonstrators would find something else to criticize. Then Hays implied that he had carried some sort of weapon in his car yesterday. If a demonstrator had tried to stop him, his would have been the last car the demonstrator ever touched. Great applause from the House hawks.

Hays has an acid tongue, and as I listened to his remarks I felt an almost uncontrollable rage surging through my body. Last month, on the floor, referring to a newspaper item about me, he accused me of saying that most congressmen were dumb and uninformed. He pointed to a magazine and said, "There is a picture of Mr. Riegle here and also one of Gloria Steinem, and I'm glad they have them labeled because otherwise I could not tell one from the other, from the hair." He continued in this vein for several minutes. Then he said: "I do not have to defend this body. I have been here a long time, and I have met kings, queens, prime ministers, generals, privates, authors, actors, farmers and merchants, and some of the smartest people I have ever met are right in this chamber. In the twenty-two years I have been here, the only member I have ever seen referred to in *Time* magazine as a 'potato-head' was the gentleman from Michigan." Some of the old-timers told me later that his was one of the most vicious personal attacks they'd ever heard made against another member. He had violated the rules of the House then, and I couldn't help thinking of that as I rose to respond this time.

I was restrained, but I spoke with a good deal of feeling. Not all the demonstrations would stop if the war ended tomorrow, I said, but many of them would. And wouldn't it be nice to find out how many? Hays was complaining about the work stoppage here in Washington yesterday, but we in Congress have engaged in a work stoppage on the war for the past ten years. There hasn't been a single vote to authorize the war in either the House or the Senate. So wasn't it time for *us* to get back to work?

As I walked from the well of the House, I was aware of scattered applause. All of it seemed to be coming from the balcony. Then I noticed one enthusiastic member who was standing and clapping furiously. Bella and I are on the same wave length.

Meredith White and I had lunch together on the grass by the Bell Tower today. Egg salad sandwiches, Cokes and potato chips. We leafed through a book of poems she'd borrowed and read some soft and touching verses and just leaned on each other for a while. She's probably my closest friend now. She is fresh, sunny and warm, and her calmness makes the turbulent world almost seem serene.

After graduating from the University of California at Berkeley, Meredith spent a year living and working in London. On returning to the United States, she stopped to visit her sister, a lawyer in Washington. She decided to stay, joined my office staff and worked here for a year and a half. During that time she was engaged to a Berkeley classmate who was in Vietnam. We developed an easy and natural exchange, and became important human reference points to each other.

Meredith left our office to return home to New Mexico and get married. But time had changed things both for her and for her fiancé, and they never were married. Meredith later came back to Washington. One evening last summer I felt very alone and invited her to dinner. I remember how tanned she looked against her white silk blouse. We talked and laughed for hours. We had talked many times before, sharing the deepest confidences as trusted friends. But that night was somehow different. It was as if all the hundreds of disconnected impressions and feelings that I had about Meredith were merging, coming into a single focus. At one point we were talking about feelings, how each of us had always had trouble sharing deep feelings with someone else. I explained that I didn't know why—whether I was afraid to or just didn't want to. As I spoke I gradually became aware that I was conscious of this fact only because my feelings were now out in the open. Something had changed. Then the full force of it hit me with a jolt. Meredith and I made each other work. We had somehow unlocked each other and I knew for the first time in my life that I was only *half* of something. I knew it because the other half was sitting across the table from me. I realized that I loved the soft, gentle spirit behind the green eyes. That was the clearest and strongest moment of my life.

When I returned to the House floor after lunch, I found I'd missed a roll-call vote. The bill in question was unimportant—something to do with letting the U. S. Postal Service receive two-dollar fees for executing passport applications. It was approved overwhelmingly and I would have voted for it. But if you're absent for a vote, it implies that you don't have a position. It suggests you don't care, and when you do care, that's enormously frustrating.

In the Republican cloakroom I bumped into McCloskey. He hadn't eaten lunch, so we walked to the sandwich stand in the corner of the room. Then we went back to the floor. Pete sat down beside Chuck Whalen, and John Rousselot, another Republican from California, joined the conversation. "Don't worry about the United Republicans," Rousselot said, "they don't have any clout." Last weekend the United Republicans of California, a predominantly right-wing group, met and passed a resolution asking Pete to leave the party because he'd decided to challenge Nixon in some primaries. Rousselot pointed out that the same organization had almost approved motions lambasting the President for his "liberal" policies and urging him not to run again.

John is a passionate conservative, a former member of the John Birch Society, but he's also a good friend. He and Pete went to high school together near Los Angeles and, during the 1970 campaign, Pete went into John's district to speak in his behalf. John was saying this afternoon that he'd try to return the favor.

Pete and I left the chamber, got into my car, drove over to the Longworth Building and talked for another ten minutes. He said he'd rented a campaign headquarters on Pennsylvania Avenue and committed himself to hiring a girl who will be responsible for scheduling and volunteer operations during the primaries in both New Hampshire and Rhode Island. I stressed the need to establish a tight organization to plan and implement the campaign. I asked what he thought of the suggestion that we have a campaign staff meeting early each morning.

At that, he shook his head. He looks forward to spending that time with his family, before his kids leave for school, and this has become a time they all treasure. I didn't push him; his mind was working on the problem, and I've learned that when dealing with a mystical Irishman you don't recommend a course of action directly. Rather, you raise the issues in such a way that he can reach that judgment on his own. Then you hope for the best.

At seven this evening I pulled into the driveway in McLean and all three children came to the car. Laurie and Donny crawled inside and it was hard for me to say to them that Cathy and I were going out for dinner alone. At the age of twelve, Cathy feels our separation more deeply than the other kids, so there is a special need for us to find ways to stay in touch. I called Cathy to the car. She came running and we left.

I suggested we go to a restaurant that served international food, and Cathy decided she wanted to try La Fonda. Each of us ordered the Mexican Special—a combination plate. There were two Mexican singers and Cathy was delighted by that. She really enjoyed her dinner and ate slowly and gracefully. I couldn't help thinking that she was eating slowly on purpose to make our time together last longer, and that made my heart ache.

We had a long and sensitive talk about life in general and the situation at home. I said that if at some later point I established a new home, then Cathy could perhaps live with me. There was no way she could stay with me now because I was gone so much of the time and that would be an unhappy situation. When Cathy is sad, the tears just well up in her eyes and start to spill out. She looks away. I stop and we have to let a moment pass before we can go forward again.

At one point I offered to write her a letter citing my reasons for leaving McLean. I said I'd keep the letter until she was older because there were things she'd understand better then. She said she didn't want me to do that.

The moment that touched me most and burned an impression on my brain came when Cathy said, "We were talking about the things we learn and understand as we get older. One thing I have learned is that you don't really appreciate someone until they've gone away." Both of us began to cry. We reached across the table and I put her head into my hands and then we held our heads together for a minute there. We looked at each other and kissed each other and didn't speak for some time. When we left La Fonda we drove to Georgetown for dessert. We took our ice cream cones and walked along Wisconsin Avenue with our arms around each other and it was a very close time.

Wednesday, May 5. There were some 1500 anti-war protesters on the Capitol steps this morning and they were addressed by four House members. Even before the speakers were finished, police began making arrests. The center of attraction seemed to be a bearded young man who had taken off all his clothes and stood naked smoking a joint. A person like that discredits the entire peace movement. He performs an act so outrageous that most Americans turn against him and all the others opposing the war, and turn instead toward Richard Nixon because they think it's a way to express their displeasure at that kind of behavior. This just buys Nixon time, and everything that buys him time costs Asian and American lives.

Thursday, May 6. After a meeting of the full Appropriations Committee, I headed toward the Cannon House Office Building where some high school students from Flint were waiting. They were exhausted, as are so many student groups who tour the capital. They stay up all night and run out of gas during the day, and these kids were pretty droopy by the time I talked to them. We had our pictures taken in the rear of the Capitol. I'll have some copies made and sign them and send them to those students to keep as souvenirs.

This afternoon I got a call notifying me that members opposed to the war were having a meeting in the Rayburn House Office Building. At the meeting we decided we had to bring pressure on the House leadership, make Speaker Carl Albert our primary target and try to force him to bring the war to a vote. Then John Conyers, a Democrat from Michigan, added a worrisome note. Having brought about a vote which we'll likely lose, he said, we should then prepare ourselves for more radical steps. We should think in terms of obstructive tactics—if necessary, shut the House down.

I was not at all enthused about Conyers' approach. Yet as John spoke I couldn't help thinking that I may come around to his point of view. Although I'm leery now about the use of disruptive tactics, there have been other times when people suggested things that seemed to go too far, were too radical for me. Then, as time went by, I had to agree that more drastic steps were required.

For example, I remember when it was first suggested that those of us who oppose the war should vote against the full Defense appropriations bill, since some twenty-five to thirty per cent of the money in the bill would be used in Vietnam. I was reluctant to do that because I felt that much of the non-Vietnam defense money was really necessary; what I wanted to do was register my specific opposition to the war in Vietnam. Then I changed my mind. I decided that I couldn't in good conscience any longer support the full Defense Appropriation as long as it contained funds to continue the Vietnam war. So what I've done for the past few years has been to vote "present." To me, that's almost the equivalent of voting no.

Friday, May 7. In Detroit this morning I joined a congressional panel looking into nursing home conditions in Michigan. The testimony was crammed with references to unsanitary wards, the lack of nutritional foods, the physical abuse of patients and the type of inadequate care that results in bedsores.

A number of senior citizens spoke with eloquence. They desperately want to stay connected to society in a meaningful way. They don't want to be boxed into little rooms where no one is interested in them. In my opening statement I said that, while we were there to discuss the problems of nursing homes, we had to realize that they were just part of a larger set of problems facing elderly people today and that we couldn't begin to solve those problems until we ended the war. Surprisingly, the senior citizens vehemently agreed.

After returning to Washington, I decided to take a nap. When I woke up, it was dark and blustery. I wanted to get out of the apartment, so I called Meredith and we walked through the rain to see the film *Summer of '42*. It was sad but moving, and it brought back memories of growing up in Flint. It reminded me, too, of the note I'd written my parents earlier this week, saying how discouraged I was that, because of the divorce and some other matters, we were having trouble communicating with one another.

I remember my mother as she was during my childhood much more clearly than I do my father, partly because Dad was so involved in local politics. He first ran for the City Commission when he was twenty-four and then he ran subsequently in six or seven different elections. He lost the first five times, but then, at the age of thirty-three, he was elected mayor of Flint. Dad was someone I respected and feared; I loved him but didn't know him very well, I didn't feel close to him. The things I remember most are the things we didn't do. We didn't play baseball. The two of us seldom went places together. The number of times we sat down and talked about things were few.

Once the family went on a picnic and a neighborhood kid criticized Dad. I was only seven or eight, but I sailed into the guy and we began to fight. My father just assumed that I was at fault. He took me over behind the car and started spanking me. Another time, while we kids were playing ball, someone provoked an argument and I wound up in a scuffle. My mother was troubled because I was fighting in a Cub Scout uniform. She said she was going to telephone Dad and have him come home and discipline me, and I remember standing there in mortal terror for what seemed an eternity.

Both Mother and Dad were pleased when I received a partial baseball scholarship to Western Michigan University. At that moment in my life my main desire was to be a big-league ball player. A young pitcher named Jim Bouton was on the team my first year there; our starting shortstop was Frank Quilici, who went on to play for the Minnesota Twins. We were undefeated that year, and I remember one game when Bouton was pitching a no-hitter and some batter smacked the ball eight million miles into left field. The ball just kept going and going and I don't remember whether there was a fence or not, but it was one of those times in sports when you make the impossible play with no margin left at all. It preserved Bouton's no-hitter. There were quite a few major league scouts trailing the team and after the game they huddled with him. Later he signed with the Yankees for $30,000. No one seemed interested in talking to the left fielder.

I wanted to return to Western Michigan and play ball the following year, but the birth of our first child was imminent. I couldn't leave home, so I enrolled at the Flint College of the University of Michigan and eventually graduated with a degree in business and economics. I was all set to take a job with the AC Division of General Motors when a friend named Andy Paton suggested I go on to graduate school. Andy had taught at Michigan State. He made some quick telephone calls and somehow arranged for me to receive a graduate fellowship: $2200 per year, and an opportunity to earn an MBA in finance.

I'll never forget the evening I heard the news about the fellowship. I was having dinner with my in-laws. They had been happy about my decision to get a job at GM and remain in Flint. Then the telephone rang. When I came back into the room I was so excited that I couldn't contain myself. I repeated what Andy had said, and it was almost as if I'd just announced that someone in the family had died. Long faces looked back at me. That was a rare moment of insight into the conflict between what I wanted to do and what others wanted me to do. I began to understand some things about myself.

Going to Michigan State was one of those opportunities that changed the course of my life. At one point in my senior year at Flint College, I'd held down five part-time jobs simultaneously. There were times when I sat down to eat and couldn't because my metabolism was racing too fast. But now I was away from the Flint setting, all the Flint reference points, and it was a great awakening process. There was enough money to pay the bills and enough time to study and think. I found my mind opening up, generally expanding in terms of things I saw and felt and understood.

After one year in East Lansing, I'd completed my MBA requirements in finance. I stayed on to complete them in marketing as well. My father came to visit me; often, we'd have breakfast together. We began to discover each other. When I left Michigan State, I took a job with IBM in White Plains, New York, and I began my daily commute up and down the Saw Mill River Parkway. My first assignment was in something called Plant and Lab Accounting Co-ordination. After several months of that I was transferred to Pricing —the area of IBM where people go through special gyrations to justify charging substantial rents for the use of their computers.

On one occasion I was sent home for wearing a blue shirt instead of a white one to work. But the incident that finished my IBM career occurred in November 1963. I was on the telephone when word rippled through the building that President Kennedy had been shot. People dashed out of their cubicles, but nobody could get any information. There were no radios or TV sets in the building and the IBM intercom hadn't said a thing.

I ran out to the parking lot and turned on the radio in my car. I was facing this long, low, modern building with all the windows on one side and I could see people continuing to work inside. What struck me was how few of them left the building to find out what was happening. I was dumfounded and I thought: "Why aren't more people concerned enough to turn on their car radios? Why doesn't the need to know just shove them out that door? How can they be content with fragments of information?"

The horrifying details kept spilling from my radio. The President had indeed been shot. Half his head was blown away. He was in critical condition and there was some question as to whether Lyndon Johnson had been shot too. I was stunned—it didn't seem possible. After a few minutes of this I went back to my office. Just then the intercom reported the news of the shooting. Nobody knew the circumstances, the voice kept repeating; he would have another report when there was something further to say.

I felt the deepest kind of personal shock and I just had to go back to my car. Minutes later the word came through: Kennedy was dead. I didn't want to believe it. I looked back at the building and it was business as usual. In my division a presentation was going on in the comptroller's office. I could see the guys with flip charts talking and gesturing as though nothing at all had happened, and I was never more struck by the meaninglessness of what they were doing.

By some crazy distortion of events and relationships, IBM had removed itself from what was really important in the world. The world was at a crisis point, but IBM continued to roll along. It was one of those rare moments when you suddenly realize that what you're a part of is very different from what you really are; that there is no basis for a partnership between these separate entities; that it just isn't you and that you are just not it.

I returned to my office. Thirty or forty minutes passed and then the man on the intercom said the President was dead. But IBM continued to shuffle papers. Nobody missed a stroke. I finally telephoned one of the company's executives and said I thought it was inappropriate for us to continue to work—that out of respect for the late President we ought to close for the rest of the day.

"Well, you know," he replied, "we've checked the precedents on this. Franklin Roosevelt also died on a Friday and there was a national day of mourning the following Monday. So we'll have a holiday next Monday; you'll have that day off."

It was the classic organization-man response. His tone was even, rational, and we might as well have been talking about how many vacation days I'd earned. But he had missed the point completely. There was nothing more to say, so I hung up.

That experience made me realize that I simply wasn't cut out to be that kind of organization man. The problems I cared most about were on the public side; the idea of becoming a problem-solver in government began to dominate my thinking. In the fall of 1964, I left IBM and went to the Harvard Business School to earn my doctorate in business-government relations. If I could distinguish myself academically, I thought, that would give me the credentials I needed to break into the Washington arena.

That was really my second choice. My first choice was to be elected to office somewhere. But I seemed blocked by several handicaps. I was young and I had no name. I had no money and, because I was moving around, no political base. I had no desire to start at the county commissioner level; that would take too long. So the decision to go the staff route into government problem-solving was a very practical one.

Partly because of the headlong dash through the years—Michigan State, where I was working almost all the time; IBM, where I had to put in long hours; and Harvard, where my work load was almost overwhelming—the time I had to relax with my family was virtually non-existent. Life was high-speed, jammed full of work. Commitment. Responsibility. "The only way I'm going to succeed," I kept telling myself, "is on the basis of brains and hard work." After my first year at Harvard I ranked second in my class.

One day in January 1966, I received a telephone call from a young man in Flint. He said his name was Larry Ford. He had run for the state legislature, unsuccessfully, and had met my father, who had told him about me. With a father's pride, Dad had described me in almost superhuman terms. Larry said he felt as if he knew me well already. At the time, he was in charge of finding candidates to run as Republicans in Genesee County. The slot he was having most trouble filling was the congressional slot. That was understandable enough. The incumbent was a Democrat and former state highway commissioner named John Mackie. Although a lackluster performer in Congress, he had money, contacts, a well-established name and the support of organized labor. He had won 66 per cent of the vote in 1964 and he looked unbeatable. Larry said the Republicans had drawn blanks everywhere. They didn't even have a "nice guy" who was willing to run and lose. He was calling me as a last resort. From what he knew of my background, he said, I was a guy who could and should run. At least it was something I should seriously consider.

I had been away from the state for the past five years—three at IBM in New York and two at the Harvard Business School—

and I knew little of Flint's political situation. So I flew back to Michigan two weekends in a row and talked to key people in the Seventh District. The more I thought about the race, the more I concluded that Mackie was vulnerable. Maybe there was a way to put it all together.

I asked a group of personal advisers to a meeting in Cambridge. Carl Blake, a friend and former IBM associate, drove over from Poughkeepsie to help evaluate the opportunity. Another friend at the meeting, Dick Tozer, suggested I get in touch with Howie Phillips, who had worked for the Spencer Roberts organization, a campaign management firm in California. Phillips knew someone named Vince Barabba at Spencer Roberts. On the spur of the moment one night, we called him and asked if Spencer Roberts would possibly be interested in helping a Riegle campaign. At that time, Spencer Roberts was trying to broaden its base beyond the West Coast and expand nationwide by winning "impossible" races in other areas of the country. George Romney was an obvious though unannounced candidate for the presidency. Nothing would please the Roberts firm more than a chance to win a big victory on Romney's home turf. Vince Barabba flew to Flint, assessed the situation and concluded there was a long-shot chance to win. I needed consulting help. Vince offered a bargain rate. It was a vital connection.

All of this meant that I'd have to take a leave of absence from the doctoral program at Harvard. I'd have to give up my faculty appointment as research assistant to Professor Paul Cherington and postpone writing my thesis. Nonetheless, I realized that this was the time and place to run, the first and probably the last chance I'd ever get to run for Congress. On March 12, at Bishop Airport in Flint, I announced my candidacy.

I flew back to Boston and spent the next four weeks studying day and night for my doctoral special field examination. I passed it and, next day, returned to Michigan. Dave Brunell, a friend at Harvard, resigned his faculty position at the Business School and arrived in Flint early in June to take over as campaign manager.

From then until November 8 we invested every gram of energy and imagination we had in the campaign. Hundreds of volunteers pitched in to help. My family was great. No one worked harder than my parents and sister, Dee Ann, or Nancy and her brother and sister. There were a few turning points. Mackie accused me of being a member of the John Birch Society. Governor Romney defended me. I held a press conference on the lawn of the UAW-CIO headquarters to protest their endorsement procedures. On a TV show, I cut a raw steak in half to illustrate how food prices were rising and viewers' dollars were buying less and less. The rest was a blur of shaking hands at plant gates early in the morning, endless coffees, TV ads, speeches, brochures and bumper stickers. On election night, I recall, I stood on the steps of a polling precinct in the rain shaking the last hand possible. I looked through a window and saw that the hands of the clock stood at two minutes past eight. For the first time in eight months, there was nothing more to do.

Mackie had taken us for granted too long. When all the returns were in, I'd received fifty-four per cent of the vote. I thought I'd win and so did my dad, but that margin exceeded our greatest expectations. At six o'clock next morning I was back at plant gates to thank the workers for their support.

Saturday, May 8. I was up at six-thirty because I had to fly to Michigan and give a keynote address to the annual toastmasters' convention in Midland. Bill McMillan of the toastmasters met me at the airport in Saginaw and suggested that I could rest for a while on the studio couch in his den. After making a couple of calls to the local news media, I tried to take a nap. I'd had two or three cups of coffee on the plane and wasn't able to sleep. My mind kept turning as I lay there; it was just one of those times when ideas you've been thinking about subconsciously begin to jell in your head.

I had a rough outline of what I wanted to say to the toastmasters, but the program started late. I knew I had to catch a plane, so I felt pressured by the clock. I spoke more quickly than usual and didn't say things I'd meant to say. The audience was not responsive. There was no spontaneous applause and it was hard to tell whether or not I was getting the message across.

Bill McMillan drove me back to the airport in his wife's Mustang. It was a warm, sunny day and I felt really spent. I was damp under the arms, sweating so much that it was almost embarrassing. Bill said he was going to hang a bronze plaque in his den announcing that "Don Riegle slept here." I thought he was kidding, then realized he was serious. "Well," he said, "if you get to be President, it might be nice to have that plaque there." I promised him that if that happened I'd make it a point to stay there again. "But," I said, "don't hold your breath."

As I was waiting for my plane, a Midland businessman recognized me and sat down to chat. I was tired and not really interested in talking to him. I listened as politely as I could; then, when the plane was ready to receive passengers, I sprang to the gate and quickly walked up the ramp. But he kept pace with me. It would have been awkward to sit anywhere other than beside him, so we sat together. I don't know what he'd had for lunch, but his breath was very unpleasant. I had to look straight ahead.

Finally, in desperation, I used a system I save for situations like that: I exhaled when he exhaled, inhaled when he inhaled. He just kept talking, and after another few minutes of this, I said as nicely as I could that I needed to take a nap. I leaned back and closed my eyes. When I woke up, he was gone.

This evening Meredith and I decided to see *Mad Dogs and Englishmen,* a Joe Cocker movie playing in Georgetown. We lost control at the candy counter, spent two dollars on popcorn and chocolate mints, and sat through the movie twice. It was better than *Woodstock, Gimme Shelter* or *Let It Be,* and I remember saying how absolutely dumfounded my mother or her friends would be if they witnessed this. It's easy to see why older people have so much trouble understanding their children's attitudes.

Sunday, May 9. Dave Brunell stopped by the apartment this afternoon to talk about the political situation in Flint. Dave is thirty-five, of medium height and solid build, and his hair is thinning on top. At the moment, he's growing a bushy red beard. He's been one of my two administrative assistants since I came to Congress and he's the chief political strategist on my office staff. He's also my closest male friend. Our relationship is so natural, open and honest that we're almost closer than brothers. His calm demeanor contrasts favorably with my own tendency to seem a bit frantic at times. His approach is more thorough and painstaking, although I sometimes get frustrated at his seeming inability to conclude a telephone call in anything less than thirty minutes. Like the day at the Detroit airport when he got so engrossed in a phone call—in sight of the plane ramp—that the departure time came and the plane left without him.

Originally from Long Island, Dave earned an undergraduate degree in engineering at R.P.I., served in the Navy and then enrolled at the Harvard Business School. We first met there and found that our interests were remarkably similar.

In the Boston School Board elections of 1965, Dave was campaign manager for the slate that opposed the backlash candidate, Louise Day Hicks. On election day he rented a horse and a Paul Revere outfit and rode all over the city trying to drum up support for his slate of challengers. That slate wound up with forty-two per cent of the vote, a remarkably good showing.

When I decided to leave Harvard and run for Congress I asked him to become my campaign manager. Dave took the job. The 1966 campaign was as grueling as a campaign can possibly be, and in the course of that joint effort we developed absolute confidence in each other's abilities. Since then we've gone through three more campaigns—one primary and two general elections—and Dave has been chief overseer of all my activities.

Dave will spend days planning and engineering practical jokes—once he had himself sealed in a huge crate and delivered to the Washington office on April Fool's Day.

His finest hour was a prank he pulled on me in the last election. I tend to be a worrier and had asked Dave repeatedly if we'd pinpointed and reserved the choice billboard locations for the general election. He kept telling me not to worry—he was handling it—but he seemed awfully casual about it.

Late in the year I received a letter from the manager of the sign board company, confirming our contract for billboards. Attached to it was a map of the district with the agreed-upon locations marked with small gold stars. Given my earlier apprehension, I quickly began to study the map. I realized in an instant we'd been assigned the worst possible boards—some on dead-end roads, others overlooking vacant lots. I could feel my blood pressure skyrocketing. I called Flint immediately. Dave was there, and he and Paul Visser, my district office manager, got on the line as I began burning the wires.

After I'd stormed for four or five minutes, they told me we'd been too late—my opponent had beaten us to the best locations. I was ready to commit mayhem. After another minute or two Dave interrupted to tell me it was all a joke. He'd arranged with the sign company to send a dummy map—we actually had the best locations reserved. For a moment I was speechless. Then I vowed to get even. I'm still trying.

Today Dave is ultimately responsible for service to my district. He helps Angela Hogan, my staff assistant for federal aid programs, take care of the Washington end of our urban problem-solving efforts. He handles all my communications: newsletters, press statements and TV appearances. He also helps me maintain my relationships at local, state and national levels with the Republican Party. That's what was on his mind this afternoon. Those relationships, he said, have deteriorated seriously over the past five years. We've got to find a way to nurse them back to health.

Any improvement, of course, is going to be difficult as long as I'm associated with the Republican insurgency. In the midst of the 1970 campaign, McCloskey and I concluded that the emerging profile of the Nixon Administration was a distressing one. The war continued in Vietnam. There were incursions into Laos and Cambodia and the Administration's election tactics hinged around the unfortunate Southern strategy. Reluctantly, we decided that Nixon was not the man we'd hoped he was. We felt that his record would catch up with him and that he couldn't be re-elected in the face of a first-rate Democratic challenger. Even more worrisome was the fact that citizen faith in the whole self-government process was continuing to deteriorate. At that time our heads were not yet into the notion of challenging him in the primaries. Then, last February,

Pete made his impeachment comments at Stanford University. We began to consider the challenge seriously.

What we wanted initially was to persuade someone to head the insurgency effort—not so much with the idea of carrying through with it but rather with the hope of forcing Nixon to change course. If we could bring pressure to bear on him in the primaries, we could catch him eight or nine months out of phase with his November elecion timetable. Two months ago, McCloskey, Illinois Representative Tom Railsback and I flew to New York and tried to convince John Lindsay to remain in the Republican Party and lead the challenge to Nixon's policies. It was obvious from our conversation that he was deep into the question of whether or not to switch parties. He wasn't ready to make any commitments.

To make the challenge to the Administration's policies credible, Pete has been saying, "I'll run against Nixon myself if no one else steps forward." He offered a list of names he could support: Lindsay and three senators—Mark Hatfield of Oregon, Chuck Percy of Illinois and Mac Mathias of Maryland. Neither Pete nor I nor anyone else seriously thought he would become the candidate.

The crucial event was Pete's performance in Boston last March at a Ripon Society meeting. He was superb, better than I'd ever seen him. That's when I realized that the best guy to head the insurgency was McCloskey himself. This isn't to say he doesn't have handicaps. He does. Some worry about his health; he has ulcers. I worry about his habit of sticking his foot in his mouth and saying things he doesn't mean. But what makes him better on balance than any other candidate is that he has a fire burning in the pit of his gut. He knows more about the Vietnam question than Lindsay; he's much less a product of big city politics and certainly more credible as a citizen-statesman. In terms of honesty, ability and sensitivity, he's just as good pound for pound as anyone else around.

Politics is changing in this country. So are people's attitudes toward politicians. The time has come for the first-rate unknown to knock off the entrenched, old style politician. We saw that in 1970 with Jimmy Carter, the new governor of Georgia; with Reubin Askew, the new governor of Florida; with Dale Bumpers, the new governor of Arkansas. Nobody knew them when they began their respective campaigns. They just hit people right. And Pete is the perfect man to do that on a national level.

So in my own head, once I was past the question of "Who?", the next obvious question became "Will it really have to happen?" Or can we persuade Nixon to change course between now and the time when we have to commit ourselves? At this point Nixon's troop withdrawal schedule makes a primary challenge inevitable. He clearly intends to keep U.S. forces in Vietnam well into 1972 and probably beyond. To enter the primaries, we'll have to have a formal organization in the field by the end of this year. It looks as if we'll be slugging it out in New Hampshire next March. I don't know what the challenge will do to my personal life. I just hope it doesn't boil over and consume us all.

Monday, May 10. On the plane to Pittsburgh this morning with the anti-war barnstorming tour, I sat next to McCloskey. He was reading some highly classified information from the Pentagon which someone had slipped him. Congressmen ought to have official access to this sort of information; very often they don't. We began to discuss the data in these Pentagon papers when a reporter, Saul Friedman, stepped up from the rear of the plane. Pete hid the papers immediately and began talking about the weather. Saul didn't suspect a thing.

We had a couple of rooms reserved at the William Penn Hotel and some of us went upstairs to relax before the press conference began. I thought my driver and I were the first to arrive, but then I heard coughing from the bathroom, someone trying to clear his throat, and it turned out to be Fitz Ryan, a Democrat from New York City, who has had surgery for cancer. He still has difficulty talking and the medication he takes doesn't help him very much.

Bella Abzug burst into the room with the force of a Sherman tank, still indignant about the arrests of those May Day demonstrators in Washington. She was even more upset at her liberal House colleagues who had "taken a walk," shied away from defending the demonstrators. "They're chicken," Bella said. "Everybody's chicken."

Later, Pete and I had one of those brief but very direct eye-to-eye conversations and said some basic things to each other.

"It seems we've got two problems," I began. "Number one, do you really want to be President?"

He replied, "I want to be competent to be the President," indicating to me that at least he sees the possibility of pursuing this thing all the way. That forced the second question: "How long do you say you're willing to defer to some other Republican who may wish to step forward?" Pete said there are only two men to whom he'd defer, Lindsay and Hatfield, and he isn't sure about Hatfield. The more he sees of other potential challengers, the more inclined he is to think he should try to do the job himself.

Tuesday, May 11. At ten-thirty this morning I was scheduled to speak to a group of political science students from American University. When I arrived at the room in the Cannon Building, I found about thirty-five students. They had already heard from two other members. I sat on a table in the front of the room and began to describe the workings of Congress from my vantage point on the Appropriations Committee. Before I got very far, a tall, dark-haired fellow wearing a gray sweater raised his hand. I had planned to answer questions at the end, so I continued talking. He kept his hand in the air. Finally I decided I'd better take his question.

He stood up and said: "For the last hour we've been listening to the standard congressional bullshit. And you're giving us more of the same. Is that all you've got to say?"

I sensed that others in the group were wondering the same thing. I thought to myself, "He's right. Bullshit is an occupational hazard around this place." So I said, "Let me try to tell you about this job as I see it, and then I'll open up the discussion to Q & A later on.

"Doing this job," I began, "means wanting to go to work for 500,000 people. It means listening to them, understanding their worries and needs, studying the issues and then expressing your own best judgments on how to act in their behalf. To do this right means building a working relationship with your people. It means being available on a regular basis to talk face to face with them—even if you don't happen to feel like it that particular day. It means an active district office where every citizen feels welcome to bring any governmental problem he or she can't solve. It means a hot-line phone in that office, that people can use to call me in Washington free of charge. It means regular newsletters and public statements setting forth positions on the issues—and going to the extra trouble of making them lively enough so that they don't put people to sleep. And it means regular detailed questionnaires which allow citizens to give me their opinions.

"Above all," I continued, worrying that I might be sounding too virtuous, "citizens must feel that they can believe their congressman and that his *only* interest is to do the right thing. Then they can accept some honest differences of opinion, even honest mistakes. They can have that faith only if they're dealt with openly and honestly. That faith is what lets a congressman take 'lead' positions on the issues—unpopular stands where only the passage of time will prove whether or not he's right. You have to build that bond of faith, and if it doesn't exist, then the job isn't worth a hell of a lot.

"There are times when there's a direct conflict between popular opinion in the district and what a detailed assessment of the facts shows to be the right course. Different congressmen deal with this problem in different ways. My own view is that you take the right course, which is what the majority of your people would do if they had the same facts. Your job then is to get those facts to them, so they can understand why you took the position you did."

I answered questions for another thirty minutes. As I left the room, several students walked over to introduce themselves, and one offered to do volunteer work in the office. But the tall, dark-haired fellow in the gray sweater stood at a distance. I could feel his skepticism. I had failed to reach him.

Later this morning Dave Brunell and I met with McCloskey in his office. Pete had told someone to Xerox copies of three key documents. That person hadn't done the job and Pete was really irritated. He raged on at full boil, directing most of his anger at his top aide, Robin Schmidt. Robin wasn't the man he'd asked to Xerox those copies. He was just an available target.

Dave and I were troubled by this and so embarrassed that—for

Robin's sake—we left the room and waited outside in the hall until McCloskey cooled down again. The session was supposed to be small, but when it finally began, a dozen people filled the room. Pete had drafted a memo to all potential volunteers and Republican members of Congress setting forth his reasons for running. He read that memo aloud and asked, "Well, what d'ya think?"

All of us suggested changes. Then Pete said he was feeling heat from the financial types, who were insisting on an organizational follow-through to make sure their money was well spent. So we discussed the sort of organization McCloskey needs. Organization is not his strength. He's a lawyer, not a business manager. He runs his day-to-day operation with a smaller staff than mine; he delegates authority to fewer key people than I would ever do. His style thus far has been adequate for the congressional job, but now he needs a brand-new kind of organization around him. And he needs to delegate power.

Many Republicans in the House are strong Nixon supporters. Others who have doubts about Nixon are scared to death to rally behind Pete because of their fears of reprisal, the flak they'd take from the Administration. Still others disagree with Pete on certain key issues. Some question whether he's anywhere near as competent as Nixon. Almost all think the effort is doomed—and who wants to board a leaky boat? Pete doesn't plan to ask any Republican members to identify themselves publicly with us now. He doesn't want to put them in the position of having to say yes or no. Our first priority is to build support at the grass roots.

Wednesday, May 12. There was a piece in this morning's Washington *Post* about an effort to "Dump McCloskey" in his California congressional district. It's an ominous sign. If it's "Dump McCloskey" today, how long will it be before it's "Dump Riegle"? I met with the Genesee County Republican Policy Committee two weeks ago and set forth my views on the issues. There's still concern about me in that group, but the local criticisms haven't yet reached the level that they have for Pete.

At noon today Pete and I were discussing staff people when the quorum bells rang. I asked someone to let us know when they were in the H's on the second roll call so we could leave at that point and arrive in time to vote. We broke away at the last minute and ran to the elevator. Rain was pouring down outside; I looked for my car alongside the Longworth Building, couldn't spot it and then remembered that I'd parked behind the Capitol today. By this time we were very late. We ran the length of the Longworth Building, crossed the street and dashed through the door of the Capitol, stumbling upstairs into the well just in time to answer our names. Pete is older than I am; the run just had to be tougher on him, and when we reached the Capitol door he turned to me and huffed, "You're showing me something, Riggly." I replied, "Save your breath for New Hampshire."

I walked off the floor of the House and into the Republican cloakroom. The regulars always sit in large, overstuffed leather chairs and order lunch on wooden trays that fit across both arms. There is a short-order counter in the corner, and the women serve bowls of soup, hot dogs, cottage cheese and sandwiches. I spotted Dan Kuykendall, from Tennessee; Elford ("Cedie") Cederberg, from Michigan; and Bob McEwen, from New York. They began kidding me, asking if I were the force behind the "Dump McCloskey" drive. Their jabs were aimed at what they consider to be my own presidential ambition.

Les Arends from Illinois, the Republican whip, stepped up and asked if I would vote with the Administration to reinstate funds for the SST. I said I couldn't. Then he asked if I'd be willing to serve as a "live pair" with an absent Democrat who would have voted for the money. That's a gimmick where I would initially vote no—and later withdraw my vote, "pairing" myself with the absent Democrat. They often use this tactic to reduce the number of votes opposing a bill the White House wants. I refused again.

We went out on the floor and lost the SST vote, 201 to 195. Several weeks ago we'd won a similar vote by a dozen ballots. Today we lost by six. The lobbying pressures from the White House and the business community have been so intense lately that some members had to buckle. That's discouraging. But I don't think they'll be able to succeed in the Senate, though; I'll be very surprised if they do.

My Treasury-Post Office Subcommittee heard testimony today from Herb Stein, one of Nixon's top economic advisers. I felt particularly aggressive and in my cross-examination pushed him about as far as one can. He was sweating, fidgeting, showing the strain he felt. This is a guy who spends part of every day with Nixon. He has to have some awareness of two guys named McCloskey and Riegle. I couldn't help thinking it was time he got a taste of what we're like.

Opening the Washington *Evening Star* tonight, I was distressed to read Pete's statement that he didn't really expect to win, didn't even "give a damn." That's one of those classic McCloskey comments which only those close to him can ever understand. What he meant to say, of course, is that it's more important to make the challenge and to put the issues in focus than to worry about winning or losing. What troubles me is that you simply can't ask competent people to support your candidacy unless you're out there running to win. McCloskey's statements are self-defeating. I wrote him a memo and urged him to knock it off. Any successful public figure has to develop an automatic filtering mechanism between his brain and his mouth. Pete doesn't have that mechanism yet and it's his greatest single weakness.

Thursday, May 13. We had a meeting of my office staff this morning in the Speaker's private dining room which lasted longer than I expected. I explained my state of mind on the insurgency: why I thought it was necessary and what it would mean for them. I said that Pete and I were shoving our chips onto the table, playing for keeps, and that this could end in tragedy. We had to take it a day at a time and be ready for anything. I said that, as pressures increased, some might feel they had to leave to preserve their sanity. I would understand that, of course, but I hoped we could make the fight together.

A dedicated, competent staff is absolutely essential for anyone who wants to win and then retain a seat in Congress. Every member of the House receives some $150,000 per year to pay the salaries of as many as fifteen employees in Washington and in his home district. If he chooses, he can allot all of that money to people and projects whose main task is to get him re-elected. Some members are shameless about that.

Because the money is limited, I stretch it by hiring people willing to work long hours for modest pay, people moved mainly by a strong desire to serve others. The staff is like a family. Everyone is on a first-name basis, and everyone is treated equally, regardless of salary or seniority. Each staffer has a specific job: legislation, solving problems for constituents, federal aid programs. Each is responsible for organizing his or her own work and producing results on time. In cases where the citizen has a complaint against the government, we always assume the citizen is right until facts prove otherwise. Experience has shown the citizen to be right about ninety per cent of the time.

On the floor of the House this afternoon I talked with a colleague who has just returned from a long, busy weekend out of town. He was exhausted but he still had strength enough to give me a running account of his sexual exploits. Over the weekend he had "scored" with four different girls—and almost "scored" with two more. Congressmen on the make around here usually lead active lives. The fact that a member might be married makes no difference at all.

One of the prevailing myths about the House is that many congressmen spend their time accepting money, gifts or the favors of call girls from omnipresent lobbyists. No doubt it happens from time to time, but I have not seen or heard an instance of that happening in the time that I've been here. Members—even elderly members—who want girls usually don't have to rely on anybody to get them. The life that congressmen lead brings them into contact with large numbers of people, including women. And many of these women are attracted to politicians and power in much the same way that others gravitate to baseball players, professional entertainers and movie stars.

At five o'clock I flew to Michigan to address the Detroit Bar Association. I was met at the airport by a tall, somewhat distant man who handles public relations for the DBA. He drove me to the Sheraton-Cadillac and I checked into a suite on the nineteenth floor. I'd had an upset stomach all day and realized that I needed to spend at least ten minutes in the john. Often, in this business, you don't have that much time. In any case, I made the head call and was able to get squared away before the PR man announced the press was waiting for me downstairs.

After a brief session with them, I entered the main dining room. I felt relaxed and ready to speak, not apprehensive in any way, and I began by cracking a joke. It fell flat; there was hardly a ripple of laughter. I decided this audience was going to be tough. I shifted gears and began talking about the need for congressional reform. We had too many lawyers in the Congress, I said; 301 of 535, and—on balance—they didn't represent the best people in the legal profession. We needed more people from other backgrounds—medicine, business, labor, science, education. I described how Congress didn't work properly, how the seniority system kept us from coming to grips with problems. Then I got into the war and my disagreements with Nixon.

I didn't table-pound, as I sometimes do, but I spoke with feeling and force and I heard afterward that some trial lawyers thought I'd kept things at an emotional peak too long. You can judge an audience by applause or laughter, but you can also judge it by how people listen. These people listened well.

After the speech I had a beer with Bob Pisor of the Detroit *News*. He asked what I thought my future was in Michigan politics. I replied that it looked bleak. I didn't see any avenue open to me and I wasn't sure that things were going to change that much. He didn't say so, but it was obvious that he agreed.

Friday, May 14. Because I knew I had nothing scheduled in Washington today and was, in fact, going to take a day off, I hadn't bothered to pack a suitcase for the trip to Detroit. I regretted that decision when I woke up in Detroit this morning because I didn't have shaving gear, a toothbrush or clean underwear. Putting on the same clothes I'd worn the night before gave me a scudgie, picked-over feeling. I hoped I wouldn't run into anyone I knew before I could get some Life Savers to improve my breath.

Saturday, May 15. This afternoon I took the children to a movie and then to the playground at Haines Point where they always want to go. I watched them play on the swings and sliding boards. At one point Donny and I were romping together—I have a tendency to hold onto him, carry him on my shoulders and give him hugs and kisses. We were lying on the grass, and he fell on me and said, "Daddy, I really missed you last night." I said, "Well, I missed you too, Donny." Then he said, "Well," and he paused, "well, I *really* missed you last night." I thought about that later; the sadness just doesn't go away.

At seven o'clock I took the kids home. The house in McLean has a painting I've always liked. I wanted to take it to my apartment so the kids would have something familiar to recognize when they come to visit me. But it's always awkward for me to leave McLean with something under my arm. I feel I shouldn't do that.

Monday, May 17. I stopped by the Washington Hilton tonight to attend a reception given by the Michigan Plumbers Association. I got into a heated discussion about the war with three plumbing contractors from my district, particularly one fellow who said we just couldn't leave Vietnam because we'd spent too much money there. He'd rather fight the "Commies" in Asia, he said, than in America.

It was an angry confrontation. I was tired and more argumentative than usual and, at one point, I said that men like him who continued to support the war were just as responsible for the deaths of our kids in Vietnam as anyone in the Administration. His face turned beet red and I thought he was going to hit me.

Tuesday, May 18. I woke up this morning feeling that things are moving too fast; the pace of life is just too frantic; the need to rush here, rush there, attend this event, appear at that banquet. It was hard to get out of bed, dress and head toward the office.

The first item on my schedule was a meeting of the Treasury-Post Office Subcommittee. While I was listening to witnesses drone on about our inadequate civil defense procedures, I received a telephone call. The message was worrisome enough. Yesterday, in the House dining room, a Democratic member overheard two conservative Republicans discussing a plan to remove me from the Appropriations Committee. The member wanted to warn me about this. Two or three days ago Jerry Ford was quoted as saying the party would not purge McCloskey, Riegle or anyone else associated with our effort. The party was big enough to encompass differences of opinion. If Jerry meant what he said, then the conservatives won't be able to force me off the committee.

On the floor this afternoon, McCloskey came up and put his arm on my shoulder. He said he appreciated my latest memo and thought I was right in urging him to put the lid on self-deprecatory comments and begin to talk only in terms of winning the nomination. "You know me," he said. "I haven't ever entered anything without the thought of winning."

"Sure," I replied, "but that just ought to come through more than it does today."

Then I said it was important that he start to think of himself as a President, behave and speak as a President would.

Pete laughed. "You mean I have to give up girls? That I can't like girls any more?"

"No," I said. "To the contrary. That's one of the key reasons why you could be President. You have an appreciation for girls."

Once back at my apartment, I got a telephone call from Flint. The executive committee of the local Republican Party had just met and voted on a sharply worded resolution disavowing the positions I have taken and cutting off any future party financial support for me. After harsh debate, the measure was defeated by a vote of 21 to 17. Jim Smith, a Republican state legislator, spoke on my behalf and argued that "this resolution demonstrates the suicidal tendencies of this party." Conservatives are heavily represented on the executive committee, and winning this vote won't make the problem go away. I'll have to try harder to explain my actions to Seventh District Republicans.

Thursday, May 20. Yesterday afternoon I taped a "Capitol Cloakroom" show with three CBS reporters. I discussed the insurgency and mentioned that Nixon had told me back in 1968 that he'd end the war in six months if he were elected. The show was aired last night, and this morning I got some feedback from two members of Congress. Andy Jacobs, a Democrat from Indiana, went out of his way to say nice things. But Tom Pelly, a Republican from Washington, seemed upset. I said, "I hope it didn't spoil your dinner," and he replied, "No, I'd already eaten, but it did affect me in such a way that I wasn't able to sleep very well." He didn't seem to be kidding.

Laurie had a dance recital rehearsal at her school this afternoon. I left Capitol Hill about three and drove to McLean to see it. After the rehearsal I suggested to her that we have dinner at the Capitol. The House had recessed for most of the afternoon and was due back to consider a supplemental appropriations bill. She thought that was a great idea, so we drove to the Capitol and went into the House dining room. We ordered sandwiches, then split a butterscotch sundae. Debate was winding up on the bill. Laurie was due back at school for the actual dance recital. They started the roll call at six-forty; my name came up at ten to seven and as soon as I had answered, Laurie and I ran to the car. I drove like a madman to McLean.

All the other parents were seated and waiting for the show to start. Cathy helped Laurie slip on her costume and she was ready in a matter of seconds. I went to the phone booth, called the House floor and found that another roll call was beginning on an amendment. It would increase the money the airlines would receive as refunds for their down payments on the SST. The vote would be close—I intended to vote no.

The guy in the cloakroom said the clerk was calling the B's the first time around. If I left immediately, I had a chance to make it on the second roll-call vote. I'd have to miss Laurie's recital. I didn't want to do that, but I was also reluctant to miss the vote. It was just beginning to rain; I ran to the car and drove as fast as I could and made it to the Capitol in near record time. I took the House steps six at a time. A man was going through the revolving door and I went right over him and nearly knocked a policeman down as I ran to the floor. Only one member remained in the well, Ancher Nelsen of Minnesota. I was the last Republican to vote. Five seconds later they gaveled the end of the roll call and announced the results.

We won, but I feel awful about missing Laurie's performance. Perhaps I should have stayed and watched it and let the roll call go. If I had it to do over again, that's what I would do.

Friday, May 21. The House was not in session today—hooray—and there was no committee work either, so I slept until eleven and just puttered around the apartment trying to install two window air conditioners. At five-thirty I flew to Detroit to address the graduating class at the Hurley Hospital Nursing School in the heart of my district.

On the plane I saw Max Fisher, a wealthy Republican who's personally close to Nixon. We talked about the insurgency and, in a nice way, Max rebutted all of my arguments. If Nixon winds down the war, he said, and gets the economy moving again, people's memories will be short. They'll re-elect him easily. We agreed to disagree.

Paul Visser met the plane and we drove up to Flint. At thirty-six, Paul is a tough and able administrator. He lost a heartbreaking state legislative election in 1966 by a hundred votes—but bounced back and accepted the job of serving as my district representative. For the past four years he's done a terrific job.

As I was leafing through the Detroit *News,* I came across an editorial headlined, "Riegle Masquerading in GOP." "If anyone ever writes a sequel to *Profiles in Courage,*" it began, "then the name of Rep. Donald W. Riegle, Jr., won't be in it." It went on to suggest that I was a traitor to the party, that I ought to get out. That bludgeoning editorial style delights some conservative Republicans—and helps explain why it's so hard to carry on a dialogue with them.

I hadn't prepared my remarks for the nurses, so I asked Paul what I should say. I should skip Vietnam, he replied; everyone knew my views on that. I hadn't thought of that, but the suggestion made sense to me. I scribbled out a short speech about what I thought it meant to be a nurse.

We stopped by the district office, had a hamburger next door, then drove to Whiting Auditorium. The nurses were waiting and when I arrived we marched in together. I sat on stage with the graduates and when it was my turn to speak I was thankful for

Paul's advice. I spoke from the heart and received long and sustained applause.

Saturday, May 22. I didn't sleep very well last night. I kept tossing and turning in my bed at the Durant Hotel, so at one-thirty I got up and dressed and walked down to Herrlich's Drug Store, which is open all night. I bought a quart of milk, two blueberry doughnuts and a jelly roll. I figured that if I ate enough I might be able to eat myself to sleep. I was wrong.

I had an eight-thirty meeting with the people who run the Genesee County welfare program. They were forty-five minutes late but, when the session began, it was fairly productive. They said the Mills welfare reform substitute doesn't get at the basic problems, and I agreed to have someone draft a summary of the changes they thought ought to be made in the Mills bill. Then came some radio interviews and a visit to a clothing store to find a replacement for my tie, which didn't go with my brown suit at all. After lunch I drove out to visit my uncle Clarence, who's dying of cancer. This was the first chance I'd had to see him since his illness was diagnosed. I had a hunch that Mother would be there but didn't expect to see Dad. We had been estranged so long; this was the first time we had met in months. I was just so moved to see him; we held each other for two or three minutes.

My uncle looked very frail. He's lost a lot of weight. It's frustrating and sad to think about the cancer at work inside his body causing him to waste away. In the background, the Tigers were playing the Senators on TV. He hasn't lost his love for baseball or his sense of humor. He kidded me, telling me I was working too hard. He turned serious and said he wanted to get into the Ann Arbor Hospital. Maybe they could arrest this thing. I told him I'd see if I could do anything to get him in the hospital.

This afternoon I met with Saul Seigel, who was one of the first members of my "kitchen cabinet." Saul said he's been trying to defend me among people in the district, but he doesn't have a clear idea of what I'm doing or why. He asked if I intend to run for reelection because it appeared to him that I just don't give a damn about that. I told him that I do plan to run, that I will be running to win, and that anyone who thought otherwise was wrong.

At the City Club tonight, there was a buffet for Republican financial contributors. Senator Griffin was there with some businessmen and the sentiments of those guests were hardly enthusiastic toward me. Later we went downstairs for a GOP auction and there were about four hundred items on the block. One was a "Riegle dartboard" and it wound up going for $22.50—to Gordon Suber, one of our City Council members. I was surprised and a little hurt until he told me he had purchased it "because I wanted to be sure no one got to throw darts at it." His gesture made my day.

Sunday, May 23. I flew to Minneapolis this morning for a voter registration rally and spotted McCloskey at the airport. He had just arrived from California. "Riggly!" he yelled. I flashed the peace sign in return. With Pete was Chuck Daly, his combat buddy in Korea who'd been active in several Kennedy campaigns. Someone directed us to a helicopter; we landed at the Sports Arena in another five minutes' time.

Despite the rain, the place was jammed with a crowd of about 27,000. As I watched from the third-floor VIP enclosure, Al Lowenstein came onto the platform below. Al headed the "Dump LBJ" movement before serving one term in Congress as a Democrat from New York. He spoke effectively. After I'd gone down to the main floor, I began looking for Pete. Someone motioned toward the men's room. It was deserted except for one of the stalls. All I could see was a pair of shoes and his pants down around his ankles. I didn't know if we'd find time to talk later so I started talking. He was trapped and had to listen.

The Administration, I said, was in greater jeopardy today than I'd thought possible a month ago. I listed several reasons why I thought so. Pete came out of the stall and nodded; we didn't have time to continue the conversation.

Originally, Gene McCarthy had asked to be the final speaker on the program today. He wanted to wrap up the rally by presenting his fourth-party idea. A special arrangement had been made to satisfy his request. Once the speaking schedule had been locked in, we made our respective travel plans. But as the rally continued, it dawned on him that he would have to wait for Pete and me to finish our talks. He requested that he be put in McCloskey's place and that Pete be dropped to last. He said he had to catch a plane. The switch was made and he was slated to speak after me. I was waiting for John Kerry, the head of Vietnam Veterans Against the War, to conclude his remarks; I was just about to go on when McCarthy changed his mind again. He insisted that he be allowed to speak next and, when the program chairman objected, he turned abruptly and walked onto the platform.

I'd heard he could be arrogant, but I had never seen it first hand. He was going to do what he wanted to do, no matter what. At times he is a very disarming, gentle-seeming person; at other times he's a man with a vast ego who has little concern for anyone else.

What troubled me most was the fact that I'd seen the text of his speech. It would take him forty-five minutes to deliver. To interject a statement of that length after so many others had already appeared was unreasonable. He did it anyway. His presentation was rhetorical, very low key, and it turned the crowd off. People were beginning to drift away and move toward the exits.

Al Lowenstein appeared. Al helps run these voter registration rallies, and I explained what had happened. We talked about how to deal with McCarthy and I said perhaps the best solution was to take his fourth-party idea and drive a silver spike through it, try to demonstrate that it was just a copout approach. Al said he thought that was the thing to do.

McCarthy finished, finally, and I was introduced. As I walked onto the platform, I kept thinking about the fact that 27,000 people was the largest crowd I'd ever spoken to. I took off my coat and rolled up my sleeves. The place began to quiet down and, when I challenged McCarthy's fourth-party idea, I got a great response. I was right, the crowd was right, everything worked. When I had finished, I tried to shift gears, calm down and introduce McCloskey. "He's decent," I said. "He's honest, he knows what love means, and he understands the problems. This is the guy I would pick to be President."

I wanted to stay and hear Pete but I had to leave immediately in order to catch my plane. It was still raining when we lifted off for Washington.

Tuesday, May 25. There was a meeting of the House Republican Conference at ten o'clock this morning to discuss the consolidation of VISTA and other volunteer agencies into something called AC-TION, to be headed by Joe Blatchford. As the session was ending, Ed Derwinski, a conservative from Illinois and one of the few members in the House to wear a crew cut, asked for the floor to support the party's position on this. Before Blatchford took over as head of the Peace Corps, he said, many of the volunteers wore their hair down to their shoulders. Those Peace Corps volunteers, he said, "made Don Riegle look conservative."

I was determined to give Derwinski some of his own medicine. "Speaking of hair styles," I said, "the other night, at the Press Club dinner, Mr. Derwinski was one of the featured speakers. In fact, he was introduced as the only member who wears a Polish Afro."

I'm glad we can still laugh with each other.

Wednesday, May 26. We had one roll-call vote today on the question of whether or not to create an energy committee in the House. Apparently the bill's sole purpose was to create a chairmanship for Richard Fulton, a Democrat from Tennessee, who, presumably, would use it to launch his campaign for the Senate next year. The bill was just too blatant and it failed by a wide margin.

On the floor this afternoon as I was reading an early edition of the *Evening Star,* I felt a nudge on my arm. It was one of my younger Republican colleagues.

"Look up there—in the third row," he said, motioning furtively toward the visitors' gallery.

Sitting there was an attractive redhead in a green dress. What my colleague was directing my attention to was the fact that one of her thighs was fully exposed. He had already tipped off several other members, all of whom were casting appreciative glances at the gallery. Some, in fact, had moved to other locations on the floor to get a better view. Thigh watching is one of the most popular diversions in the House.

Thursday, May 27. Walking to the Capitol from the Longworth Building, I found myself waiting at a traffic light with Omar Burleson, a Democrat from Texas. He's a quiet man of sixty-five with a pleasant face. Although we've served together for almost five years, we've never had an occasion to speak to each other directly before. We began chatting about the weather; it was a warm, sunny day and the sky was azure blue. Our conversation drifted to getting time off to relax. In recent years, Burleson said, he hadn't been able to find much time to play golf or even use the House gym.

As we squeezed into the Capitol elevator he observed that life in the Congress had changed enormously during his thirteen terms here. I asked him what he thought was the biggest single change. "People's growing awareness of what goes on in Washington," he replied.

Saturday, May 29. McCloskey appeared tonight on the David Susskind show. Susskind was friendly and Pete did well. At one point, however, he was asked how Cubby, his wife, was coping with the strain of a candidacy. Pete observed that she would "rather play tennis and drink beer." I couldn't quite believe what I'd heard. I knew what he meant, but that's a pretty abbreviated summary of Cubby and the way she operates.

Sunday, May 30. This morning was humid, rainy and dreary. Pete and I appeared together on ABC-TV's "Issues and Answers" and then I had to get back to the job of preparing commencement remarks for American University. I didn't feel very productive, so I just walked around my apartment and wound up losing track of the time.

I've never liked wearing a watch. I hate being a captive of time and that's precisely what I am. This job involves watching the clock and living by a schedule card and I am bothered by the thought of having to live so close to the line. Not wearing a watch is a small expression of rebellion. The price I pay for that, of course, is often being late.

That's what happened this afternoon. Commencement started at four o'clock sharp and I arrived a few minutes afterward. But when the time came for me to speak, I felt up for it and received a good ovation when I finished. Mother and Dad were in the audience to see my sister graduate and also to hear me speak. I suggested to Dee Ann that she ride to the reception in my car. I'd bought her a silk scarf and a turquoise ring as graduation presents and put them in a glass jewelry box. While the degrees were being awarded, I'd written her a note expressing some thoughts I'd wanted to share with her for some time. As we drove to the reception she read the note and put her head on my shoulder. She began to cry and I guess I was crying too.

III. JUNE

Tuesday, June 1. Shortly after noon today my dad and I went to lunch at Jimmy's on Pennsylvania Avenue. He was disturbed about my personal situation, but we didn't talk much about that. We've been over the subject a million times; there's just no new ground to cover and it's painful for both of us.

Dad said he liked the article in the current issue of *Look* which contained separate statements by Lowenstein and me under the heading of "The Dump-Nixon Campaign." He'd torn out the article and carried it in his breast pocket. He said he referred to it whenever he got into political discussions with his friends. Dad and I have had our share of disagreements in the past, but let someone else challenge me or disagree with a stand I've taken and Dad will defend me ardently.

This week *Time* gave a page, with pictures, to the Republican insurgency. The tone of the piece was fine. It said we had a long-shot chance—like the old Brooklyn Dodgers. If I remember my baseball history, the Dodgers won their share of games.

The piece was a far cry from my last appearance in *Time,* in July 1970. At the time the House was considering the Cooper-Church amendment to cut off funds for U.S. military operations in Cambodia. Jerry Ford had asked if I'd be interested in offering the "motion to instruct" the House conferees to accept the amendment. I replied that I was. When I offered the motion, Wayne Hays moved immediately to table it, apparently by pre-arrangement with anti-Cooper-Church forces. This cut off further debate and forced a vote on the tabling motion. It avoided a direct yes or no vote on Cooper-

Church itself. Although Hays's tabling motion prevailed by a vote of 237 to 153, we had our first record vote in ten years about the war in Vietnam.

Time's congressional correspondent, Neil McNeil, is a veteran House reporter. Because he depends on senior members as news sources, he is a potential conduit for any angry member who wishes to ax a colleague anonymously. Someone in the House—not identified by McNeil—had called me a "potato-head." He argued that I had been duped by Ford into offering the "motion to instruct" and suggested that personal resentment toward me on the part of some colleagues might cause them to oppose automatically any motion I introduced. McNeil went on to say that my thirst for "center stage" had prompted me to offer the motion anyway.

It was an interesting notion, but that isn't the way things work around here. House members are too smart to cast an important record vote on the basis of personal pique against a sponsoring member. Congressmen invariably vote their own consciences—or to protect their own skins—on highly visible roll calls. When the story appeared, I wondered if McNeil had checked his facts. He hadn't talked to me, and it turned out he hadn't talked to Ford either.

Predictably, my opponent in the Republican primary reprinted the *Time* piece and urged voters to "unload old potato-head." An anonymous colleague had the article reprinted in brochure form with a picture of me and the caption, "A funny thing happened on the way to the White House." A few of these brochures turned up on the floor of the House. When Ford found out that my opponent was using the story in his campaign, he wrote a blunt letter to the Flint *Journal* refuting the *Time* account. Forty other Republican House colleagues signed a similar letter to the *Journal*.

After my initial distress, the whole affair seemed pretty funny. My staffers nicknamed me "Spud" and my friends couldn't resist giving "potato-head" the business for weeks afterward. On election night 1970, my volunteers dumped a hundred-pound sack of potatoes on the floor of our campaign headquarters.

Thursday, June 3. Norton Simon, a California financier and unsuccessful candidate for governor, has expressed an interest in helping the McCloskey campaign. During a two-hour session in Pete's office this afternoon, Robin Schmidt, Pete's campaign director, ran through the pitch he'll give Simon in terms of organization, financial plans, budget and control systems. Pete was very tough, almost hostile, in reviewing the presentation. It was almost as if he expected to find mistakes and that put Robin off balance initially.

I'm not sure what it is in Pete's background and personality that accounts for this. But it worries me.

Another worry: Pete had written four or five memos to his campaign staff. One of the points in one of these memos had been overlooked in the shuffle. It involved precinct data from New Hampshire and Rhode Island and Pete was very upset to find that it hadn't been treated in the manner of a commandment from the mountain.

Dave Brunell said, "Look, don't worry about trying to put detailed precinct manuals into the hands of volunteers now. The primary's eight months away. The volunteers don't expect it." Pete was adamant. He said he was going to be meeting people in both states this weekend who would offer to help him. He wanted to be able to give them specific information.

So we had an impasse. There was Pete saying, "God damn it, this is what I want and I told you guys two weeks ago and it still isn't here." And all of us replied, "Look, we've had a hundred things to do and we've done ninety-five of them and nobody knew this precinct data was so important to you."

The argument was heated at times, and it exposed one of our principal dilemmas: to what extent is Pete the candidate and to what extent is he the campaign manager? Because he's a lawyer and a "line-item man," he has this tendency to jump into the details of everything, and that's a drain on his time. It drives the competent people around him crazy. Anyway, I made it a point to kid him as much as I could. If there's one thing he needs to do at this point it's to laugh at himself.

I think he's making progress. At the end of our session he was walking around the office with his head down muttering about his advisers and their crazy suggestions. Suddenly he threw his hands up and said, "Damn it, I don't know why the hell we're doing this.

I'd much rather write poetry, put a flower in my teeth and go out and grab those young girls out there."

That broke the tension considerably.

Friday, June 4. The House session began at ten and will end early today so most members can catch planes. One quorum call and the vote on final passage. I must remember to have Kathleen Sadler give me my voting percentage. It should be between eighty-five and ninety per cent.

This afternoon Kathleen came in for a long talk. She's been troubled about her working relationship with Carl Blake and suggested that perhaps she should leave the staff. I told her I needed her. She's a trusted confidante and a crack executive secretary. She's almost indispensable. I asked her to rise above these problems. I said I encounter frustrations daily that make me want to scream or lash out. Sometimes I feel I *have* to blow, but I almost never do that any more. It's wasted effort.

Saturday, June 5. The New York *Times* this morning said the whole-sale price index rose four tenths of one per cent in May and that unemployment had risen to more than six per cent. How the Administration can continue to put a hopeful face on such statistics is beyond me. The economic "game plan" is an utter fraud.

I was angered to read also that the governor of Alaska vetoed a bill that would have established an early primary. The White House, Pete told me, promised the governor anything he wanted in return for that veto.

Sunday, June 6. Al Lowenstein called this morning to say he thought we should get together. He was in town for the annual gathering of Robert Kennedy supporters at Hickory Hill. His wife Jennifer (or Droopy, as he calls her) was due to fly in this afternoon for a memorial service at Arlington Cemetery. He and an aide, Jay Jacobson, arrived about noon. Meredith took care of the salad and tuna fish sandwiches while Al talked about recent political developments.

He's facing a dilemma, he said, with respect to the anti-war rally

on Long Island next week. Gene McCarthy wants to speak and
the problem is to find some means to keep him away gracefully.
Apparently McCarthy told a reporter recently that he was glad
Lowenstein was gathering audiences that he, McCarthy, could use
for his own purposes.

We talked about other possible speakers. George McGovern is
flat on his back recovering from a hernia operation. Ed Muskie and
Birch Bayh will be speaking in Rhode Island that day. Ted Kennedy
is unwilling to accept any engagements that might suggest a candidacy. Ramsay Clark wants to avoid any activities that might
interfere with his defense of the Berrigan brothers.

Hubert Humphrey? No. Harold Hughes? Probably not the right
speaker for this crowd. It's a dilemma—with the problem further
complicated by the fact that it's Al's home territory. Al paced the
floor, racking his brain to come up with other possible speakers.
There was a long silence.

I suggested Lowenstein's driver could pick up McCarthy at the
airport and then get lost on the way to the rally. Laughter; the joke
was real—Lowenstein's drivers don't always know where they're
going. Then Al found the solution: tie the rally to the McGovern-
Hatfield end-the-war amendment, make it a rally to promote Senate
passage of that measure. Typically, McCarthy opposes McGovern-
Hatfield. He won't come for that reason.

There are some new entries in the Democratic sweepstakes. Al
said he got a call from Congressman Jim Howard of New Jersey,
who apparently began by saying that "none of the challengers are
exciting people," so "you or I should run." I told Al I thought the
Democrats would do better with *Frank* Howard of the Washington
Senators.

Monday, June 7. McCloskey's weekend trip to New Hampshire and
Rhode Island was a hectic affair, or so Dave Brunell told me this
morning. Pete kept involving himself in campaign management,
which made it impossible for Dick Rykken, his advance man, to
function properly. Dave was angry about it.

As they're starting to pull together the type of organization they
need to make a sustained challenge, they're finding that Pete himself

is the variable. It's difficult as hell to subject him to regimentation, impose any discipline on his activities, commitments and public statements.

He says, "I don't want you guys getting between me and the people. I want to talk to volunteers, give them assignments and get thoughts from them, be able to change my schedule on the spur of the moment. I don't want a campaign produced by professional politicians."

From watching McCloskey operate, I gather that there's just a certain amount of system he'll submit to. Then his instincts and emotions take over.

Wednesday, June 9. On the Capitol steps this morning, I addressed a group of federal employees opposed to the war in Vietnam. As I was waiting to be introduced, Bella Abzug joined me. She was upset about a story in today's Washington *Post* that insinuated she'd left an anti-war rally because she was angry at its organizers. In fact, she left only because some constituents were waiting in her office. "You know," she said, "I feel pretty badly about it. I'm really a very sensitive person." I put my hand on her shoulder and told her she shouldn't let things like that get to her. She's so forceful in expressing her views that most people here don't realize what a gentle, vulnerable person she is.

The man whose power within the Congress probably counts for more than all the other members put together is Wilbur Mills of Arkansas. He's the man who writes the tax bills that come out of the Ways and Means Committee; he writes them the way he wants them or they just don't come out. His power is enormous. After lunch I spotted him and asked if I could see him privately in the next day or two. Although I didn't say so, I wanted to urge him to support the Nedzi-Whalen amendment to cut off funds for the war. He was extremely gracious. "You don't need an appointment," he said, "and if you don't know that yet, well, it's time you found out. You just look me up on the floor tomorrow and we'll step off the floor and talk for as long as you need."

Later this afternoon I ran into Bill Steiger and we had a chance to chat. Both of us were twenty-eight when we first came to the Congress in January 1967, but our respective styles and adjustments have differed enormously since then. A diabetic, Bill is probably the thinnest man in the House. He's deadly serious, a tough, able "inside man" who's very much at home with the internal legislative process: the day-to-day piecemeal adjustments, the perfecting amendments, the above-average participation in the succession of floor statements on pending bills, the base-touching and necessary courtesies to senior members, the laughing at their unfunny jokes. He's a dependable team player and he's learned how to dissent occasionally without burning his bridges.

His is the chip-away method—the occasional reform of consequence, the steady, methodical attempt to make small but regular incremental impacts on the flow of legislation. It's a necessary function and it serves a useful, if limited, purpose.

In my opinion, though, that approach will not enable America to beat the train to the crossroads. A continuation of business as usual in the Congress won't help us stave off approaching disasters. We're trapped by a traditional momentum that makes it impossible for us to shift into an emergency state of mind and operation and come to grips with urgent problems.

After being here for a while, I learned what the limitations are in terms of making things happen. The legislative process is slow and has a million roadblocks in it. The seniority system plays a big part and there's almost no way a newer member can affect the shape of legislation. There's damn little you can get your hands on, make happen or influence.

Even your vote doesn't count for much. Since I've been here only one major bill has been decided by a single vote. If you try to evaluate your incremental impact, you have to decide that, unless you're Speaker, chairman of an important committee or part of the House leadership—and all these assignments are a function of seniority—you just can't have much impact on normal congressional operations.

There are three approaches you can take. The first is to play the game and be one of the boys. Essentially, that's what Steiger is doing. Avoid major controversy, get yourself re-elected time after time and accumulate power slowly. The second is to leave the House when you see the barriers to getting things done. If you're John Lindsay, you run for mayor of New York. If you're Mel Laird, you become Secretary of Defense. If you're Don Rumsfeld, you leave to head OEO. In these positions it's possible to have an incremental impact.

The third approach is to stay in the House and become an outside man. Develop ad hoc initiatives, mechanisms that lie outside the established, traditional paths. By dramatizing the public debate on some critical issues, you force the legislative and executive branches and the press to deal with realities more quickly and more honestly than they'd otherwise prefer.

Congress is really a body of followers, not leaders, and it's often necessary to build a significant public mandate to get Congress to move. Congress usually won't face up to a problem until it has to, before it's forced to. By using these outside methods to bring pressure on your colleagues, you tend to burn your bridges behind you. You can become an "outsider" within the club.

But if the country is in jeopardy and you're not prepared to try to force a change, then your political future doesn't mean anything on moral or practical grounds. It doesn't stand for anything. If you choose the role of outsider, you just can't worry about what happens to you as a consequence. That philosophy is a violation of the traditional rules around here. That's why some people think I've lost my mind.

Thursday, June 10. Nancy Dickerson of NBC came by the office at noon today. She's doing a news item on the insurgency and asked if I was Pete's campaign manager. I said no, that I was just one of many helpers. Later she asked, "Well, would you like to be Vice President?" I had to smile at that. I'm thirty-three; not old enough.

This afternoon Dave Brunell told me that Norton Simon is coming to Washington next Wednesday. I should set aside time to meet with him. Apparently Simon has said he'll consider financing a $750,000 TV package that Charles Guggenheim would pull together—if he can get answers to a few questions about Pete's campaign. He's also willing to foot the bills for the first month's operation. We'll be ready for him.

At four-thirty I left the office and drove to Sherrill's Bakery on Pennsylvania Avenue to buy a cake for Meredith's twenty-sixth birthday. A few minutes later I picked her up at her office at the Smithsonian Institution. We went to my apartment where I had just fifteen minutes to light the candles, sing "Happy Birthday," blow out the candles and share a quick piece of cake. Then I had to rush to the airport and catch a plane to Michigan. I had to give the commencement address at Carman High School in Flint tonight.

The seniors had decided that I was the person they wanted to hear; that gave me a special incentive to be as frank as possible and say some hard things that people don't particularly want to listen to. Later the graduates stepped up to receive their diplomas. One young kid was pretty far out. He may have been stoned; I don't know. Anyway, he looked at me with a distant expression and said slowly, "Hey, man, that was some heavy speech."

Tuesday, June 15. I bumped into H. R. Gross on the floor today and congratulated him on his designation as the ranking Republican on the House Post Office Committee. I told him why I insisted on a secret ballot in the Republican Conference this morning and didn't allow the unrecorded vote to be taken. He said he approved of that. He said if he'd been there, in fact, he would have requested the secret ballot himself.

This was the first time H.R. and I have ever spoken at any length. For twenty-three years he's been a maverick. He's opposed the leadership often and, as a result, he's been punished. Years ago, he said, members were more independent, more willing to oppose both party and President on matters of conscience. Today, he said, he could count on the fingers of both hands the number of men who vote their consciences in each and every instance.

H.R. is short, with heavy eyelids, and as he looked up at me from under his bushy brows he added, "You know, I made a living before I came to Congress. There are lots of things I could be doing now and the only thing that makes this job worth while is being able to say and do what I think is right."

As I was leaving the floor, I passed Leonor Sullivan in the hallway. A Democrat from Missouri, she's a distinguished, matronly woman with silver hair whose dresses are hemmed well below the knee. I noticed that she had stopped and, with an arched and critical eye, was watching a pretty young girl who was walking past in one of the shortest skirts I have ever seen. Mrs. Sullivan stood very erect, puffed up her chest and sniffed, "Why, she's showing everything she's got!" With that, she turned on her heel and stalked into the chamber.

Wednesday, June 16. Norton Simon's people phoned to say he couldn't make the meeting today. That was disappointing as hell. But they promise he'll set a new date soon.

Thursday, June 17. The guy in the Michigan delegation who keeps showing me more and more is Jim Harvey from Saginaw. I've always liked him personally, but as time passes his essential honesty and good judgment are moving him further away from the status quo positions of the other more senior Republicans. At the delegation's weekly breakfast session this morning, he sounded a strong warning about the war issue and the President's re-election chances. The real point of the discussion, however, was Nixon's handling of the Pentagon papers. Bob Griffin and Cederberg defended the President's decision to try to suppress the data. Harvey and I argued that people's faith in their government is at issue here and that it's time to give the public full access to the Vietnam material. We didn't change anyone's mind.

At ten-thirty I had an appointment with Jerry Ford in the Capitol. He was on the phone when I arrived at his office, but in two or three minutes he opened the door and ushered me to an overstuffed leather chair. Jerry said he was harried; he had to be at the House TV studio in the next fifteen minutes, so I gave him a quick runthrough of my thinking on the insurgency. I said I thought Nixon was doomed next year unless he institutes a dramatic shift in over-all policy. It isn't too late for reconciliation. But if our challenge goes forward, we'll try to force Nixon out along the way. Jerry fondled his pipe and listened attentively.

"Don't ever underestimate the capacity of a President to change the political environment," he said when I finished, "and be assured that this President will use that power as much or more than his predecessors. This President wants to be re-elected. He will do everything he possibly can to maximize his chances. All Presidents do it. This is the big leagues," Jerry continued. "Nixon has a hundred times the number of chips you do." As we moved toward the door he made a parting comment that sticks out in my memory: "Don't be too surprised if the rug is pulled out from under you."

In the men's room this afternoon I passed the Speaker, Carl Albert, who was standing at a sink with a comb in his hand. I remarked that I didn't know Speakers had time to comb their hair.

"We don't," Albert said. "All of us ought to be like Speaker Rayburn. He didn't have a hair on his head."

The floor maneuvering today on the Nedzi-Whalen amendment to the Military Procurement Act was long and inconclusive; it influenced few votes. Both Lou Nedzi, a Democrat from Michigan, and Chuck Whalen spoke effectively. Then Les Arends moved to limit all further debate. Future speakers would receive no more than two minutes. I felt ashamed and outraged that my party should be the one to stifle debate on the first direct vote this House has taken on the Vietnam war in the past ten years. I said as much when it was my turn to speak. That probably burned another bridge or two.

At one point in the proceedings I sat next to McCloskey. He was wearing a stainless steel POW bracelet which an imprisoned pilot's wife gave him recently. Listening to the debate had put him in a foul mood. He muttered under his breath, "Old men babble while young men die."

The final vote came at seven-thirty. We tallied 158 ayes—nowhere near the necessary 218, but certainly pointed in that direction. Ed Derwinski, the conservative Republican from Illinois, walked up the aisle as if to support the amendment. At the last second he turned aside, chuckling into his cupped hand at his own humor. Bella Abzug clapped and yelled, "Yea!"—letting Derwinski know she didn't want him on our side anyway.

Friday, June 18. Irreconcilible conflicts today. Because I'd already accepted some commitments in Flint, I had to miss the House session and two recorded votes. At the airport in Cleveland, I bumped into Charlie Vanik, a Democrat from Ohio. We talked about yesterday's vote on the war and I said I thought Wilbur Mills was the key to setting a cutoff date. Vanik nodded. He lunches with Mills regularly and said that Mills is serious now about the presidency. We agreed that Mills was probably giving serious thought to supporting a move to cut off funds for the war and decided to press him on this.

At a press conference in Flint, I predicted that Congress would set a cutoff date this year. The conference was well attended and the subsequent coverage was good. After lunch with some key supporters, Bob Breeden came to my hotel room for a prearranged meeting.

Bob and I first met early in 1966—and immediately hit it off. In all my campaigns no one worked any harder or more effectively than Bob—as personal adviser and fund raiser. His whole family pitched in. He's one of my closest and most trusted friends. He and his wife Bess are Donny's godparents. Slight and bespectacled at fifty-three, Bob is a successful executive, the manufacturing manager of General Motors' Buick Division. When a conversation becomes intense, he paces back and forth across the room and uses his hands to punctuate his arguments. He got to the point immediately.

I'm wrong to challenge the President, he said. What I'm doing to Nixon reminds him of what Ralph Nader's been doing to General Motors. The GM guys—and Bob is one of them—all hate Nader with a passion, so that was really strong medicine. Then, looking me straight in the eye, Bob said he may have to "oppose" me next year. That hit home and for a minute or two I had absolutely nothing to say. Here was my best, most steadfast supporter saying our partnership may be over.

My first thoughts were: "He means it; I may not be able to change his mind; this may be the issue that splits us apart." I was reminded of what was said about the Civil War: the differences were so great that they split families in half. Further conversation just then seemed futile. We shook hands quickly and Bob left.

At dusk I sat in my room and tried to prepare some remarks for this evening's high school commencement. It was a struggle. My mind was barren and kept coming back to the Breeden confrontation. I reread copies of other high school commencement addresses, but none of them seemed right.

Then came a knock on the door: Pete Kleinpell, president of the school board in Flint and a long-time supporter. Driving to the commencement, we discussed the issues and the insurgency. Then

Pete offered some advice: examine my personal situation and see if a way can't be found to patch up things with my family. I was non-committal. But he delivered his message skillfully; my affection for him deepened.

Saturday, June 19. I arrived at my father-in-law's this morning to pick up Cathy, who was to spend the day with me. We had breakfast together in a downtown restaurant. The weather was pleasant, so after breakfast we walked to the district office, holding hands along the way. There we met two people from my staff and all of us drove to the small suburban city of Davison. Periodically, I mail about 15,000 postcards to constituents announcing that I will be in a certain area at a certain time, inviting them to drop by and discuss anything that's on their minds.

We set up a card table in front of the Rexall Drug Store on Davison's main street. Business was modest but steady. A West Point appointee and his father stopped by to say thanks for my help with his application. Henry Auld, an early supporter, said there's concern about my separation. A young college grad who needed advice about applying for conscientious objector status said he'd been given the run-around by his local draft board. I agreed to look into this. An older woman said she was burdened with huge medical bills. It wasn't clear that I could find any additional help, but I promised to try. A female high school graduate said she couldn't find a job. Could I help her? I said the situation was bleak everywhere today; that was why we simply had to end the war. She didn't see any connection between the two.

On the plane to Washington this afternoon, a young General Motors executive told me of a recent internal memo ordering an across-the-board cost cut in all operating units of the company. This, he said, is going to mean numerous layoffs. I thought that if the GM planners see the economy this way, so will other corporations. That will just depress the chances for economic recovery. Breeden must have known of this cost-cutting mandate when he talked to me, but he didn't mention it. Why can't he see that Nixon's failed, that the absence of confidence is pulling the whole country down? He believes I'm making a bad situation worse by focusing attention on it.

I'm saying the situation will remain critical regardless of what I say or do.

GM's internal managers are getting whipped harder and harder, being driven by almost impossible management objectives and the external curse of Naderism. Old reference points are crumbling. With Breeden, the changing attitudes of his three children are just adding to the turmoil that he must try to understand and deal with.

Given the pressures on both of us, I'm not sure that I'll be able to reach Bob. Somehow, I've failed to reach him, let him understand my reasoning. Perhaps I haven't appreciated all the pressures that businessmen are facing. But if we fail to resolve our differences now, I wonder if we'll be able to find each other later—after the war is over.

Tuesday, June 22. This morning I answered a letter from Republican State Representative Quincy Hoffman of Applegate, Michigan. He had written to say he was "ashamed" that both of us had been "elected under the same political label." The party that I should belong to, he said, "is not legal" in Michigan; I was nothing more than "a political prostitute."

What can you say to people like that? The note I sent him won't change his mind at all. It probably won't even calm him down. It's sad to see a man so consumed by vitriol.

After lunch I called McCloskey, only to learn that FBI agents were in his office quizzing him on Daniel Ellsberg and the Pentagon papers. I dashed upstairs. Reporters and photographers jammed his anteroom. I sent him a note saying that I was outside and willing to sit in as an independent witness. His door opened a few minutes later. The FBI men shouldered their way through the crowd and disappeared down the hall. Quorum bells rang. Pete and I walked to the floor, but we still couldn't talk; reporters kept tagging along in our wake.

Later, in his office, he removed a copy of the Pentagon papers, which Ellsberg had given him, from his safe and handed them to me to read. They were carefully written and exhaustively footnoted, and I was struck by the unprincipled nature of U.S. intervention in South Vietnam, particularly our role in the coup against President Ngo Dinh Diem.

The quorum bells rang again and I rushed off to cast the first of two votes on the welfare reform measure. Then I walked across the Capitol to the Senate chamber to watch the vote on the Mansfield amendment. Griffin seemed quite harried as he voted no. Strom Thurmond hurried in, smoothing down his remaining hair, and also voted no.

Nonetheless, the measure passed, setting a nine-month deadline for American withdrawal from Vietnam pending release of the POWs. For what turned out to be an historic moment, the chamber and the gallery were surprisingly low-key. I got a copy of the amendment and hurried back to the House. Wilbur Mills was controlling the time. I told Bella Abzug and John Conyers about the result in the Senate, then mentioned it to Mills himself. He was cordial but said he had no time to yield. Bella was still scolding him because he hadn't given her a chance to speak earlier.

After the final vote on the welfare reform bill, I drove to the Washington Navy Yard. Secretary of Defense Mel Laird had invited several of us from the House for a cruise on board the yacht *Sequoia*. It was a balmy evening and as I walked through the pier gate with Garner Shriver and Burt Talcott, a Republican from California, I realized that all of this evening's guests were members of the House Appropriations Committee.

Talcott seemed uncomfortable about being seen with me and said so. He may have been kidding, but he lagged several steps behind us anyway. Shriver said, "I'm happy to walk with Riegle. We've walked around most of the world together." Talcott smiled but kept his distance.

Burt is very proper, very dignified. Soon after I came to Congress he sent a letter to all the members chastising them for being ill-mannered and ill-kempt on the House floor. There were too many guys reading newspapers, he said; too many guys slouching in their seats; too many guys wearing loud clothing. Many members made fun of this. That he would take it upon himself to write that kind of letter puzzled people here.

But that's the way Burt feels. He doesn't smoke, he doesn't drink and he's very religious. He *does* try to bend a little. If you're watching the news ticker in the Republican cloakroom, he's apt to walk up to you, smile and ask disarmingly, "How in *health* are you?" Once in a conversation with McCloskey, Burt indicated he never takes a position on a controversial issue. By doing so, he told Pete, you only create enemies. As long as there is no *requirement* to take positions on the issues, why weaken yourself unnecessarily?

Aboard *Sequoia,* young Navy men saluted smartly. The yacht was humming; it seemed presidential. On the top deck, surrounding Laird, Deputy Defense Secretary David Packard and other DOD aides, were about twenty-five of my committee colleagues. Mel was wearing a blue and yellow ascot. He seemed fully recovered from his hernia operation. We shook hands, exchanged pleasantries, then I stepped on past.

Some of my colleagues occupied the deck chairs; others were standing. Party labels do not interfere with personal friendships among the members of this committee, so the conversations were animated and friendly. Most of the members are conservative on all key issues; they've shared so many experiences that they're very much like members of a close-knit family.

As I glanced around the deck I couldn't help being conscious of the generation gap on the Appropriations Committee. Otto Passman, a Democrat from Louisiana, and others are in their seventies; most members are in their fifties and sixties, a few are in their forties, and there are only two of us still in our thirties. Then, too, by temperament and choice, most committee members are "inside" men. They labor in the bank vault of Congress, drawing their satisfaction from having a hand on the purse strings of the federal government. Other committees write laws and devise new programs—our job is to divvy up the money. This gives the subcommittee chairmen considerable power and influence. The committee itself has to work on the basis of accommodation: accommodation within the subcommittees, within the full committee; then accommodation with the Senate— and finally accommodation with the executive branch. We accommodate ourselves right down the drain.

After walking the length of the deck, I joined Laird and four colleagues in discussing the Mansfield amendment vote today. They discounted it, saying it was only "a sense of the Senate" resolution. Tactful Riegle interrupted, saying that they were wrong. The way the amendment is worded—if the President signs it into law, it will become official United States policy. Some of my colleagues disagreed, but I persisted and then asked Laird if he could safely remove our forces if the amendment did become law.

"Yes," he said. "We might have to leave some equipment behind, but we can get the people out."

The Navy enlisted men stood ready to cast off *Sequoia*'s lines. The radar antenna was revolving, the engines began to change pitch. Suddenly a car pulled up at the gate of the pier. Doc Long, a Democrat from Maryland, and Gunn McKay, a Democrat from Utah, hurried toward the yacht. *Sequoia* was just beginning to head out into the Potomac channel.

"Reverse the engines," someone yelled.

"No," Burt Talcott said. "Go ahead without them."

Sequoia returned to pick them up.

As we headed out into the Potomac again I noticed Otto Passman and John Rooney, a Democrat from New York, huddled together on the top deck aft. Cederberg, Silvio Conte, an affable Republican from Massachusetts, Laird and others had moved forward. My first drink, a martini, was so dry and powerful that it could have propelled me to Mount Vernon. On the second go-around I ordered a gin and tonic. Waiters circulated with trays of spicy hot dogs, bacon-wrapped liver bits and cheese-covered Fritos.

Mel Laird, who had left the committee to run the Pentagon, was with old chums tonight and everyone was going to enjoy nothing but the best. The dinner included roast beef, split lobster tails, browned potatoes, salad and wine, with melon balls and fresh fruit for dessert. During dinner I talked to Joe Evins, a Democrat from Tennessee, about the end-the-war amendment. Evins is chairman of one of our subcommittees, a hard-working man with a steel-trap mind. He said he sensed the public was shifting on Vietnam. Congress may have to pass a cut-off; he may have to support one.

Minutes later I caught up with Garner Shriver and Jack Flynt, who's from Georgia. Flynt was the first Deep South Democrat to oppose the war and tonight he said his only regret is that he didn't do it earlier. He and I bet a beer that Shriver will switch later this year and vote to cut off funds for the war. Flynt said he won't. I said he will.

After a run or two up the river, we steamed back to the dock. By this time Laird was in fine form as our social director. He encouraged a quartet to sing a few chords of "Let Me Call You Sweetheart." He called on George Andrews, a Democrat from Alabama, for a couple of stories and gravel-throated George, the best raconteur in Congress, obliged happily. Bob Michel, a Republican from Illinois, sang "Edelweiss" and led the chorus in beginning "When Irish Eyes Are Smiling." Finally Charlotte Reid, another Illinois Republican, gave us "September Song." She used to be the vocalist on Don McNeill's Breakfast Club.

Wednesday, June 23. The full Appropriations Committee met this morning to consider the HUD-Veterans Hospitals-NASA bill. When I arrived, twenty minutes late, Transportation Subcommittee Chairman Eddie Boland, a Democrat from Massachusetts, was explaining what the bill contained. I found an empty chair next to John Rhodes, a Republican from Arizona, in a corner of the room.

No one can accuse this committee of living in luxury. The meeting room is spartan, drab. The tables are old; so are the brown swivel chairs. Six or seven faded scenic prints look down from light green walls. This is the room where our committee divides up $200 billion each year.

Boland spoke rapidly and knowledgeably about our HUD appropriation. In the ensuing discussion Ed Patten, a white-haired, ham-fisted, former high school teacher from New Jersey, took the floor. Standing five feet ten, weighing at least two hundred and fifty pounds, he resembles the stereotype of an effusive, cigar-chewing U.S. congressman. Drawing on what he called "personal experience," he gave an impassioned description of the virtue of public housing programs.

When he finished, Boland said, "Love that boy from Perth Amboy." Friendly laughter rippled across the room.

Doc Long raised a question about the treatment of drug addicts in veterans' hospitals. Chairman George Mahon, a Democrat from Texas, was hunched over talking to Jamie Whitten, a Democrat from Mississippi. At the appropriate point, I sought recognition to ask about the funds that the subcommittee had considered to finance home-ownership counseling services for low-income families. Boland said the money was in the bill.

Charlie Jonas from North Carolina, the ranking Republican on the subcommittee, rose to present figures showing that the various federal housing programs have created obligations forty years into the future. He pointed out that with this bill we were further obligating the government to pay some $80 billion over the next forty years. His facts were sobering.

Boland completed his explanation of this very complicated bill. Mahon led the applause and there was general table-thumping. Then came a moment of conflict. Del Clawson, a conservative Republican from California, rose to offer an amendment that would strike out the money for home-ownership counseling services. His staff had uncovered a booklet describing an endless number of existing counseling agencies. Why, he asked, did we need another one?

Boland disputed Clawson, but not too energetically, so I sought recognition and urged the committee to keep the money in the bill. Counseling funds, I said, are vital to the success of the program, and I cited the difficulties we've had with the low-income housing program in my own district.

Mahon called for a show of hands. Clawson's amendment passed, 20 to 18. Sid Yates, a Democrat from Illinois, demanded a record vote and the roll call began. Most Republicans voted the way they had informally, but now that the results were going to be on the public record, some of the Democrats switched. On this second go-around, we defeated the amendment, 22 to 19. Burt Talcott challenged the tally, but it was accurate. George Andrews moved the bill for adoption by the committee; it passed and members got up to leave, having approved the expenditure in the next fiscal year of another $18 billion.

Thursday, June 24. At one point yesterday afternoon, McCloskey was talking in his office with the father of an American POW. He was talking, specifically, about the ways to persuade members of Congress to change their minds and vote for a cutoff date on the war. He began to describe what he thought happened in members' minds and as he spoke he opened a window into his own mental processes.

"The thing you have to understand about most congressmen," he said, "is that even if they're wrong they won't admit it. They'll go home at night, think about what you said and then it may be a matter of weeks before they'll change their minds."

What he was really doing, of course, was talking about himself. He's just not a guy who can easily admit to an error in judgment, even if all the facts are clear. Unless he becomes less dogged in his approach to some things, he may not survive as a candidate.

Monday, June 28. Angie Hogan, my staff assistant for federal aid programs, told me at nine o'clock this morning that I was due to testify on community schools before the District of Columbia subcommittee today at ten-fifteen sharp. I was annoyed that she hadn't told me earlier. We looked each other square in the eye; then she left to pull together all the relevant data. An hour later she returned and briefed me informally. She'd done a superb job and I had everything I thought I needed. In the subcommittee room, Chairman Bill Natcher motioned me to take a seat beside him. The room was familiar; I served on the subcommittee my first four years in the House, before being transferred to another committee.

Natcher introduced me and then, to my surprise, turned the meeting over to me. I described the history of community schools in my district—how the Mott Foundation had originally funded two pilot schools to try the Flint concept in Washington, and how the number had grown to thirteen. I told how student test scores had improved, vandalism was down, PTA membership up, and afterhour programs well attended. I urged that the funding of the program be continued—despite a general budget cutback. The coffee wagon arrived and I was vaguely conscious of someone setting a cup in front of me. For the next hour or so Bob Giaimo of Connecticut and John Myers, a Republican from Indiana, asked probing questions about the community school program, and I responded as well as I could.

At the appropriate time Natcher took charge again and systematically persuaded all the people in that room, including subcommittee members, to commit themselves on the record to the community school idea. He also committed himself to the program, as he has from the outset, and his support was vital. Natcher is a consummate craftsman, and I marveled at his skill.

Lunch in the Republican cloakroom was a stand-up affair: two hot dogs, a plate of cottage cheese and a Coke. I wolfed it down; we were debating the Mansfield amendment and I wanted a chance to speak. Armed Services Committee Chairman Eddie Hébert, a Democrat from Louisiana, controlled the time. I asked for two minutes and saw my name go on the list.

Scribbling notes on the back of an envelope, I heard Hébert call my name. I moved to the well of the House, thanked him for yielding and began to speak. The bill is reasonable, I said. It's operative only if our POWs are returned. The claim that it would undercut negotiations in Paris is a sham. Because I'd had so little time to prepare, I wasn't well organized. I didn't do any better than 6 on a 10 scale. That was pretty frustrating. Still, most members knew how they were going to vote before the debate started.

We lost by a margin of 219 to 176. John Anderson, a Republican from Illinois, spoke forcefully against the amendment. I'm really disappointed in him. That's one I won't be able to forget. At one point I was talking to Al Johnson, a conservative Republican from Pennsylvania, urging him to support a cutoff date on the war. He's not quite ready yet but is moving in that direction. Then we got into a conversation with H. R. Gross, who said flatly, "It's time we got the hell outta there." Johnson seemed very surprised and listened attentively. I'd like to think that old H.R. moved him an inch or two.

Tuesday, June 29. In the Congressional Record, I checked the vote on the Mansfield amendment. The 176 ayes included a high-water mark of 33 Republicans. Another 15 members were "paired for" and that means we're only 27 votes short of an absolute majority. Few people realize it, but we're on the verge of winning.

At three o'clock this afternoon I passed Wilbur Mills in the Rayburn Room. He stopped, shook hands and said, "I've told Eddie [Hébert], 'You've just got to bring back something on this bill.'" He was referring to the bill to extend the draft. Privately, he had urged Hébert to reach an accommodation with the anti-war advocates—and work out some kind of an end-the-war compromise with the Senate.

God damn. I wanted to scream for joy. If Mills is ready to support a cutoff date on the war, we've finally got the votes to pass it in the House. I had to fight back a sense of euphoria. I telephoned Pete. "God, that's exciting," he said.

Wednesday, June 30. This afternoon there was a Senate-House conference on the Treasury-Post Office appropriations bill. We convened on the Senate side in the old Supreme Court chamber. This was probably my tenth or eleventh conference there, so the room was familiar: the old broken clock with the hands at high noon, the large bronze eagle clutching the faded red ribbon, the four old fireplaces that used to warm the room, the old seating charts on the walls explaining who sat where when this was the Senate chamber more than a century ago, and on the charts the names of Henry Clay and Daniel Webster.

Eight House members and four senators were present. There were several items of disagreement, most of them in areas where the Senate had added money to the House-passed bill. We yielded on most of them. Our chairman was Tom Steed, from Oklahoma. Theirs was Joe Montoya, a Democrat from New Mexico. He said he had a plane to catch and he was curt, abrasive, demanding. I resented his rudeness and, at the first opportunity, challenged one of his assertions. We battled to a draw. One by one, the twenty or so items of disagreement were resolved. Finally we reached agreement. I signed the conference report and left, stopping at the cloakroom for a sandwich before walking onto the floor to listen to the debate on the HUD appropriation.

In the well, Del Clawson was offering his amendment to strike the funds for counseling services from the home-ownership program; it was the same amendment that we had defeated in the subcommittee. I walked over to Eddie Boland and said I wanted to speak against Clawson's amendment. When the time came I spoke with considerable feeling and think my remarks may have had some effect. Pete Peyser, a Republican from New York, said that I had convinced him. We defeated Clawson's amendment by just seven votes.

IV. JULY

Thursday, July 1. Mike Mansfield, the Senate majority leader, was out of his office when I called him this morning, so I left a message and went to the Foreign Operations Subcommittee to hear and cross-examine Secretary of State William Rogers. Mansfield returned my call several minutes later. He said he was free. I left the subcommittee and walked to his office on the Senate side of the Capitol. Although it was our first meeting, he was relaxed, called me "Don" and offered me a cup of coffee.

I pointed out that the House vote in favor of his cutoff amendment had not been just 176, but really 191 because of the 15 "paired" absentees. We were just 27 votes short of a majority. I thought we could set a cutoff date soon and urged him to stand firm on the amendment's language. He said he isn't about to compromise. He likes the language of his amendment, he said, and he seems pretty firm. Mills is the key in the House, I said. It seems he might be about to cross over, but he needs encouragement. Mansfield nodded and smiled.

I hurried back to the subcommittee but found our session with Secretary Rogers was an empty exercise. The House has long since abandoned its responsibility to dig into policies of the executive branch. While he can be a scrooge on specific items in the budget, Otto Passman makes it clear he has little interest in pursuing "policy" questions, and today he used the "reform" rules to effectively squelch any penetrating cross-examination of the Secretary. Under these rules, each member has just five minutes to question a witness. Then the chairman can cross-examine for as long as he wants. When the chairman is finished—if any time remains—the other subcommittee members can vie for it, according to seniority. Once the five-minute periods were exhausted, Otto used all the remaining time.

Rogers is a pleasant, unassuming man, not particularly complicated or profound. He just plugs away at his job, and things don't change very much. He's ring-wise on subcommittee appearances, however, and for him a House Foreign Ops session is a piece of cake—compared, for example, to the hostile questioning and publicity of a Senate Foreign Relations Committee meeting. Our sessions are closed to the public and press. An Administration witness can strike out any or all of his testimony before it's printed in the record. Beyond that, he knows that he isn't likely to have more than a five-minute skirmish with a contrary member. So Rogers was relaxed and agreeable. He let Otto do most of the talking. He nodded and smiled for nearly two hours and offered generalities that provided us less insight than this morning's Washington *Post*.

When my turn came to cross-examine, I thanked the Secretary for his initiatives in the Middle East, then asked immediately about his testimony before the subcommittee last year, which had been stricken verbatim from the public record. Rogers had appeared before us six days prior to the U.S. move into Cambodia. At that time he had indicated, rather forcefully, that the U.S. was not contemplating sending troops into Cambodia. He had said emphatically that such a move would "destroy our Vietnamization program."* If circumstances changed, he added, and the Administration decided to enter Cambodia, either he or someone else would surely inform Congress in advance—and seek congressional authorization.

Six days later the U.S. did precisely what Rogers had said the U.S. wouldn't do. The Congress had been misled. So this morning I read portions of last year's classified transcript aloud and asked

* While this direct quotation was officially classified—and deleted from the public record—another subcommittee member, Clarence Long of Maryland, released the quote to the press, thereby making it a matter of public record.

Rogers why his testimony had been so unreliable. Then I asked, "Has sufficient time passed for this material to be declassified and printed in the record?"

Passman fidgeted and came to the Secretary's defense. That testimony should remain classified, he said. It was necessary to protect "national security."

I continued to press Rogers, asking for explanations. He smiled and hemmed and hawed and offered only vague and indirect responses.

"The gentleman from Michigan," Passman interrupted, "has now consumed *seven* minutes."

Rogers knew my time was up and that I'd have no further chance to cross-examine him this year. He smiled at Passman appreciatively.

Sunday, July 4. It promised to be a beautiful day in Washington, and I wanted to loaf. But I had to fly to Michigan. En route, I noticed a squib in the paper to the effect that Nixon has nominated Charlotte Reid to the Federal Communications Commission. This will take away one more senior Republican from the Appropriations Committee and move me up a notch. More important, I'll now be the second-ranking Republican on the Foreign Ops Subcommittee. The seniority system grinds forward inexorably.

Two young men on my district staff, Bob Niles and Jim Gordon, met me at the airport and during our drive to Flint gave me some early results of a poll we've been conducting. There is some dissatisfaction with me among hard-core Republicans. That means a probable primary challenge next year.

We drove to Fenton for the Fourth of July parade. Before it started we stopped at a Stuckey store for a chili dog and a Coke. The counter girls recognized me, so we signed them up as volunteers for 1972. I always walk in the Fenton parade on Independence Day, crisscrossing the street, shaking hands. The weather was hot, muggy and overcast, so this year's parade attendance was modest.

There was a pretty good number of smiles and waves, a few outbursts of applause along the two- or three-mile route. I also sensed some reserve, but I was determined to keep walking and, in effect, back up my statements and positions with my physical presence. If people wanted to disagree, they could do it in person. I could think of only four or five hundred things I'd rather be doing today.

Monday, July 5. In this morning's mail came a letter from an anonymous fan in Los Angeles: "Keep shooting your goddamn mouth off about President Nixon, you bastard, and you and that other political pimp McCloskey are going to get your teeth knocked out. You're both fronts for that lying murderer, Kennedy. Since William Douglas is against the death penalty, I hope he gets his throat slashed from ear to ear."

Wednesday, July 7. There was a meeting for key McCloskey campaign people in Pete's office this morning. All agreed that Pete should announce his candidacy in California Friday. We need to stop the tide of new voter registrations going to the Democrats, and only a formal candidacy can begin to pull some of these new voters to the Republican side. Unless Pete is in to stay, we're going to have trouble attracting funds and volunteers. Then, too, the momentum of this "inside" campaign has evolved into the sort of challenge that needs a declared candidate.

Pete was attentive but edgy. The events he's set in motion have reached the inevitable point of requiring a clear decision from him. Obviously he still resents having to face two gut issues that make him uncomfortable. There is the question of his congressional seat. Should he abandon it for the presidential challenge? Despite his frustrations here, he loves the Congress; the last month has been particularly rewarding for him and the thought of leaving Congress isn't appealing at all. He knows the rug can be pulled out from under his presidential bid any time, in which case he'd like to stay on and press the fight in Congress.

Also, Pete is troubled by his belief that declaring for President sounds "arrogant." He was self-effacing on this point and said he wished he'd had more experience. He's still not confident enough in his grasp of the issues to be able to come right out and ask people to make him President. He has a low opinion of Nixon and believes he could outperform him. Still, instead of measuring himself against Nixon, Pete insists on measuring himself against the ideal, "the kind of man who ought to be President." This humility, this sense of limitation, is one of his most attractive features. But it promises trouble, too.

The meeting accomplished its purpose. Pete agreed to declare for New Hampshire and California on Friday. He will be non-committal on the other primaries. It's not a flat-out dash for the nomination. It's a measured, limited challenge. Privately, Pete told me that he thinks September would be about the right time to say that he is going to stay in the race regardless of what Nixon does. And he was encouraged about the session he had with Norton Simon the other day. Originally scheduled back in June, that session was postponed twice. But Simon finally came and made some financial commitments.

As today's meeting was breaking up, Dick Rykken asked why these sessions always had to proceed as if the staff were the enemy. Pete replied that he believes in "the adversary procedure of coming at each other." This method, he said, tends to produce the best results. I wondered if he recognized that it also drains morale.

Later this afternoon I learned that Eddie Hébert had vowed that no end-the-war date would come out of the draft-extension bill conference committee—not while he was serving as chairman of Armed Services. The more I thought about this, the more enraged I became. Who the hell is he to block the setting of a date? Nearly eighty per cent of the American people, the polls say, want a date set for our troops to leave Vietnam. So do 191 members of this House. Why should more young men have to die because Hébert says so?

Suddenly I felt an urge to smash Hébert in the face. To know that such feelings are flowing through me is disturbing and depressing.

I'm sure that from time to time other members have felt the same way about each other—perhaps even as a result of something I have done—but it's rare that they try to vent their frustrations physically. The last reported fist fight here occurred in 1963 between Ed Foreman, a Republican from Texas, and Henry Gonzalez, a Democrat from the same state. It started when Foreman, who was extremely conservative, charged that Gonzalez' voting record was ultra-liberal and left wing and furthered "the Socialist-Communist cause." Gonzalez was very upset. He confronted Foreman in the Speaker's lobby and reportedly socked him on the shoulder. "My fist went into him three inches, he's so soft," Gonzalez told reporters later. "I asked him to take off his glasses, but he wouldn't. In fact he put on his glasses as soon as he saw me coming. I'd still like to have it out with him man for man, but he's a *jate*—that's Spanish for a yellow-livered sissy."

Foreman was a husky six-footer who weighed about two hundred pounds and had played football in college. He was anything but a sissy and afterward he explained that he didn't believe in settling differences with his fists.

Thursday, July 8. There was a full Appropriations Committee hearing today· on the transportation bill, but it produced nothing spectacular. Silvio Conte and Bob Giaimo squabbled about the funding for air traffic control operations. Someone kidded Doc Long about the money in the bill for a subway system in Baltimore. Long had fought subway money for Washington, D.C. Doc rose and replied that he also opposed the funds for Baltimore in this bill. He has a curious mannerism of hooking his little finger in the corner of his mouth and sucking on it, running his tongue slowly past it. Other members joke about this, but never to his face.

Saturday, July 10. I drove to McLean this morning and signed the financial settlement, then signed and initialed each page and each modification. I felt shell-shocked. It was hard to realize that the neat stack of papers had any relation whatsoever to the long, difficult months of discussion and compromise. Nancy and I talked about the kids, visitation schedules, and it occurred to me that I need to buy a hide-away bed for my apartment.

Laurie and Donny were waiting in the car for me when I left the house. We stopped at Dulles Airport—Donny's big on planes —then at my office and finally at the park behind the Longworth Building. The water looked so inviting that I encouraged the kids to wade in. They splashed around until a Capitol policeman came by and asked them to stop. "That water," he said, "is full of germs."

Back in McLean, we played catch on the front lawn for a while. At five o'clock I kissed the kids good-by, held them and told them to have a safe trip driving to Michigan with their mother Monday morning.

Monday, July 12. I couldn't sleep last night. I kept thinking of the kids piling in that car and driving off to Michigan. It's a trip we've often made together. On the spur of the moment this morning, I decided to return to McLean, say my good-bys once again and, if possible, help load the car for the trip to Flint. I took a brown bag and filled it with candy, Crackerjack, fruit and some baseball trading cards I've been saving for Laurie. Then I got into my car and arrived at the house about seven o'clock.

Their car was already gone. I knocked at the front door but knew instinctively that I had missed them. I sat on the steps for a while thinking they might return, but of course they didn't. I drove slowly through McLean hoping to spot them at a gas station. At that hour, most of the stations were closed. I didn't see anyone. At eight-thirty I returned to my apartment and put the brown bag in the cupboard.

On the House floor this afternnon, McCloskey engaged in a special order debate about the Indochina war with Charles Gubser, a conservative Republican from California. I've urged Pete to ignore Gubser and not even give him the time of day. I warned him that Nixon hopes he'll spend his time battling the Gubsers of the world. But Pete wouldn't listen. Gubser had come into his district and attacked him personally. He was determined to meet the challenge head on.

It was a stacked-deck situation. Each man had an hour to speak, but Gubser retained the right to speak last and he demagogued his way around all of McCloskey's arguments. Conservatives cheered Gubser's performance and guffawed every time he drew blood.

Pete was tough and stood his ground, but he was trying to play the game by gentlemanly rules. Gubser wasn't, and Pete's staff people in the gallery were dying a thousand deaths. I spoke to them later and told them not to let what had happened discourage them. No real damage had been done and the lesson that all of us had to learn from this was to avoid stacked decks in the future. The House chamber, I said, isn't the relevant battleground. We will win or lose this fight in the primaries.

Tuesday, July 13. The House voted this afternoon against a proposal to censure Dr. Frank Stanton of CBS for refusing to give the Interstate and Foreign Commerce Committee the "out-takes" of the controversial TV show called "The Selling of the Pentagon." In doing so, it rejected the advice of Committee Chairman Harley Staggers, a Democrat from West Virginia. This was a meaningful victory; still, the anti-media feeling that pervades the House is worrisome to me. The members who wanted to censure CBS—181 of them—yelled out their votes; their spite for the networks stops just short of hatred.

Later, on the floor, the Gubser-McCloskey "debate" continued. At one point Gubser's demagoguery was just too much to bear. I asked McCloskey to yield and, when he did, challenged Gubser to join us in asking the Defense Department for official photographs of villages in Laos that U.S. bombs have devastated.

He tried to slide away from making a commitment on that, so I interrupted him and asked him to say—yes or no—whether he would assist in our quest for the pictures. We battled back and forth on this. Finally, showing his anger, Gubser said yes, he would. His tactics drew some snickers from the spectators' gallery and that just provoked him even more. After my exchange with him, I had to leave the floor. Listening to a man like that—and not being able to do much about it—is just too frustrating.

Wednesday, July 14. I had to speak to a Detroit Rotary Club luncheon today and it wasn't until my plane touched down at Metropolitan Airport that I realized I'd left my wallet back in the apartment. My pockets contained just twenty cents. I promptly splurged a dime on the Detroit *News*.

The Rotary Club turnout was good. Between four and five hundred members had come to the luncheon in the Detroit Hilton and I couldn't see any empty chairs. I skipped eating in order to polish my remarks. By tradition, Rotary speeches end at one-thirty sharp. I began at twelve fifty-three and finished right on the button.

The applause was adequate, no more. Later, probably a dozen Rotarians offered compliments. But John Nagel, an old friend and financial supporter, didn't even say hello. One of the men at the head table told me afterward that John was troubled about some things, including the length of my hair. He was serious. John owns a brass company. He's a strait-laced man, a fiscal conservative, but he's always been with me in the past. I can't afford to lose supporters like John and Gladys Nagel, especially for a reason like the length of my hair. And it isn't even *that* long.

I was hungry by the time I reached the airport and had some time to spare, so I decided to grab a sandwich. Then I remembered that I had only one dime in my pocket. I went to the candy counter, but everything there cost fifteen cents. There was nothing for a dime.

Thursday, July 15. At this morning's Michigan delegation breakfast, Jerry Ford made a curious comment. He stops at the White House every day to talk to Nixon or his advisers. "Something's up over there," Jerry said. "Something special."

Later, in the House bank, I bumped into Charlie Vanik, from Ohio, and we got into a conversation about the Maryland shore. Occasional two-day excursions there with his family save his sanity, he said, and he urged me to try one myself. I guess I wasn't hard to convince. Early this evening I set out for Ocean City. I needed to get away from this place and feel the sun again.

Friday, July 16. President Nixon announced on television last evening that he had accepted an invitation to visit mainland China sometime before May 1972. It's a bold, encouraging move.

Sunday, July 18. Late this afternoon, Meredith and I drove around Capitol Hill and looked at funky old houses. We stopped and walked around several neighborhoods. In one we found a large gray and white old English sheep dog. Meredith loves shaggy dogs, especially ones that can't see. Maybe she identifies with them. Her whole family is nearsighted. Meredith got her first pair of glasses when she was nine and she remembers driving home and noticing separate leaves on trees for the first time. Before, they had just blended into a green blob. When she put on her glasses at the dinner table, she also noticed moles on her father's face. That was a huge shock for her.

Monday, July 19. A lady promoting the school prayer amendment stopped by the office this morning and we discussed its pros and cons for half an hour or more. She wanted a commitment from me for her newsletter, which I was not prepared to give.

Sitting alone this humid evening in the living room of my apartment, I started thinking about the job and where I stand after nearly five years here. In some respects, it seems that I've been here too long. My initial enthusiasm and idealism have long since been tempered by the frustrating realities of day-to-day existence. The constraints are hard and mean and making the right thing happen is damn near impossible.

Had I been here longer, the seniority system would have provided some additional influence. But increased influence in the House isn't really the answer. Suppose I became chairman of the Appropriations Committee tomorrow morning. I could load up Flint with federal projects. That's about the size of it, though. As chairman, I still couldn't turn the country in a new direction. That's why my thoughts keep returning to McCloskey and presidential politics. That one man at the top has a potential to lead and inspire that no other figure or organization can possibly match. The right idea expressed by the President at the right time and in the right way may be worth all the votes that I could cast in this House in the next forty years.

And so, I'm not quite sure what to do just now. I'm wondering how best to gather my talents and resources and channel them into the most productive avenues. Essentially, I'm groping for direction.

The McCloskey campaign offers part of the answer. But only part. Ending the war, pushing voter registration, helping the elderly— so many of these crying needs extend so far beyond the boundaries of a single campaign.

Much of my restlessness and sense of drift stems, of course, from the great changes in my personal life. I'm not the upward-bound, goal-directed hotshot that I used to think I was. I guess that what's occurred to me—and to so many others, as well—is the fact that, so often, winning is losing. Either the compromises you have to make to achieve your goal wind up destroying you or you find when you finally reach that goal that it's far too late to do anything about the issues that used to motivate you.

So often the tangible signs of success—elaborate offices, expensive cars and lavish homes—just don't mean anything by themselves. Getting them and having them guarantees nothing. That's why it's so sad to see people abandon their values in order to reach their material goals.

Much of the blame, it seems to me, rests with our educational system. So little of what I learned in school focused on the individual, on his need to develop a clear, calm, balanced sense of self, to think freely and pursue those things that *really* interest him. Too often, it was a lock-step exercise. Usually there was just one answer to a problem and it was *their* answer. The turmoil in the country today shows how relevant their answers have become.

Tuesday, July 20. After a vote on the House floor to establish a Joint Committee on the Environment, I walked back to the Longworth Building and stepped into McCloskey's office. Pete had been "delayed" somewhere, a secretary said, but Al Lowenstein was there. We grabbed each other behind the neck and half hugged each other. Special friendships are rare and beautiful things.

When Pete arrived, Lowenstein chided him about his performance on "Meet the Press" last Sunday. "Issue-wise," he said, "I thought your candidacy was blooming. Now I gather it isn't."

Pete replied that he'd probably spent too much time discussing the war. The show's ground rules, however, had kept him from straying too far away from the question. And moderator Larry Spivak had warned him beforehand to be "brief and to the point." Al said he had received a similar warning before his own appearance, but he had ignored it and instead followed Robert Kennedy's advice. "Keep talking," Kennedy had once told him. "Get off their questions quickly and get onto the points you want to make. You can't talk to twenty million people every day."

I never met Robert Kennedy, although we passed each other one day on a small stairway in the Savile Book Store in Georgetown. I almost introduced myself but hesitated, and the moment passed. It never came again.

Thursday, July 22. The full Appropriations Committee met this morning to consider the HEW bill. Subcommittee Chairman Dan Flood, a Democrat from Pennsylvania, was ten minutes into explaining this rather complicated measure by the time I arrived. Nearing seventy, Dan is thin; he's had several serious operations and often seems to be in great pain. Nonetheless, he's smart and witty and ranks as one of our most entertaining members. He's the only member to sport a pencil-thin waxed mustache. He still retains the bearing and manner of the Shakespearean actor he once was. And I could tell that he was in very good form today.

One section of the bill appropriated money to combat alcoholism. Flood said he was "concerned" about the problem but thought the measure as written probably allocated sufficient funds to deal with it. "I had an uncle who went up San Juan Hill every day," he said, "years before Teddy Roosevelt ever heard of the place." There was a pause to acknowledge the appreciative chuckles. "He was a drunk, an alcoholic." Pause. "I've seen these things and there's enough money in this bill to do something about it."

Working from a sheaf of typewritten notes, Flood reviewed each item on his list, defending the choices his subcommittee had made. "I've been in subcommittees," he said, "where we've had blood all over the floor. This is no game for boys."

Glenn Davis, a Republican from Wisconsin, began coughing uncontrollably. He had choked on a piece of cellophane from his cigar wrapper. In one corner of the room, Charlie Jonas from North

Carolina was talking softly with a staff member. Burt Talcott and Garner Shriver huddled in another corner. Doc Long stepped into the room and walked to an empty chair.

Flood began discussing the funds in the bill for venereal disease control. "Now we're picking up," someone muttered under his breath.

"Gonorrhea is absolutely rampant," Flood declared. He said it again for emphasis. "Now you'd better be careful."

Laughter rippled through the room.

"Okay," Flood said. "Okay. But you'll be laughing out of the other side of your mouth after another seven days."

John Rooney, a short, tough member from Brooklyn, stepped into the hearing room and found a seat in front. An aging Napoleon.

"Don't tinker with these numbers," Flood was saying, more seriously now. He moved on to cancer control and referred to Nixon's sudden decision to spend $100 million in fighting the disease next year. "I have spies," Flood said. "I have spies. How else do you think I know what's going on? And my spies tell me that the first draft of the President's speech didn't contain a word about cancer. Not one word. Then, bam, $100 million for cancer."

Throughout the morning Flood chuckled, exhorted, warned, scolded and pleaded. Finally he was nearing the end. "The total for this bill," he said, "is $20,364,746,000." He turned to Bob Casey, a Democrat from Texas. "Do you hear that, Casey?" He repeated the figure. "Do you think we're moth-eaten, hunched-back chiselers? We're up two and a half billion since last year." Then he added sarcastically, "You want to add another $500 million? We have another thirty minutes here. Why not add a billion?"

He paused to let the figure sink in. No one challenged him. Flood smiled. "There are no magic numbers," he said. "Houdini couldn't do it, couldn't pick the right numbers. So the Lord asked Flood to do it."

Then he added in the various trust fund amounts: Social Security, railroad retirement and the like. He came to a grand total. "Eighty-three billion in the bill," he said. "It's bigger than Defense. You hear that? HEW is bigger than Defense."

At one point in Flood's presentation, Doc Long rose to question him about some funds for a research project in Maryland. Flood gave him assurances that he needn't worry; the problem would be solved. But when Bob Michel from Illinois made the minority presentation, Long stood up again. He asked the same questions and sought the same reassurances.

After the meeting I passed John Rooney on the floor of the House. He was miffed about Long's discourtesy in not accepting Flood's word. Just then Long walked up to us. Rooney stopped him and gave him a passionate tongue-lashing. He had never seen such a discourtesy, he said, in all his years in this House. A few minutes later I asked Rooney if he thought Long had gotten the message.

"You know," Rooney said, "we always have trouble with those professor types during committee sessions." He shook his head. "Professor types," he mumbled again, and went on his way.

Saturday, July 24. Late in the morning I picked up Donny and brought him back to the apartment. The high point of our time together came when we took a shower. Donny's had a fear of showers, of getting his head under the water. But he seemed anxious to give it another try, so we peeled off our clothes and stepped under the tap. The water was warm, not hot, and I made sure that the spray wasn't too strong. I told him to watch as I soaped and rinsed myself. Then we changed places. He backed his little fanny into the stream of water slowly. It felt so good to him that pretty soon he straightened up, let the water hit his shoulders and run down his back. When we finished with our showers we were clean and happy. I couldn't remember anything I'd enjoyed doing more. Donny was lyrical.

Monday, July 26. There were no votes on the floor today, so I worked in the office on odds and ends. In midmorning I received word from Flint that my uncle Clarence had died. I tried several times to call my aunt, but her line was busy. I did call Mother and talked with her for some time.

Tuesday, July 27. At three o'clock this afternoon a constituent of mine, Bob Williams, stopped by my office. He makes plastic pipe and his company's sales have zoomed from ground zero in 1964 to almost $18 million last year. Today his firm, Genova Products, is Genesee County's second largest employer—second only to General Motors. Trim, tanned and smiling at fifty, a born marketeer who talks with his hands, Bob is one of those rare men who have a sure sense of the public mood. He's one of my strongest backers in a shrinking circle of financial contributors.

Earlier, he had asked me to arrange a meeting with John Dingell, a Democrat from Michigan. He said he thought that Dingell, an important subcommittee chairman, might be "anti-plastic pipe" and wanted the chance to persuade him otherwise. Dingell was courteous; he and Bob had a direct and useful exchange of views. I thanked John for taking the time.

Back in my office Bob leaned forward on his chair and—as if he were grabbing opportunity out of the air—urged me to keep slugging. Most of the people are with me, he said; the hard-core Republicans will understand that later. He feels that Griffin is a "dead duck" and that I should challenge him in the primary. Bob is a winner in business and his approach to politics is the same: fight to win. Running "sure losers" galls and frustrates him.

I mentioned my recent conversation with Breeden, repeated his comment that he may have to oppose me next year and confessed that I don't really know what to do about that. Bob thinks that perhaps the best way for me to get through to Breeden is to point out that the destruction of the Republican Party would necessarily mean the end of the competitive free enterprise system. Breeden still supports me, Bob thought; I haven't burned *all* my bridges there.

Later this afternoon, on the floor of the House, Al O'Konski took me aside and told me that the Senate-House draft bill conferees have reached a tentative secret accord. They will take the "date certain" out of the Mansfield amendment and make it "the sense of the Congress" that the President should announce a date for final U.S. withdrawal from Vietnam at the earliest practicable date following the release of all POWs. Apparently the White House has agreed to this. A few days after next October's elections in South Vietnam, Nixon will announce a final withdrawal date.

This was big news, and it seemed essential that I tell Pete as soon as possible. I tracked him down in the Rayburn Building speaking to some interns from Princeton. When he finished we walked back to the floor together. On a pledge of secrecy, I repeated what O'Konski had said. Pete has expected something like this. He gave me a tough half-smile and it was clear to me then that he's in the race to stay.

Wednesday, July 28. Meredith and I talked about funerals last night—apropos of my flight today to Flint for Uncle Clarence's funeral. Neither of us wants one, each preferring a simple memorial service instead. I said that I want mine to take place outside, probably in a park. It should last no more than fifteen minutes and consist of two parts. The first would be some brief remarks I'd have written beforehand on the beauty of life and an appeal for those present to savor life and try to help others. Meredith smiled. "A little speechifying at your own service?"

I chuckled and said that I'd like to have Dave Brunell read the remarks. The second part of the service would be musical—probably a song from *The Sound of Music*. (Meredith wrinkled up her nose at that.) Then everyone would leave. No shrouded rooms or funeral flowers and no futile gloom. Instead, a fresh-air service with the sun shining down; one or two uplifting thoughts and it would be over.

I thought about that discussion this morning as I was flying to Flint. I knew Uncle Clarence's funeral would be a rerun of others I remembered well: those of my maternal grandparents and my great-grandmother. All took place at a drab funeral home on Third Avenue: the same room with the same odors, the same solemn funeral attendants, the same hushed family gathering. The only time the whole family gets together today is at funerals or weddings. There haven't been many weddings lately.

In many respects my mother's family was permanently scarred by the Depression and World War II. This big land of opportunity just missed them, passed them by—and hundreds of thousands of others like them. They came from the farm to the city and life in the city was lean and hard. Both Aunt Eunice and Uncle Clarence deserved more than they received. I guess I'm bitter about that.

Thursday, July 29. At six-thirty this evening eight of my summer interns arrived at my apartment for an informal dinner of tacos, refried beans, salad and cheesecake. I extended the invitation because I thought this might be my last chance to spend some relaxed hours with them. The House was still in session considering the public works appropriations for fiscal year 1972. But I knew that, living just four blocks from the Capitol, I could rush over to vote when it was necessary. As it turned out, I had to leave three times during the meal.

At one point Joe Loveland, a student at the University of North Carolina, asked me a searching question about McCloskey's values. Unfortunately I had to leave before I could answer him. The vote was on final passage and as I was leaving the floor I bumped into Pete. I mentioned Joe's question and urged him to come back to the apartment and answer it himself. We ran through the rain to my car. The interns were absolutely floored to see McCloskey in the flesh.

For the next forty-five minutes Pete talked about himself, his values and experiences, his reasons for challenging Nixon. He mentioned the great influence that the life of Oliver Wendell Holmes had on him and compared the famous jurist's wartime experiences with a few of his own. During the Korean War, for example, his platoon was taking enemy rifle fire from a small village. He was ordered to call in air strikes. After the planes had made a series of bombing and strafing runs, he and his men entered the village. The enemy riflemen had already slipped away. Of the eighty villagers who had chosen to remain, fifty were dead or badly wounded, most of them women and children. Pete said he realized then what an air war did to civilians.

Friday, July 30. I called Bob Breeden this afternoon. We agreed that we needed to spend some uninterrupted hours together and settled on September 5. I told Bob of my deep personal feeling for him and said it was separate and apart from our political relationship. I said I felt it was worth it to keep struggling until we can again understand each other as friends. He obviously wants to reach me as much as I want to reach him. He agreed, so we will. One thing I must do on the fifth is *listen* to him. I must not concentrate so hard on defending my own positions that I prevent Bob from stating his.

This was the day of the vote on whether the government should guarantee a loan to rescue Lockheed Aircraft from its financial troubles. There were some early parliamentary skirmishes and procedural maneuvers, but it wasn't until late afternoon that the House got down to business. The final vote was very close. The chamber was hushed so everyone could hear each response. Several members kept running tallies on the backs of envelopes.

After the first roll-call vote, the nays were ahead by two. As the clerk began calling the remaining names again, activity picked up on the floor. Jerry Ford was moving about, looking for potential switches, trying to glean additional votes. Majority Leader Hale Boggs, a Democrat from Louisiana, was doing the same thing on the other side of the aisle. Then I noticed something very interesting.

Bill Steiger hadn't answered on the first roll-call vote. Yet he had been standing on the floor and obviously had heard his name called. Bill is a party man; he's careful to play the game by the established rules. He knew the Lockheed loan wouldn't be popular in his district. Hence he wanted to vote against it. But at the same time he's close to the Republican leadership. They wanted him to vote aye. So he intended to vote for the loan only if it developed that one or two votes were needed to pass it. He'd go with the party and thereby earn the leadership's gratitude. Either way, he'd score numerous brownie points.

The clerk was completing the second calling of the roll. "Steiger of Wisconsin." Again Bill didn't answer. The vote was a virtual dead heat. Plainly, the issue was going to be decided in the well of the House—the open space between the members' seats and the raised Speaker's platform. Once the roll has been called twice, those who haven't yet voted or who wish to change their votes can stand in the well and be recognized for that purpose. Because the Democrats control the House, the Democratic side of the well is the first to be "cleared." Democrats are recognized before Republicans—and women are recognized before men.

When the Democrats had voted, the clerk turned toward the dozen or so Republicans who were waiting to be recognized. Steiger was standing in the far corner of the well so he could vote at the end of the line and be absolutely certain that his vote was needed. Because the leadership of both parties wanted this bill to pass, announcement of the final vote result by the Speaker, Carl Albert, was going to be delayed. That would give Hale Boggs, Jerry Ford and Les Arends more time to round up additional votes.

At this point, only four or five members remained in the well. The margin of ayes was big enough to let Steiger vote no, and with a look of obvious relief on his face, that's exactly what he did. The bill passed by three votes, 192 to 189.

Saturday, July 31. Today I had to make an in-and-out trip to the district. The morning flight to Detroit was smooth enough and Bob Niles was waiting at the airport gate to drive me to Flint. After a stop at the district office, I left for my scheduled round of "office hours" at area shopping centers.

At the Dort Mall shopping center I noticed that increasing numbers of individual blacks are coming to me with personal problems. That's encouraging. Most whites can't comprehend how hard it is for most black people to approach a white person, especially a white politician, and confide anything. Such is the record of white indifference—if not treachery—that even in 1971 it takes a long time to break through.

I noticed, too, that there is serious concern about the economy. Unemployment is high in the district. One mother told me she has a job but is barely paying her bills. Her two teen-age children want to work; they just can't find jobs. She said she doesn't want to go on the welfare rolls but feels there's no alternative. There was also an unemployed Vietnam veteran and a county health worker who had been let off after six years on the job. Both were bitter. The most depressing case of all was a seventy-four-year-old woman who arrived with her dependent daughter. A proud, self-reliant woman, she had come in desperation. She said she received $141 a month in social security and a hospital pension of $26. She and her daughter couldn't make ends meet any longer. As she spoke the tears ran down her face. Later, I told the district office staff to keep working on her case until we found her some additional income.

At Dort Mall there was substantial anti-Nixon sentiment. Three lifelong Republicans told me they wouldn't vote for him again. At Swartz Creek there were many retirees concerned about rising property taxes. At Flushing, a young AWOL serviceman asked for help in getting things straightened out with the Army.

Back in Flint, I met with the Black Republican Action Movement at the home of Bob Jackson, a high school friend and football teammate. Nancy West of my district staff heads the group. Its members are interested in finding more black candidates to run as Republicans. Finally, I had to leave for the airport to catch the 7:50 flight to Washington. I made it with five minutes to spare.

V. AUGUST

Monday, August 2. The AP and UPI ticker tape machines stand about twenty yards apart from each other in the Speaker's lobby off the floor of the House. They print a constant flow of news items on long white sheets of paper. Periodically, these sheets are taken from the machines and hung from a long wooden board. Late this afternoon, there was an angry buzz as several members stood by that board and read an item coded "UPI-48 (Dellums)."

Milwaukee—Rep. Ronald V. Dellums, D.Cal., says he thinks most Senators and Congressmen "are mediocre prima donnas who pass legislation that has nothing to do with the reality of misery in this country. The level of mediocrity of the leaders in the country scares the hell out of me," Dellums said Sunday.
   Dellums said both parties "are just opposite sides of the same coin" in Washington and charged that it was the lobbyists and not Congressmen who run the nation.

Doc Morgan, a Democrat from Pennsylvania, was standing next to me. He's chairman of the House Foreign Affairs Committee and also a practicing physician who somehow manages to treat patients in his district two days a week. A large man, he looked at me and with a half-smile asked, "You think he's talking about you or me?"
   "Probably both of us," I said.

Wednesday, August 4. This was the day for the vote on the Draft Bill Conference Report. I was opposed to the final compromise. The

Senate-House conferees had taken the "date certain" out of the Mansfield amendment and watered it down in other ways as well. I don't think it's right to require men to fight in wars that are not declared. One hundred eight of us voted against the bill, but we lost by a lopsided margin. As a result, 15,300 servicemen will be sent to Vietnam this month and the draft will be extended for another two years.

On the floor this afternoon Charlie Diggs, a Democrat from Detroit, intercepted me to say that he had heard feedback from Lansing about a new redistricting plan that the state legislature is considering. It would require incumbent members to run at-large state-wide. He'd heard that the conservatives in Lansing felt they could eliminate me this way. They didn't think I'd fare well in a state-wide Republican primary.

That was the first I'd heard of the plan and I told Diggs that I thought it would probably backfire. But it was interesting to learn that I had Republican enemies in the state legislature. My friend Quincy Hoffman is probably leading the pack.

Saturday, August 7. Meredith and I drove over to play tennis at Langley High School in Virginia this afternoon. She's trying to make me feel thirty-three again. When we arrived at the courts, however, we found that the gate was locked. She was skinny enough to wriggle through; the little fat boy had to climb over the fence.

Sunday, August 8. The House began its summer vacation last Thursday and this is a week that I'm going to spend with the children. I picked them up in McLean this afternoon and noticed immediately that Donny was having a delayed reaction to an automobile accident he'd been in last week. He kept thinking of reasons why I should stop the car: he'd forgotten something; there was a stop sign just ahead; wouldn't it be fun to stop and get out here? He stood behind me in the back seat and I could see his face in the rear-view mirror. He was watching the traffic intently. I stopped the car four or five times and tried to reassure him.

When I was seven years old our house in Flint burned down and our family barely escaped. Before the fire trucks left the scene, a mailman arrived and handed my father his draft induction notice.

The evening after the fire, I was so frightened that I kept begging for permission to sleep at the fire station. I nagged my father, then nagged him again. Finally he just exploded. Because I remember my own sense of terror so vividly, I knew what Donny was feeling today.

Tuesday, August 10. Early this afternoon we drove from Washington to Ocean City, Maryland. We spent an hour at the beach, another hour at a nearby amusement park. Then we found a miniature golf course. Laurie took an early lead. Jumping about like an acrobat, she led all the way, although toward the end Cathy produced two shrieking holes-in-one. After the match was over I gave Cathy the standard speech on how it was great to win but that the real thrill came from playing the game, doing one's best, win or lose. Cathy conceded that. But the real issue, she told me, was "losing to an eight-year-old little sister." I could see her point.

While Cathy and Laurie are highly competitive, they occasionally work as a team. Playing in the breaking waves and trying some of the scarier rides at the amusement park, they helped and supported each other. I was pleased about that. Most of the time, however, Laurie feels that she should match her twelve-year-old sister stride for stride, and Cathy resents any encounter where Laurie's abilities exceed her own. The rivalry is sometimes a little wearying, but I know they'll work it out as they grow older.

Wednesday, August 11. I heard on the radio today that John Lindsay has switched parties and become a Democrat. I feel bad that he left without making a fight of it. He never issued a direct challenge on behalf of the liberal Republican point of view he represented. With his media credibility, he was the guy best positioned to force Nixon to modify some of his policies. But he had special problems to deal with, including the fact that he lost the Republican nomination in his last race for mayor. I could appreciate his dilemma. I'm sorry he's gone—he's a good man and the fight will be tougher without him.

Thursday, August 12. I talked with Tom DeFrank of *Newsweek* today about a story he's writing on Lowenstein's voter registration effort. I made the point that it's more than a "Dump Nixon" drive or an alternative to "revolution"; it's really an attempt to win the allegiance and commitment of a new generation of young people to the idea of self-government. If we lose this generation through cynicism and loss of faith, then we'll probably have lost the chance for meaningful democracy in the years ahead.

Later, at my apartment, Donny and I were lying on the bed and I noted that he would be returning to his mother tomorrow. He seemed to be reflecting on that, so I reminded him that he'd been lonesome to see her. He lay quiet for a minute, then he said, "When I'm with Mom, I'm lonesome to see you—and when I'm with you, I'm lonesome to see Mom." With a child's insight and clarity, he had —in one step—taken our discussion to its ultimate limit.

Friday, August 13. Early this evening Dave Brunell stopped by the apartment with his three-year-old son Paulie. He wanted to give me vacation advice. Paulie, verbal and active, reminded me of my own kids. After forty-five minutes or so, I asked them to leave. The tension I feel tonight is enormous.

Monday, August 16. Banner headlines this morning announcing Nixon's sudden decision to freeze wages and prices for ninety days —and take several other dramatic steps. It means a whole new ball game on the economic front. The old economic game plan, based on traditional Republican dogma, appears to be dead and gone. He argued that the sudden policy reversal would produce "a new prosperity." I hope so. We need some, and soon.

High unemployment, continued inflation, a deteriorating balance of payments and a depressed stock market all combined to force some dramatic change in policy. But the advancing 1972 presidential election imposes its own practical deadline, and McCloskey's challenge now means Nixon has to begin producing results before the New Hampshire primary. Economic recovery—and political survival—impose the same demand: emergency action to try to break the downward spiral of the economy. Despite the months of drift, Nixon has now moved vigorously, and he deserves credit for it.

Tuesday, August 31. The office was clicking along when I returned this morning from a two-week vacation in Maine and Nova Scotia.

Before I left Washington, I was pretty strung out. I needed rest and distance from the Capitol, from noise and telephones and the demands of the job. I needed a change of pace. This was the first time I'd ever spent two weeks away from the telephone. The longest period I'd ever given myself for the sole purpose of relaxing. During that time I didn't maintain my diary, but all I would have said was that I recognized a sense of calm returning. I was actually beginning to relax.

Back in harness again, I reviewed the mail, worked on my personal budget, wrote and mailed some checks. I talked to Carl Blake, then settled back into the routine. Pretty soon the phones were ringing, and the job began to push in on me from all sides again. At lunchtime Meredith and I drove to Karl's Delicatessen on Connecticut Avenue for minestrone soup and pastrami sandwiches. Later she trimmed my hair for my appearance tonight at the Linden Centennial.

The afternoon was a mad rush. Kathleen told me that I had already exhausted the congressional allowance of one expenses-paid trip to the district for each month the House is in session. There was no money in the office account, so I would have to pay for the trip to Linden myself. I didn't know where I'd find the eighty or eighty-five dollars that the air fare alone would cost and knew I didn't have that much in my personal account. Kathleen offered to pay for the ticket with her American Express credit card. That way, the bill won't come in for another several weeks, and I'll have time to try to line up some speeches with honorariums. I don't like the idea of having to go into the hole for the plane fare to the district, but if I am going to meet my commitments, that is something I'll just have to do.

I left the office at four-forty and stopped briefly at the apartment to change into another suit, shirt and tie. There was no time to pack an overnight bag. I took the steps two at a time, tucked in my shirt along the way and arrived at National Airport with just enough time remaining to grab a paper en route to the ramp. An aide, a former Peace Corps volunteer named Dean Wilkinson, was waiting for me at the gate in Detroit and we drove to Linden in just over an hour. Linden is a quiet town of about 5000 people and a centennial is a big event. After shaking hands with the mayor I was directed to an antique Buick that was going to lead a two-car procession onto the high school football field.

The evening was cold and damp and got progressively colder. In my haste to leave Washington, I had neglected to wear a T-shirt and this was a growing regret as the evening unfolded. The program featured the crowning of a queen and an historical pageant. The first hangup occurred when our old car chugged out onto the field. The crowd in the grandstands was sparse, so we circled the field, then stopped to wait for a signal to "officially" arrive and step out of the car. That was at seven-thirty. Forty minutes later we were still waiting. The air grew colder; the crowd huddled closer together. Finally, mercifully, the signal came; we rolled out onto the field and got out of the car.

There was another unexpected and unexplained delay. Five, ten, fifteen minutes. Suddenly a short, stocky, mustachioed man with a clipboard under his arm appeared in front of me. He was the show's producer imported from the East at a cost of more than three thousand dollars, and he performed as if he were stage-managing the opening of a Broadway production, making snap decisions and barking orders. I submitted to detailed instructions on how to walk out on stage and crown the radiant queen. Ten minutes later I was "on." Firmly but carefully I placed the rhine-stone crown on the queen's bouffant hairdo.

At the end of the coronation a pageant depicting the last hundred years of life in Linden began. I sat in the grandstand steps for another forty-five minutes until my teeth began chattering. I couldn't take the cold any longer so I found Dean Wilkinson and drove to my new district office in Flint's Metropolitan Building. It was bright, efficient-looking and thoroughly unfamiliar. Leaving the office a few minutes later, I locked the door behind me. Only then did I realize that I'd left my briefcase inside. The building was deserted. As I was leaving for Detroit at five o'clock in the morning, I needed to get my briefcase tonight. So I had to roust out the building manager. Now it's one-thirty, and I'm about to sink into bed. It's going to be a very short night.

VI. SEPTEMBER

Wednesday, September 1. There was a staff meeting this afternoon at Pete McCloskey's home in McLean. Pete looked tanned and rested. He sat on his couch wearing a faded pair of pants and a dark green windbreaker and I thought that what he's doing must be agreeing with him. Unfortunately, the news he had to relate was bleak. There's a money crunch. Campaign expenditures are running about $60,000 per month, far outstripping the present level of contributions. Pete weighed four budget alternatives; each indicated who would be let go at succeeding levels of cuts. After much debate, he finally decided to keep his present staff intact —at least until the end of the month.

Although he detests deficit campaign financing, he bit the bullet and said, "We have a moral obligation to make this fight even if we go into debt. This thing has gotta be done." He continued, as much to himself as to the others in the room, "Riegle's too young . . . Lindsay's a Democrat . . ." It was the old Marine again coming out of the trenches and bulling his way up the hill. Someone suggested that a poll be taken in New Hampshire immediately. It would cost $9000. Dave Brunell said that it was absolutely essential and my instincts told me the same thing. I felt we needed to understand people's feelings on the issues better, and how they are perceiving Pete. But Pete questioned its value. He didn't think we could afford it.

Beyond that point the meeting proceeded aimlessly. We'd be discussing grand strategy, and switch to fund raising, then to scheduling and staffing, then to precinct organization. At one point Pete was saying, "We win in New Hampshire; we pick up a couple in Illinois; we make one helluva smash in Wisconsin." He wants to reach out to all America. He's driven by the mission, the need, the possibilities. He wants to make the fight everywhere, but he simply can't. Unless he reins in quickly, he won't be able to fight anywhere. Everything keeps coming back to New Hampshire. In order to win, we'll have to raise enough money between now and next March just to stay alive. We'll have to know the state so well that our strategy will be right ninety-five per cent of the time. Nixon will have to damage himself seriously before March 7 and we'll have to be lucky as hell. That combination makes Pete something less than a sure bet.

The meeting ended pleasantly and I stayed on for half an hour more to talk further to Pete and Cubby. While Pete scanned some working papers, I brought Cubby up to date on my personal situation. I told her I was anxious for her and Meredith to meet and get to know each other.

Friday, September 3. The House was not in session today, so I puttered around the apartment and waited for some teak dinner chairs to be delivered from the Scan furniture store. I was mindful of how I was starting over again from scratch. The last table-and-chair set I'd purchased was in McLean. I deployed the antique bottles I'd bought in Nova Scotia in my sunniest windows and wondered where to place an old brass ship's clock. Glancing around the apartment, I realized how much my taste has changed in the last twelve or fourteen months. But there are still some old pieces that I bought years ago.

Early this afternoon I picked up the children in McLean and we played together for several hours. Laurie has a new two-wheel bike and she flies like a bird on it. I loved watching her.

Saturday, September 4. I drove Meredith and her old friend Sue Barton out to Bethesda tonight for dinner at the Sir Walter Raleigh Inn. We enjoyed the salads and steaks, but unfortunately I found it hard to relax. My mind kept focusing on tomorrow morning's trip to Flint and my crucial meeting with Bob Breeden. Two beers helped a little, but I still felt apprehensive about the trip to Michigan.

Sunday, September 5. Chuck Chamberlain, a short, intense Republican from the congressional district adjoining mine, was also riding the early plane to Detroit this morning. We've been cordial in the past but never particularly close. Each of us preferred to sit alone, read the Sunday papers and work on the material in our briefcases. At one point he came back to my seat and we talked about redistricting, Griffin's chances for re-election and the possible repeal of the auto excise tax.

Chuck has always been a painstaking "service-to-the-district" man and he was returning to Jackson this morning for a homecoming celebration. He said he had no speeches to give; all he had to do was "smile." The fact that Chamberlain, after fifteen years in Congress, would feel compelled to fly to his district on a Sunday morning more than a year before the 1972 election speaks volumes about Republican prospects in the state. Michigan State University lies in Chamberlain's district. The state Supreme Court has just ruled that its 40,000 students will be eligible to vote on campus next year. Chuck has been an unswerving hawk on the war. He's probably wondering how to explain that stand to his new constituents.

Detroit was sunny and clear. Bob Niles is a steady driver and as we rolled on toward Flint I thought about my upcoming meeting with Bob Breeden. In my pocket were notes from Dave Brunell, Kathleen Sadler and Angie Hogan. All urged me to listen before I began to talk. I resolved to hold my fire until Bob had had a good shot. At nine-thirty we reached his home in an exclusive subdivision in the town of Grand Blanc.

Wearing an open-necked shirt and slacks, Breeden met me in the driveway. We exchanged warm hellos, then walked into his den. For a while we talked about our respective personal lives. Slowly, pleasantly, we worked our way into deeper water: the pressures facing General Motors, our feelings about Nixon, the barriers to effective performance in the Congress. There was a bowl of pistachio nuts on the coffee table and as our discussion grew more intense we sat on the couch furiously cracking those nuts, getting red dye on our fingers. At twelve-fifteen we broke off for turkey sandwiches that his wife, Bess, had made. We agreed that I'd return later to talk further and spend the night. Then I drove away to a meeting with Bob Williams, the president of the plastic pipe company.

Williams was friendly and to the point. He thought I had the potential for bigger things and wanted to discuss with me the pros and cons of switching parties and challenging Griffin as a Democrat. I was in such trouble with the Republican establishment, he said, that I had to consider making a move immediately. I gave him my rationale about making an all-out fight in the GOP. I added that I felt committed to helping the McCloskey campaign and that I could only do that as a Republican. Forty minutes later Williams was agreeing with me. He said he thought that I should stay and slug it out in the GOP.

After the meeting with Williams, I drove into Detroit for an appearance on the Lou Gordon TV show. Lou has deeply chiseled features and is as probing an interviewer as I've ever encountered. As we waited for the count-down he mentioned an item in today's New York *Times* to the effect that George Romney had made his suicidal "brainwash" comment on this show four years ago today. I wondered what mistake I'd make. A cameraman pointed at Lou; the red "on camera" light blinked and Lou began the introduction: "Today we have with us Flint Congressman Don Reagan—eh, cut it, boys, and let's start over." We laughed and shifted in our chairs.

Once under way again, we talked about my split with Nixon, the McCloskey challenge and the Michigan Senate race in 1972. Toward the end of the interview he asked a pointed question about my personal ambition and quoted an anonymous Republican leader as saying I was "opportunistic and completely self-interested." I did an instant burn and asked him who had said it. He declined to reveal his source. I pressed on to say that if someone wanted to make a comment like that he ought to have courage enough to come on the show and challenge me directly. I hope I made my point to the viewers; there was no way to know.

Returning to Flint, I stopped at the Durant Hotel to give the evening's keynote speech to the annual convention of the Michigan Legion of Polish-American Veterans. I found my seat at the head table, then spotted an old friend named Pauline Smorch in the audience. Her husband died recently and I had telephoned her on the day of his funeral. We kissed each other and she said she had come tonight to give me support. "You know we love you, Don," she said. "Just keep doing what you think is right." Her comments were so deeply felt that it was hard for me to reply. That really super woman gave me an enormous lift. Half jokingly, I said that now I'd have to go write a speech just because she was there.

A color guard marched into the ballroom to present the flag. The bugler stepped up to the stage with a bugle in one hand and a bottle of beer in the other. He drained the bottle with obvious satisfaction, then proceeded to play "The Star-Spangled Banner." There were plenty of flat notes but the crowd didn't mind. Minutes later a waitress approached me to say that a lady in the audience wanted to buy me a drink. I replied that I rarely drank before I spoke and asked for a Coke instead. Still furiously scribbling notes for my speech, I reached for the Coke automatically when the waitress returned and took a long drink. Only then did I realize that the glass had been strongly spiked with alcohol. I saw Pauline smiling at me, and I winked back.

Shortly before eleven o'clock I returned to Bob Breeden's home. We picked up the threads of this morning's conversation and followed them for another three hours. Bob said he agreed with my assessment of Vietnam, Cambodia and Carswell and, to some extent, with my views about the Administration's attitude toward young people. But there were other areas where I questioned Nixon's policies that he did not agree with me.

He said he thought I was using the wrong approach to accomplish my objectives. To bring about the changes I want, I should be a more effective "inside" man, a "team player" who could use more subtle ways to influence my colleagues. What he was saying, in effect, was: Use the standard GM approach. If you think the system is wrong and you're convinced you're right, follow the recognized steps of *proving* that to the other members. As an example, he cited my cross-examination of Rutherford Poats, the former AID deputy administrator, back in 1967. That was a brilliant piece of work, he said; the kind of thing I ought to do more often. The testimony he referred to occurred in the Foreign Operations Subcommittee. Poats was our top U. S. AID administrator in South Vietnam. With encouragement from Otto Passman, I had grilled him for three and a half hours. His candid admission of the failure of U.S. policy in Vietnam was later made public and helped trigger an over-all reappraisal of the American role in the war.

I tried to explain to Bob how the Poats confrontation was a freak occurrence that had happened *despite* the way the system normally operates. For a moment, the system's constraints had failed to function properly and I had been able to accomplish something. As another example, I mentioned my most recent cross-examination of Secretary of State Rogers on Cambodia. I got Rogers to give damning testimony, but the Administration insisted on suppressing that information and it was deleted from the record. A year later, when I tried to put it back on the record, they still refused.

That was the way the system normally worked, I said. Then I got into a thing about the seniority system. I told him how members are not promoted on the basis of merit or given responsibility on the basis of performance. I tried to help him understand why I couldn't play the game the way he wanted me to play it and still hope to accomplish anything substantive. Having worked in industry, I said, I could see how business executives think that a congressman ought to be a team player. In Congress, being a team player means acquiescing without a fight. It means staying silent while the wrong things are done. Being a team player in the House means throwing the game.

Finally I felt that we were beginning to reach each other. It wasn't that we agreed on all points; rather, we were becoming more comfortable with each other's point of view. I was weary but satisfied. Once alone in the guestroom, I set the alarm for five o'clock in order to catch the early morning plane to Washington.

Tuesday, September 7. This was opening night at the Kennedy Center for members of Congress and the performance was a mass that Leonard Bernstein wrote especially for the occasion. It's the first time Meredith and I have attended a public event together. Both of us felt apprehensive about it, but we had looked forward to the mass and we were determined to go.

Bernstein's mass is long, heavy and modern—a brilliant assault on the senses—and we were thrilled by it. The wine velvet interior of the concert hall, the excellent acoustics and the Austrian snowflake chandeliers added to the almost magical quality of the performance. We sat in the center orchestra next to Ed Hutchinson, a mild-mannered Republican from Fennville, Michigan, and his wife Janet. As the mass was building to its climax, I noticed that Ed was checking his watch. He and Janet left the hall the moment the curtain fell.

Wednesday, September 8. Dick Rykken called from McCloskey headquarters this morning with some disturbing news. The voter registration rally scheduled in Pittsburgh tomorrow was about to collapse. It was losing its bipartisan coloration and was fast becoming a Democratic Party affair centered around John Lindsay. Under those circumstances, I said I'd go and urge participation in the Republican Party and would pass the word along to Pete.

The rest of the morning passed in a rush: letters to draft, staff people to see, phones to answer, papers to read and office visitors to greet. At lunchtime Meredith and I slipped away to look for a print for the hallway in my apartment. In an art gallery on Connecticut Avenue, we found a fabulous Boulanger lithograph; it depicted a little boy holding onto a balloon floating away over a city.

On the floor this afternoon, Ed Hutchinson approached me and, with an inquisitive look, asked how I had enjoyed last night's mass at the Kennedy Center. I was non-committal and asked him the same question. He smiled and cocked his head. "You know," he said, "I just didn't get the message."

Thursday, September 9. At this morning's Michigan Republican delegation breakfast, our state chairman, Bill McLaughlin, described a possible redistricting plan that would protect the seats of all incumbent members. Then he mentioned an alternative that would involve significant changes in some district lines, particularly for Jim Harvey and Bill Broomfield.

Half of Harvey's present district would be shifted to Broomfield. McLaughlin said Harvey would run from the remaining half. But Harvey quickly said that he would choose which half to run in. It meant he would preserve the option to force a primary fight with Broomfield that would result in one of them losing his seat. There was a moment of silence as everyone looked around and reflected on that. "Well, gentlemen," Jack McDonald said, "I guess this is our last breakfast together." It was just the right touch and produced great laughter.

Once I got to the office, the phones began ringing furiously. McCloskey had said he was canceling out of this afternoon's voter registration rally in Pittsburgh. The rally co-ordinator, Arnie Miller, laid it on the line for me. Pete had shared top billing with Lindsay in rally publicity. The national press was going to attend. If Pete didn't appear, it would seem that he was ducking a confrontation with Lindsay. Did Pete want to leave that impression? I began calling Pete and finally located him in a meeting of the Merchant Marine and Fisheries Committee. The problem, he said, was that a bill to regulate the dumping of wastes and pollutants into coastal waters was coming up for a vote on the floor this afternoon. The bill had originated in his subcommittee—and he was going to offer an important amendment to it.

I said I thought there was a later plane to Pittsburgh. It would be very tight, but there was a chance that he could meet both commitments. After a flurry of calls I concluded that, with luck, Pete could offer his amendment, catch a four-fifty flight and arrive at the rally site with a margin of five minutes. Everything would have to go click-click. I telephoned him and reported what I'd learned. Yes, he said, he'd go this afternoon.

By this time it was almost noon. I raced to the floor to hear Nixon address the joint session of Congress. The chamber was packed and all I could find was a folding metal chair in the final row of seats. The TV lights gave the chamber an artificial glow. I looked to my right at the gallery box reserved for the President. Henry Kissinger sat with Mrs. Nixon, Tricia and her husband, Ed Cox.

Speaker Carl Albert introduced the President and members rose to applaud as Nixon approached the microphones. I remembered other joint sessions when Lyndon Johnson had addressed us. Senator Robert Kennedy seldom clapped; he just seemed to smolder. In the next twenty-five minutes Nixon gave a well-reasoned appeal for co-operation with his new economic game plan. He summarized its high points and asked for bipartisan support. What struck me most was his assertion—midway through the speech—that it was time for America to give first priority to solving domestic problems. He even went so far as to cite the litany of feeding the hungry, tending the sick, helping the elderly. It was a passage that could have come from any speech that Lowenstein, McGovern, Lindsay or I had made in recent years. It marked a real change in tone and I felt a flash of encouragement. Despite our differences in strategies, the President was citing goals and priorities that I could embrace and support. As soon as he had finished, I hurried to my office to phone the media in Flint. I had *positive* comments to make on the President's remarks. That, I thought, ought to make news.

Only an hour remained before my flight to Pittsburgh. I left the office to pick up Meredith at the Smithsonian. We improvised a picnic on the grass beside the Potomac several blocks away. She gave me a note to read on the plane and I placed it in my breast pocket.

After I took her back to work I glanced at the clock and realized that time had gotten away from me. I raced to National Airport, parked in the congressional lot and ran the length of the terminal to the Northwest Orient Airlines gate. I had forgotten my handkerchief; so, once aboard the plane, I removed the headrest cloth from the back of my seat and used it to rub the sweat from my face.

Two motorcycle policemen met us at the airport in Pittsburgh and escorted our motorcade to the outdoor rally site. The crowd ranged somewhere between ten and fifteen thousand and when I arrived I was told that I'd be among the first speakers. I would have preferred to speak later—after the crowd had jelled—but there was nothing I could do to change the situation. When it was my turn to go on, I made the case for McCloskey and the Republican challenge. I wished John Lindsay well, I said, as he tackled Mayor Daley, Lyndon Johnson and Lester Maddox in his newly adopted party.

Minutes later Lindsay arrived, handsome as ever, in a cluster of supporters who kept ooh-ing and ah-ing him. He received a warm welcome from the crowd. Then, with studied effort, he proceeded to blow it. First, he chose to read his speech. He spoke of his concern for young workers and came down hard on the side of law and order. It was new material aimed at a blue-collar audience and he didn't read it well. Then, too, the young people in that crowd didn't want canned stuff. That's all they got. When he finished, the applause was modest. He hadn't offended anyone. But he hadn't converted anyone either.

As he was leaving the stage he walked over to shake hands. He seemed slightly uneasy, perhaps because he couldn't remember my first name, but more likely because he felt troubled about his party switch and the decision to leave liberal Republicans behind. We looked each other in the eye. "Good luck," he said, and then, in a lower voice, "You've got big balls, really big balls."

"I'll probably get 'em cut off," I said.

Lindsay grinned. "We'll probably both get 'em cut off," he said.

I turned away, then felt a hand on my arm. It was Lindsay again. "When you get up to New York, get ahold of me."

"Sure," I replied. As he walked away, I felt a feeling of warmth for Lindsay—almost a sad warmth. It's hard to be constantly pressed in a swarm of admirers, to have to smile, to put a mask on your fatigue and worries. Suddenly he seemed terribly vulnerable as he made his way through the crowd.

McCloskey arrived about six-thirty and I introduced him to the audience. He spoke off the cuff, steady and straight, but hardly inspirational. He talked about love and kindness, condemned the war and asked for support in the Republican primaries. I thought he outperformed Lindsay, but he still has to do better. And he can. Back in Washington again, I drove him to his house in McLean and stopped in for a moment to tell Cubby he'd done well. She was pleased and with a flourish produced a $1600 commission check that she'd earned selling real estate. Pete gave her a huge hug and told her to spend it on a new wardrobe.

Impossible, she said. The money was already committed to pay household bills.

Saturday, September 11. The children and I window-shopped at Tysons Corner this afternoon. We loaded up on grape slurpees and checked out an amateur art exhibit at the mall. At one point, in a toy store, I was speaking to Donny when I heard a strange voice ask: "And how do you feel about inflation, Congressman Riegle?" I turned—and found myself looking into the face of an alligator hand puppet with Laurie on the other end of it. That really made me laugh.

Early this evening Meredith and I drove to National Airport to pick up her father, who was arriving on a flight from Albuquerque, New Mexico. We parked the car and as we walked to the terminal I suddenly realized that I felt buoyant and happy, that my mood was completely different from the way it usually is when I'm dashing in and out of that airport. Today I wasn't going anywhere. I didn't have to get on a plane and fly away from Washington.

At the Trans World Airlines gate, Meredith's father gave us a wave from about fifty feet away. A tall, solidly built man, Dr. Clayton White is an M.D. as well as a physicist. He's long been involved in researching the effects of nuclear blasts and in recent years has served as president of the Lovelace Foundation for Medical Education and Research in Albuquerque. He and Meredith hugged and kissed each other, then his big hand swallowed mine in a strong handshake. We drove him to the Watergate Hotel and while he checked in picked up a bottle of sherry at the liquor store.

Later, at Trader Vic's we had a superb dinner. It was relaxed and fun. Meredith kept reaching for my hand and squeezing it just to make sure I felt at ease.

Monday, September 13. Dave Brunell and I got into a closed-door discussion this morning about the Bob Breeden situation and the present unhappy status of the McCloskey campaign. Breeden apparently told Paul Visser last week that he felt our September 5 session had strengthened our personal friendship. He had come away with a better understanding of the way I feel and he thought it was mutual. Ominously, however, he said he hadn't gotten through in terms of being able to help me. The more he reflected on it, the more frustrated he felt on that point. There was no way, he had decided, to help me change my behavior and become "more effective" in Congress.

The second half of Brunell's message was equally discouraging. After nearly two weeks of concentrated effort, McCloskey's fund raisers have come up with blanks and dry holes everywhere. It doesn't appear that Pete can generate anything approaching the $60,000 he needs to run the campaign each month; there's even doubt as to whether or not the next staff pay checks can be covered at the bank. Norton Simon has already contributed between $70,000 and $100,000 and is apparently willing to give another $100,000 if—and this is a big "if"—others can guarantee $50,000. The problem is: where do you find that other $50,000? Unless there's an enormous breakthrough soon, which no one anticipates, the campaign is going to face its moment of truth. Major surgery will have to take place to keep the effort alive.

On the floor this afternoon, I was talking with Stew McKinney, a Republican from Connecticut. McKinney is tanned, well to do and quite independent. He wears very "with it" clothes, he has a young aggressive staff and he rides a motorcycle to work—all of which separate him from the image of the traditional New England Republican. Some important constituents, he said, were waiting to meet with him to complain about the Administration's ten per cent import surcharge. Then he asked, "See what I'm wearing?" When it was clear to him that I didn't understand, he smiled and pointed out that he was dressed from head to toe in clothes of foreign manufacture. "I just wanted them to see what the President is up against in the trade area," he explained.

At that point we were standing behind the brass railing behind the Democratic side of the chamber waiting for our names in a quorum call. Most senior Republicans have an aversion to that side of the House chamber, and some even refuse to use the doors on that side. McKinney and I feel none of this reluctance. Actually, standing on the Democratic side is a convenience. After answering your name, you can dash more quickly either to the members' dining room or down the House steps and back to your office.

Tuesday, September 14. I've been having bad chest pains the last four or five days, especially at night. At eleven o'clock this morning I walked to the doctor's office in the Capitol. My weight was 177; my blood pressure 112 over 68. I was given an EKG and a chest X ray. The doctor said he thought my trouble was a virus in my chest wall; he gave me some pills to ease the pain.

There were three roll-call votes on the floor this afternoon to prohibit the establishment of detention camps and to make sure that no one could be interned except by an act of Congress. Some of the more conservative members unleashed predictable sound and fury, but the issue was never in doubt and the vote on final passage was 356 to 49. Waiting to vote, I talked briefly with Chuck Whalen. A graduate of the Harvard Business School and a former professor of economics, he's one of the House's more lucid and persuasive members. He was describing a messy situation that has developed in his district.

Several weeks ago Nixon flew to Dayton to dedicate a museum at Wright-Patterson Air Force Base. Theoretically, the ceremony was open to the public. The base MPs however, denied entry to anyone who was dressed unconventionally or who appeared to be against the war in Vietnam. They turned away a minister who wore a peace button and many young people with long hair. Since then, Whalen said, the community has been in an uproar. Chuck has spoken out against the base MPs and I can imagine the pressures he's feeling as a result of this stand. It's not popular to defend the First Amendment these days.

Wednesday, September 15. The whip of the Michigan Republican delegation, the man in charge of finding out how the rest of us are going to vote on any given bill and then reporting that to the leadership, is Elford A. Cederberg. A former mayor of Bay City, Cedie is serving his tenth term here and ranks third in seniority on the Republican side of the Appropriations Committee. He loves the House gym; he's been involved in its organization and management, and he's a regular in the cloakroom off the House floor. He has a keen sense of humor and he needles other members constantly. He's very forceful in expressing his views, which are quite conservative. Although our voting records differ sharply, I like Cedie, respect his straightforward manner, and we are cordial to each other.

I was talking to him on the floor of the House this afternoon when I spotted Tom Railsback, from Illinois, sitting at the Republican table. The quorum call was ending. I turned to Cedie and asked him to keep an eye on Railsback so he wouldn't screw up the pending floor debate on the highly controversial Equal Employment Enforcement Act. Cedie looked at Railsback and, with friendly disdain, remarked: "Railsback, you're over the hill."

"What kind of hill?" Railsback asked. Then he paused for a moment. "Cedie," he said, "you're the guy who's over the hill."

Cederberg laughed. "Sure," he said, "but at least I admit it."

"Cedie," said Railsback, "you're so far gone that you go limp at the thought of it."

A few minutes later Cederberg hailed McCloskey on the floor and asked him teasingly if he were able to keep up with Nixon. Clearly, he felt that Nixon's initiatives on China and the economy were cutting some of the ground out from under the McCloskey challenge. "You got to change direction faster to keep up with Nixon," he said, chuckling. "You ought to get some Dri-Slide to help you do it." Dri-Slide is a lubricant used on firearms.

Not to be outdone, Pete suggested that he and I nominate Ceder-berg as vice chairman of the Republican Conference. Pete began ticking off Cedie's qualifications: "Toughness, experience, ability to produce articulate bullshit . . ."

Thursday, September 16. Because there was a McCloskey staff meeting this morning, I had to miss the weekly Michigan Republican delegation breakfast at the Capitol Hill Club. At nine o'clock I arrived at the campaign headquarters on Pennsylvania Avenue and was directed to an office in the rear of the building. The office looked and smelled unused. It was full of drab brown furniture, dirty ashtrays and discarded styrofoam coffee cups. The venetian blinds were drawn.

A five-page agenda had been prepared for the meeting. We were supposed to talk not only about the campaign's financial position but also about a press representative, major speeches and media development. Instead, we spent the next three hours solely on the money crunch. Finance Chairman Al Shreck concluded that it would have to be "a fairly thinly financed campaign—something on the order of $30,000 per month." Robin Schmidt spelled out the details. As of October 1, the projected cash deficit would stand at $37,000. If the campaign folded that day, liabilities still in the pipeline would raise that amount to between $50,000 and $60,000. Accordingly, he had prepared a list of "cuts and keeps" among the staff. Of twenty-four names, twelve were slated to go. His name was among them.

Pete studied that list for a long time. He wasn't prepared to accept its verdict. "We've been aiming our efforts at the wrong constituency," he said finally. "We waited too long for a Wall Street appeal and now Nixon's economic moves have just made that more difficult." He glanced down at the paper again. "We're all on the list to be canned. Our asses are all on the chopping block as of October 1 unless we start raising money. Everybody will have to put twenty-five per cent of his time into fund raising. We need $100,000 per month to finance the operation. I don't know if the job can be done or not. We haven't tried very effectively yet." As the meeting drew to a close, he designated Robin Schmidt as the man responsible for the "over-all conception, direction and strategy" of the campaign.

Then he put Al Toffel, a thirty-six-year-old, curly-haired Californian, in charge of its "mechanical implementation."

My stomach had been rumbling all morning and by this time I was in some distress. I made three specific recommendations, and when Pete and the others accepted them, I excused myself and raced three blocks to my apartment. I arrived just in time.

On the floor this afternoon there were some close votes on proposed amendments to the Equal Employment Enforcement Act. The "liberal" version would have empowered the government to issue cease and desist orders to companies that used discriminatory hiring practices. The "conservative" version required lengthy court proceedings. The House still has little sympathy for problems facing minority groups and today's vote reflected that fact. Shortly after I had cast my ballot against the conservative amendment, I noticed a flurry of activity. Jerry Ford pointed to a Republican staff member and shouted, "Get Bill Harsha in here." The aide disappeared into the cloakroom and, minutes later, Harsha appeared. Still smoothing down his hair, he walked to the well and voted aye.

Because they keep a running tally of Republican votes at the desk, the leadership knows at a glance how each member has voted and who still has to vote. They zero in on the absentees and the potential switchers. On most issues, Ford can wring out four or five extra votes. That's what he did today. He led the fight for the conservative amendment and it prevailed by a vote of 202 to 197. A switch of three votes would have changed the outcome.

During the afternoon Brad Morse of Massachusetts asked me if I'd support Jim Harvey as the new vice chairman of the Republican Conference and I said I'd be happy to. Later, as I was leaving the floor, I spotted Harvey standing by the brass rail at the rear of the chamber. I approached him to wish him well and to say how glad I was that he was a candidate. I was a little sensitive about standing with him too long; I didn't want any antagonisms that other members feel toward me to rub off on him. At that moment Brad Morse walked by the rail and said to Jim half jokingly, "You'd better not be seen standing here too long with Riegle." I remarked that Brad was probably right, but Harvey disregarded the warning and we continued our conversation.

With great sensitivity, he went on to say that he'd worried about my personal situation many times over the past year and, on several occasions, had almost spoken to me about it. When he was practicing law back in Saginaw, he said, he always found domestic relations cases extraordinarily difficult. I took the occasion to bring him up to date and added that I appreciated his interest and concern. It was one of those rare moments in a congressional career when you achieve a special understanding with a colleague you like.

Saturday, September 18. Meredith dropped me at the airport before seven-thirty this morning. I kissed her through the open car window, then headed toward the plane for Michigan. Dave Brunell, Angie Hogan and I were flying to Flint for a surprise party in honor of Paul Visser. After running my district office for nearly five years, Paul has decided to leave and enter the insurance business.

As soon as I arrived in Flint, I held constituent office hours. An old woman whom we'd helped with a Social Security problem brought me a jar of homemade strawberry jam. She was frail, and her kindness penetrated all my defense mechanisms. I gave her a hug. A pretty girl of about seventeen came by to suggest that Congress develop some domestic alternatives to the military draft—and open them up to women. I told her I favored the idea and had been working on it for months.

My third caller was a tall, good-looking black who is working for his father as a bartender. He had been on drugs and had been divorced. He said he couldn't understand what it was that he was supposed to do. He felt all kinds of outside pressures bearing in on him but had no idea what his goal should be. He felt alone and less and less in touch with the world. He spoke in half sentences; his worries were vague and diffuse. I sat two feet away from him and leaned forward so he wouldn't feel alone with me. I told him I had faith in him, that he should have faith in himself and that we would try to help. I made a mental note to talk with him again and do my utmost to deliver on that promise.

Later, at a church fair in the suburb of Grand Blanc, Glen Wilson took me aside. A tall, silver-haired man who owns the Buick dealership in Fenton—and a lifelong Republican—he confided that the party had really disappointed him in the last several months. He'd admired the stands I'd taken; he knew my life had been difficult. He and his wife Donnie had decided to make a three-hundred-dollar contribution to my re-election fund. I was overwhelmed. It came as a complete surprise.

The party for Paul Visser tonight was an enormous success. He entered the banquet room without suspecting a thing and it took him two or three minutes to realize that the sixty-odd guests who'd been waiting out of sight were there to wish him well. Paul has ten brothers and two sisters. Since his divorce earlier this year, he has been somewhat estranged from them. But all were present this evening; I sensed that the healing process was advancing rapidly.

On the plane from Washington, I'd written a personal letter to Paul expressing my thanks to him for our five years together. During an informal ceremony I tried to read it aloud. Before I finished the first line my voice broke with emotion and I had to pause. I kept at it but had to stop often. This night marked the end of a special work relationship and the taking of separate paths. I am enormously indebted to him for the job that he has done and his faith in me. I managed to finish the last part of my letter without stopping; then Paul and I walked toward each other and embraced.

Once in my hotel room, I washed my face, brushed my teeth and then called Meredith to say good night. The day has been long and her voice at the other end was very warm and good.

Monday, September 20. I got a call today from Bill Broomfield, a Michigan Republican who's serving as president of the Capitol Hill Club. The club is moving from the Congressional Hotel to another building about a block away, he said, and it needs money to pay for interior decoration. All the other Republicans in the Michigan delegation had pledged to become life members at a thousand dollars each. If he could get a hundred per cent participation in our delegation, he could use that as a lever to pressure members from other states. So would I mind contributing my share soon?

That thousand dollars sounded like a million to me and I knew I couldn't even consider it. I replied that the financial settlement agreement I had signed made it impossible to take on any new financial commitments. I explained the facts to him.

Bill was surprised to hear the news. He was most sympathetic and said he'd think about other ways to skin the cat. He seemed grateful that my financial situation was not his own.

Wednesday, September 22. Barb Pritchard, the secretary in my district office, called from Flint this afternoon to say that she was leaving the staff. We talked for an hour and a half. The pressures she's been feeling lately have led her to conclude that she simply has to come off the firing line, relax and spend more time with her husband and three children. In the course of our conversation she said that she and the others in Flint have to cope with constituent problems every hour of every day. They need more support from Washington. There have been times when they didn't receive that support and it has been difficult for them. She went on to catalog people in the district who were bent out of shape because of my support of the McCloskey effort or who were angry at me for other things I'd done along the way. She also pointed out my strongest areas of support. Barb has done a magnificent job over the past five years and she's going to be hard to replace.

At five o'clock this afternoon there was a reception in the Rayburn Building for some British Members of Parliament who came to Washington to deliver a protest against the war in Vietnam. No sooner had I arrived than Betsy Boyce, a freckled, sandy-haired staff member of mine, approached me with a bit of bad news. Somehow, someone in the office committed me to share in the cost of an elaborate buffet. The reception's organizers had anticipated that fifty or sixty members would attend; only ten or fifteen showed up and that meant there were literally dozens of extra hors d'oeuvres on that table. My share of the bill, Betsy said, came to forty dollars. I didn't have it and didn't know where I would get it. But as long as I was picking up the tab, I thought I ought to enjoy myself. I made it a point to eat a few things off that table.

House Speaker Carl Albert, a Democrat from Bug Tussle, Oklahoma, appeared at the reception several minutes later. He was

once a Rhodes scholar and during the time he spent in England became quite familiar with the British system of government. Albert
promptly told a story about one of his former Oxford classmates.
He loved the United States, the classmate said to Albert one day.
America's only problem was that it didn't have a king. Even in recol-
lection, Albert found that comment hilarious. He rocked back and
forth on his heels. His face flushed and he laughed so hard that he
began to choke and nearly fell over. The British M.P.s smiled politely.

I never saw Albert so animated before. As I watched him, I
couldn't help thinking of the enormous physical contrast between
him and former Speaker John McCormack, who retired last January.
Albert is nearly a foot shorter than McCormack.

John McCormack was one of the most decent and sensitive men
who ever served in the House. I liked and respected him and it was
a shame that his name was linked—even peripherally—to an influ-
ence-peddling scandal involving one of his former aides. For John
McCormack was a man of integrity. Each member of Congress receives an annual $3000 stationery allowance and the federal govern-
ment does not require an accounting of how that money is spent.
Some members let the money accumulate and, when they leave the
Congress, use it for their own purposes. McCormack let his fund
accumulate too, but before he retired he turned back more than
$23,000 to the U. S. Treasury.

McCormack would always go out of his way to be kind to the
younger members. I called his office several times when I had constituents here who I thought would enjoy meeting him and he was
gracious with his time. One day several years ago my grandmother
Fitchett came to Washington. The House was not yet in session. As I
escorted her onto the floor, I spotted Johnny Monaghan, one of the
Speaker's aides, and asked if I would be able to introduce my grandmother to McCormack. Monaghan said he'd check and see if the
Speaker was free. Five minutes later the Speaker appeared. Unwilling to ask me to come to him, he had interrupted whatever he was
doing at the time, left his office and walked from the cloakroom to
the floor. That was a nice gesture for him to make to a second-term
member—and a Republican. McCormack also began the tradition of

insisting that whenever the House was not in session the children who came onto the floor were given a chance to sit in the Speaker's chair. He wanted to instill in them a sense that "This is your House; it belongs to you and your turn is coming."

On a number of occasions, at his invitation, I sat in his private office and listened to him reminisce about the years he'd served in Congress. He seemed to love to do this and he'd always say, "You know, I hope you can come back again and we'll talk further." I think McCormack had a kindred feeling for all the members in the House—especially the younger ones. He loved the Congress and extended his fairness and evenhandedness to everyone. If I had something I wanted to say that was really important to me and if I knew I'd probably exceed the one minute I'd normally be given on the floor, I'd approach him to request a "long minute." He would nod and not gavel me down at the end of my sixty seconds. Every time I asked for that favor he gave it graciously.

Since January I've asked Albert only once for permission to speak a "long minute." I wanted to nail the Administration on something and my criticism could only be interpreted as helpful to the Democrats. But Albert gaveled me down at exactly sixty seconds. The Democrats on the floor at the time just groaned; they couldn't believe that Albert would silence a Republican who was saying something helpful to their cause.

Thursday, September 23. I've been feeling pretty lousy for the past two or three days. I've had no energy at all and so this morning I walked over to the doctor's office in the Capitol. I asked him for a blood test to see whether I had some mysterious disease or was merely suffering from accumulated fatigue. The doctor's assistant squeezed a rubber band around my arm to make the vein stick out. He stabbed around in my vein for a minute or so, then apologized. The suction in his blood container wasn't working well, he said. Finally he got the amount of blood he needed.

Angie Hogan, my staff assistant for federal aid programs, has been in the district all week. She called today to report that the anti-Riegle Republicans are apparently hard at work trying to find someone to oppose me in next year's primary. They hope to find a young, aggressive candidate whose views are not controversial. As an old friend said the other day, only half jokingly, "someone who would remind the voters of what Don Riegle used to seem like—before he lost his sanity."

Late this afternoon I got a report from the doctor's office. The blood tests turned up nothing unusual. My problem is either not enough sleep or too much anxiety.

Friday, September 24. Dave Brunell and I flew to Michigan this afternoon to attend the biennial convention of state Republicans. After stops at Pittsburgh and Cleveland we landed in Detroit and headed for the private plane that would take us to Mackinac Island. Fifteen minutes later we were winging north. We encountered scattered clouds; the land looked neat and orderly below the plane's bright red wing.

I had no desire to be making this trip. For the most part, party politics is awful. Many of the people hidden in the party structure aren't motivated the way I am; they're not after the same things. The constant jockeying for position, the jealousies and backbiting leave me very cold. I'm lousy at remembering names, so I felt sure I'd have some awkward moments over the weekend as people waited expectantly for me to identify them. I expected some grumbling, too, about the McCloskey challenge—particularly after Nixon's speech last night to the Economic Club of Detroit.

But this, I rationalized, was one of those command-performance functions that you have to attend if you're going to participate in the political process. I wanted to make it very clear to the others here that my flag is still flying; I'm in the party and I intend to stay. I also hoped that they would find the real Don Riegle harder to dislike than the old "superambitious" label might suggest.

After dinner at the hotel in Mackinac, Dave and I walked downtown. The business district was deserted and we were alone except for the distant clomp-clomp of an occasional horse-drawn carriage. Years ago, while my father was serving on the Flint City Commission, I came with him to a convention at Mackinac Island. At that time, after dark, the downtown area was teeming with bats. I remember getting an empty cigar box and filling it with two dozen squealing bats. Once back at the Grand Hotel—which, to my twelve-year-old mind, seemed stuffy and sedate—I opened the lid of the cigar box. The bats flew every which way in the lobby and I laughed until my sides hurt.

Tonight Dave and I looked under the store awnings; we couldn't find any bats.

Saturday, September 25. In the lobby this morning Dave and I got into a very direct conversation with Brian Connelly about my own predicament within the state GOP. A tall, good-natured advertising executive from Ann Arbor, Brian asked about the McCloskey challenge. Dave and I outlined the situation—concluding that it was a David and Goliath confrontation. Brian thought for a minute and said: "It's more like David and twenty Goliaths—and you've only got one stone. So you've got to carom it off all twenty heads in order to succeed." He paused again and added, "The carom shot may work."

I asked Brian what was being said about me on the party grapevine. He said: "Stuff like—Riegle that goddamned son of a bitch—" I interrupted him to say "Oh, you mean it's improving?"

Brian strongly supported me on the convention floor at the Senate "consensus" meeting in Lansing in 1970. Our discussion shifted quickly to the day at that convention "when the wheels came off the buggy."

In 1970 Republicans had a difficult time trying to find a candidate to challenge the incumbent senator, Democrat Phil Hart. Several House members toyed with the idea of stepping forward, but none did. Speculation centered around George Romney, Secretary of Housing and Urban Development. For several months Romney refused to say what he would do. He made it clear that he was "keeping the door open." Given the force of his personality, his long-time dominance of the Michigan GOP and his Cabinet status, that ambiguity prevented the emergence of any other plausible candidate.

No Republican challenger could possibly wage a winning race unless he spent more than a million dollars, most of it on TV. Without the tacit approval—if not direct support—of the White House, no challenger could hope to raise that kind of money from traditional Republican sources. As long as Romney insisted on keeping the door "open," it was impossible for anyone else to seek that tacit approval. George apparently knew all along that he would not run himself; but he wanted to retain maximum leverage in determining who the candidate would be.

The nomination itself was no prize. Hart was generally popular, a decent guy who had been forthright on civil rights but non-committal on other controversial issues. He was well financed. Michigan is basically a Democratic state. The Nixon record was no plus. Then, too, the Republican Party organization seemed to be losing steam. The re-election of Bill Milliken, the incumbent Republican governor, would put first claim on its limited resources. The threat of a major auto strike around election time clouded the picture even further.

While I would much rather serve in the Senate than the House, I wasn't prepared to accept the nomination unless I felt I had a fighting chance to win. Several months earlier, Dave Brunell had begun work on what was to become our "Senate race book." This was a black, loose-leaf folder that included poll data, detailed comparisons of Hart and myself, and an evaluation of the respective party organizations. It also included sections on issues, budgets and past Michigan voting behavior.

Obviously, it was a long shot. While I'd probably run a strong race against Hart, we agreed that several key pieces necessary to ensure a "fighting chance" were missing. The most important was money; without it, I was dead from the start. Then came organization. Could I count on state-wide party support? Would the governor cooperate? Fundamental to it all was my own psychology; I would have to believe that I could win and that I could invest eight months of all-consuming effort toward achieving that goal. My staff and I decided that it was a marginal situation that had to be worked out in stages. The ultimate decision would depend on a series of interlocking events and factors. I might not be able to say yes or no until the last possible moment.

The state organization wanted to identify a single preferred candidate, give that candidate an early start and save a costly primary race. After general party agreement to pursue this approach, a "consensus" meeting was held in January and the names of roughly two dozen potential candidates were tossed into the hopper. My name was on that list. So was the name of Romney's wife, Lenore, for whom top party leaders were orchestrating a boomlet. It appeared to me at the time, and still does in retrospect, that these leaders did Mrs. Romney a great disservice by persuading her that she had more popular support than was actually the case. They were levering both ends against the middle, telling Lenore that the troops were clamoring for her while at the same time telling party workers that Lenore would run only if everyone got together and urged her to make the race.

During this period I talked with George Romney twice in Washington. At our first meeting he said he thought I would make a good candidate if I could patch up my differences within the party and raise the necessary funds. He said he'd take his own soundings on the feasibility of this. I replied that I would defer to him or to Lenore should either declare a candidacy and that, in the meantime, I would continue to do my homework. He kept his options open; so did I. At our second meeting, however, George said he felt that I could not count on broad party support. There were serious hangups about me within the Nixon Administration as well as among state party leaders. He and Lenore were concluding—reluctantly, he said—that she might have to run.

Then I received an invitation to come to the White House and talk to Murray Chotiner. I found him tucked away in a small but bustling office in the East Wing and at his request gave him my appraisal of the Michigan situation. Slightly overweight, his hair slicked back on his head, he resembled an old-fashioned bartender. He showed no trace of emotion or warmth. I had no difficulty picturing him at work for Nixon in the 1950 California Senate race, drafting the notorious pink sheet which suggested that Helen Gahagan Douglas was "soft" on Communism. He was polite but volunteered nothing, was very non-committal. I wasn't sure when I left the White House why he had arranged our chat.

The pieces soon began to fall into place. The governor sent telegrams to all potential candidates, including me, telling us that if we wanted to be considered for the nomination we should plan to address the delegates at a "shakeout" consensus meeting February 21 at Lansing's Jack Tar Hotel. Yet, as that date approached, Lenore Romney's "bandwagon" was dominating the news. No one from the first list of candidates had announced for the nomination. Outright pledges of support for Lenore fueled speculation that she would surely get the consensus designation. Harold McClure, Michigan's leading Republican fund raiser, told us nicely but bluntly that money would not be forthcoming for a Riegle campaign. It would be available for a Lenore Romney race.

Reluctantly, Dave and I agreed that the ball game was over. The party mechanism was locking itself into place around Lenore's designation. But how to respond to the governor's telegram? We decided that I would address the delegates—if for no other reason than to create the illusion of a contest and not let it appear that Lenore's selection was a back-room choice.

It also appeared that since I was going to speak I should leave my name on the list through the first round of balloting. At that point I would withdraw; Lenore would have the nomination. I discussed this plan with Jerry Ford, Bob Griffin, Bill Milliken and other party leaders. They agreed it was appropriate under the circumstances.

On the day of the meeting the Jack Tar ballroom was jammed with party delegates and members of the press. It was a convention setting; while no surprises were expected, there was excitement in the air. Under the rules, speakers were to be called in alphabetical order, which meant I'd address the delegates before Lenore Romney; Jim O'Neill, a member of the state Board of Education, would speak before me. He did—and withdrew in favor of Lenore. That touched off sustained applause.

Then it was my turn. I began by stating that I was not a candidate and that I was not in a position to say I would become one later. So I couldn't ask anyone to vote for me. Then I repeated my earlier pledge to remove my name from the list after the first ballot if Lenore said that she was in the race. Once that was out of the way, I talked about how I thought a winning campaign would have to be waged. I indicated why Phil Hart had to be replaced. I hammered away at the issues I felt most deeply about: the party's need to attract young people, civil rights and the war in Vietnam.

While there had been some applause at various points during the speech, I still wasn't prepared for the standing ovation I received when I finished. I hadn't suspected that I was striking chords capable of turning the convention in a new direction. Lenore was standing in the rear of the hall. She had heard my remarks and the delegates' response. Neither were what she had been led to expect. She didn't look well; she didn't appear to feel well either. Though normally an effective speaker, she wasn't that day. She spoke off the cuff. Her remarks wandered and at no point did she declare her candidacy. Her performance stunned the crowd. I couldn't bring myself to look up; it was just too painful. I felt embarrassment for her predicament. The moment she finished I bolted out the door and went to my room on the floor above.

After these first two speeches, someone told me later, "The wheels came off the buggy." All bets were off and we had a new ball game. The convention was in the process of turning itself upside down. Runners appeared at my door to confirm the fact that a spontaneous effort had sprung up on my behalf. Delegates were standing on chairs endorsing me and trying to rally first-ballot support. I could hear the tumult on the floor below. A chain of events had been set in motion that might end up giving me the nomination under the worst of circumstances: no funds, no support from the party leadership and a predictable backlash from Lenore's loyal supporters. Those circumstances would strangle a later candidacy. That was my rational reading of the situation.

My emotional response, however, was another story. Lenore had not declared her candidacy. Here, I thought, was my chance to be the Republican nominee for senator. All I would have to do would be to declare a formal candidacy after the first ballot; it seemed likely that I could drive to a consensus victory that day. It was an opportunity that might never come again.

The overriding constraint was money. I remember standing alone looking out the hotel window. I was acutely aware of one of the differences between the Kennedys and the Riegles. The Kennedys could finance themselves; if the moment came, they were able to

seize it. I had to depend on others; it meant waiting to line up my
ducks. I might wait forever. Then, too, my personal life was far from
settled. Could I mount the kind of campaign that would be required
under those circumstances? I wasn't sure. But I knew I shouldn't
deceive myself or anyone else by agreeing to a suicide mission.

The decision seemed clear. As I had said I would, I sat down and
wrote out a statement withdrawing my name after the first ballot.
I handed it to Bill Moeller, a delegate from Flint, and asked him to
give it to Governor Milliken. Moeller hurried to the convention floor
and handed it to Milliken. The governor read it—and put it in his
pocket.

The final tally on the first ballot was never announced. Yet it was
clear that Lenore had not received the seventy-five per cent she
needed to earn consensus designation. It was equally clear that I had
finished a strong second. Momentum was important. Shifts were taking place on the floor and self-appointed Riegle forces were gathering
delegates.

The second ballot had already started before I learned that Milliken hadn't announced my withdrawal from the race. I was *still* listed
as a candidate. I had said I would pull out after the first ballot and
I meant it. The governor's action made it appear that I was violating
a pledge. Furious, I contacted him and insisted he announce my
decision at the earliest possible moment. He promised to say something at the end of the second ballot.

Accounts of that tally varied considerably. Some held that Lenore
and I were only three votes apart. Others claimed her margin was
much wider. Confusion beset the convention. Then Milliken read
my statement. Coming when it did, that statement triggered anger
and even more confusion. My supporters groaned; they had quite
naturally assumed that when my name remained on the ballot I was
in the race to stay. They had labored feverishly for the pending third
and perhaps final ballot. Leaders of the Romney faction, badly
shaken by the turmoil but relieved that my name had been withdrawn, quickly pressed for a final ballot. Her floor manager mis-
judged the situation completely. Milliken was scrambling to control
events.

The governor called and asked me to come down to the floor, address the delegates and "clarify" my position. I replied that my statement was clear; I had nothing further to say. He called again and with much greater insistence urged me to speak to the delegates. Against my better judgment—for I had no statement to make—I agreed to do so. I walked downstairs and was directed toward the small room where I would meet with Milliken. As I neared the door, four or five Riegle supporters clapped me on the back. "We're on the verge of winning," they said. "Don't let 'em force you out."

The governor and I agreed that I would address the delegates, but only to explain my belief that no further votes should occur that day. I had, of course, withdrawn my name; only Lenore's was left. But it was my judgment that if a final ballot were taken just then she would fail to get the necessary seventy-five per cent. That would be an enormous defeat for her—one from which I doubted she could ever recover. If she were going to be the nominee, then it was important that she not be subjected to that final ballot rejection. Also, no one had any word from Lenore, and I was not sure she wanted to run. It would be best for all concerned if the final process could be suspended until some hard judgments could be made. That would enable the party to make a wise decision.

Milliken replied that he had to respond to the will of the convention; he was not in a position to halt the balloting. So I was casting about for something to say to the delegates that would make my "let's adjourn now" argument more persuasive. The only way I could do that was to say what I'd said before: that I was not a candidate and that I thought the convention should adjourn without taking further action. If the delegates agreed to this, I added, and if at some later point there was a strong consensus within the party that I should become a declared candidate, then I would consider it at that time.

That was not a commitment to get back into the act; it was the only way I saw to protect everyone's options. It would signal my backers that they should support the move to adjourn. Finally, reluctantly, I went out to address the delegates. My statement was very low key and didn't please anyone. There were further groans and moans. The Romney people thought that I was trying to hold

open a candidacy for myself. My own supporters thought I had
let them down. Having done what I had to do, I left the hall.

The delegates had two choices: proceed with a third ballot with
only Lenore's name, on which they would vote either yes or no, or
adjourn to meet later. My supporters favored adjournment. Lenore's
floor manager, having miscalculated all along, was not going to
break his stride. He was determined to force a third ballot. Milliken
approved the idea and the vote took place. Lenore fell significantly
short of the seventy-five per cent. It was a defeat for her and
George Romney was enraged. I never talked to him directly about
it, but I was told that he blamed several people—including me—for
behaving inappropriately. He apparently thought my statement had
been an attempt to sabotage Lenore and get back into the act at
a later date. Any defeat for Lenore was a defeat for George and
he was like a raging bull.

Days later, Lenore declared a formal candidacy and George
Romney pressured Milliken to endorse her. He did; and the party
then closed ranks behind a Bill Milliken/Lenore Romney ticket. In
November, Phil Hart was re-elected by half a million votes.

Sunday, September 26. The traditional GOP touch football game
started at eight o'clock this chilly Mackinac morning. For Dave
and me, this was obligatory—living proof to doubting Republicans
that we're regulars guys after all. Two dozen people were ready
to play; the ground was wet and slippery and the situation was not
conducive to much finesse. For nearly an hour we moved up and
down the field. Neither side could score. As usually happens in
these games, victory was decided by a few lucky breaks. I happened
to be quarterback at the time and completed two passes in a row,
the second for the game's only touchdown. Football is one activity
where the party honchos can't control the outcome. That's probably
why we won.

After the windup brunch I talked with a combative woman
from Oakland County who was really furious about my anti-Nixon
efforts. We differed on just about everything. She thought the two-
day session here had been "valuable." I said I didn't think it had
moved the party one inch closer to the prospect of winning in

1972. She said she thought it was important for the party leaders to get together, loosen up and let off steam late into the night. I replied that we were missing the boat, that Mackinac Island was the kind of artificial reality that tended to keep us from ever coming to grips with the issues.

After thirty minutes of this, we agreed to disagree. The woman from Oakland County was still furious.

Back in Washington this evening, I learned that John C. Watts, a Democrat from Kentucky, had died of a heart attack. I remembered reading in the paper last week a small piece that pointed out that he was second-ranking Democrat on the Ways and Means Committee. Had Wilbur Mills left the Congress, Watts would have become chairman of that committee.

What struck me was the fact that I didn't know John Watts. In almost five years here, I never had the occasion to meet or speak to him. Nor—until last week—had I read one line about him in print or heard anyone mention his name. A man can come here and serve for many years. He can be very close to a position of real power and, at the same time, be virtually anonymous.

Tuesday, September 28. I talked to McCloskey this morning and tried to get him to concur with the new ground rules that his scheduling committee has developed. As I was explaining them, we got sidetracked onto the campaign's health generally. Effective October 1, the Washington staff is being sliced in half. Those on the "cut" list have already been given the word. Everything has to focus on fund raising, Pete said. I tried to steer the conversation back to scheduling and questioned his habit of making on-the-spot judgments about when and where to appear. I urged him to let the scheduling people evaluate as many of these appearances as possible before he accepts them.

He flared at that, sitting up in his chair and saying, "Christ, Don, if we don't raise enough money now, none of this is going to matter." Eventually he agreed to the new scheduling procedure. Then he left to make some fund-raising calls that he had been scheduled to make two hours earlier. I thought afterward that Pete is right. He's fighting to keep the campaign alive and we're talking about procedures.

In midafternoon Al Toffel stopped by the office to talk with Dave and me. He was the man to fire the McCloskey campaign staffers; he didn't enjoy it but he did it and now he is thinking ahead. He showed us a revised organization chart. It's lean, but it could work. Most of Pete's closest friends in California, Toffel said, are urging him to quit the race and remain in Congress. They feel his effort is doomed and think he'll probably wind up politically discredited and deeply in debt. They've even given him an incentive to quit by promising to assume responsibility for paying off the nearly $80,000 in existing campaign debts. But Pete and Cubby are still determined to press forward, alone if necessary. What Toffel said gave me new insight into the weight of the burdens pressing down on McCloskey. I resolved to do more to help him and to write him a note saying that Dave and I are with him come hell or high water.

After Toffel left, I noticed some little red spots on my hands. They were flaking and peeling. I walked to the doctor's office in the Capitol. They're just little blisters, the doctor explained. There's no treatment for them and no one is sure what causes them. He said they were usually associated with nervous tension.

Wednesday, September 29. Two Hill staffers with families in Michigan came by the office this afternoon to urge me to switch parties, become a Democrat and challenge Griffin next year. If I do, they said, they'll "break their asses" to raise money and help me in other ways. They argued the time is right for this kind of move; a switch would be very well received. The real opportunities in the state today, they added, lie within the Democratic Party. Griffin's seat is on the block in 1972; there's the governor's race in 1974 and, presumably, a Senate vacancy in 1976. The state Democratic Party, they continued, has undergone an enormous transition. But they feel it still lacks a candidate of sufficient stature and caliber.

Dave and I listened carefully and tried to play devil's advocate. People often ask me, "Shouldn't you realize that your real constituency is in the Democratic Party? Wouldn't you be better off in the center of a party more in line with your views on the issues than in the left wing of a party less attuned to your feelings?"

Regardless of how bleak my future looks in the GOP, I replied, I intend to remain in the party and fight for my point of view. Also, I am personally committed to McCloskey's challenge and I will not abandon it under any circumstances. Party affiliation, I went on, isn't that important anyway. How I vote, for example, isn't influenced by the fact that I'm a Republican. Were I a Democrat in Congress, I'd vote the same way I vote today. I'd feel the same way about the same issues. Ideologically, I can identify with the brand of Republicanism exemplified by Abraham Lincoln, Teddy Roosevelt and Dwight Eisenhower. Then, too, I told the staffers, I started in the Republican Party. My oldest political associates tend to be Republicans. I feel connected to them in terms of friendship and shared purposes. It would be a wrenching emotional experience to pull away from those people—many of whom have helped me enormously—and move to another party. I thanked the staffers for their support but said my answer was no.

Thursday, September 30. Early this afternoon Vince Barabba, now of Decision Making Information, Inc., stopped by the office. He's gained weight since 1966 when the Spencer Roberts organization assigned him as its field man in my first campaign. Dave and I kidded him about this and he was very sensitive; he held his pants away from his mid-section and tried to convince us that he was really losing weight. Vince and I have remained close friends. He said he was worried about me. He feels I have alienated myself unnecessarily within the party and he's convinced that the McCloskey effort is a suicide mission. Dave took issue with him on that and, as is his way, asked Vince some "what if" questions about the campaign:

"What if Pete fools everybody and does better than expected in New Hampshire—say twenty per cent plus?"

"Then they'd be ready for you in the next primary," Vince replied. "And *those* guys really know how to get ready for one of these." He gave a sinister laugh.

Dave continued: "Suppose Pete goes on and does even better in Rhode Island?"

"Where does he get the money to go further?"

Dave backed away and tried another tack. "Suppose he does well in New Hampshire and Rhode Island and beats Nixon outright in Massachusetts?"

Vince laughed again. "If that happens," he said, "then give us a call."

The House remained in session until nine o'clock tonight to consider a slew of proposed amendments to the Economic Opportunity Act of 1964. We had token sessions Monday, Tuesday and Wednesday; then we had to go until nine o'clock tonight. That's typical of the regular inefficiency here. The membership just goes along, sheeplike, with a leadership that does a second-rate job. There were a number of recorded teller votes during the afternoon and they necessitated much running back and forth.

At one point, in the men's room off the floor, I noticed Frank Brasco, a Democrat from New York, standing on the scales carefully adjusting the weights. In his late thirties, he stands about five feet five and speaks through his nose with a Brooklyn accent. Ferdie St. Germain, a Democrat from Rhode Island, was sitting in the raised shoeshine chair watching Brasco intently. "Be sure to take out the cigar, Frank," Ferdie said finally, "before you weigh yourself." Brasco smiled and laid his six-inch stogie in an adjacent ashtray.

Several weeks ago Ohio Republican Chalmers Wylie introduced legislation that would allow officially designated prayers in public schools—in effect, repealing the Supreme Court's 1962 decision. His bill went to the House Judiciary Committee. Chairman Emanuel Celler, a Democrat from New York, arbitrarily refused to hold hearings on it. When a bill is blocked in committee, its sponsor can try to persuade 218 members—a majority of the House—to sign a discharge petition that is kept at a desk in the well. If he succeeds in acquiring that many signatures, the bill automatically comes to the floor for a vote.

Since 1900, members have tried to bring bills to the floor 836 times via the discharge petition. Until today, they'd succeeded only twenty-four times. Now, with Wylie's prayer amendment, they've notched their twenty-fifth victory; the amendment will probably come to the floor next month. The reason their victories have been so few is the fact that Congress runs on the committee system. And integral to that is the seniority system.

We select committee chairmen not on the basis of merit but rather on the basis of their seniority. The man who has served on the committee for the longest period becomes its chairman. At the present time in the House, we have seven committee chairmen in their seventies and four in their eighties. Eight of the remaining ten are in their sixties. One chairman, John McMillan from South Carolina, has actually gotten younger. Now in his seventies, he recently changed his biographical data in the Congressional Record to indicate that he's only sixty-nine years old. Some of these men can't hear very well, can't see very well, have difficulty working a full day. Congress is the only major institution in America that selects its leaders this way.

A man can come to Congress when he's thirty-five, serve here twenty years and emerge, at age fifty-five, as the ablest man on his committee. But because he has to wait for all the members ahead of him to either retire or die, he may have to wait another twenty years—until he's seventy-five—before he becomes a chairman. The practical and psychological implications of this are obvious. Members realize they can't afford to lose an election. They can win nineteen, lose one and find themselves at the bottom of the seniority list. They have to win twenty in a row. That means they have to do things that minimize their chances for defeat. Nearly five years ago, Cederberg gave me some of his friendly advice. "Remember, Riegle," he said, "you'll never be defeated by the speech you didn't give." In other words, keep quiet and avoid risks; if you can get re-elected year after year and outlive your colleagues, you will climb to the top of the ladder eventually. The only catch is that you may be in your seventies when the big moment comes.

Why, then, do members go along with this? The answer is that chairmen of congressional committees have enormous, almost authoritarian power, if they choose to exercise it. My own chairman,

George Mahon, for example, is chairman of the Appropriations Committee; he's also chairman of the Defense Appropriations Subcommittee. He and the other subcommittee chairmen have great influence over *multibillion*-dollar segments of the federal budget.

Analyzing the Administration's budget requests for Defense, Agriculture and HEW is an enormously time-consuming job, and while Mahon works as diligently as any man in the House, the workload is incredible. This year, for example, his Defense Appropriations Subcommittee produced nine volumes of hearings—a total of 8296 pages. Another 5924 pages were classified and taken out of the record. When a spending bill is reported out by its subcommittee, it goes to the full Appropriations Committee. As a rule, the full committee gives it only a cursory hearing. It listens to reports from the ranking majority and minority members, then reports out the bill to the floor. Once it is there, it is virtually impossible for any member to alter it.

Say, for example, that a member wants to offer an amendment to the Defense appropriations bill having to do with a certain type of aircraft. He can rise on the floor to propose his legislation; he will be recognized for five minutes. But few members ever avail themselves of this opportunity. They don't have the time or the expertise to take on the House "establishment." When the Appropriations Committee reports out a bill, it's reflecting the will of its chairman and, to a considerable extent, of the Speaker himself. Any member who hopes to offer a successful amendment has an almost herculean task.

When I first came to the Congress—and before I understood how things work around here—I offered several amendments on the floor. Most were to delete items from the Interior Department appropriation that I thought could be postponed. I was convinced, for example, that the Hirshhorn Sculpture Garden in Washington, D.C., was a luxury that could wait. The taxpayers shouldn't have had to pay for it when there were so many urgent needs for their money. However, the momentum was so strong on the side of the committee structure that none of my amendments was successful. You're playing against a stacked deck virtually all the time. In fact,

Julia Hansen, the Interior Subcommittee chairman, is still miffed at me, five years later, for challenging "her bill."

The Appropriations Committee and its subcommittees can't function properly for at least two reasons. The first is a lack of staff. Chairman Mahon has only three staff aides. For years, the Republican minority on the committee had only two staff members— although that number has recently been increased to three. Each subcommittee has from one to three staff members (five for Defense) who work for its Democratic chairman, and while these people are non-partisan they have little time to assist the other members of the subcommittee. On Foreign Ops, for example, we have one staff member for nine subcommittee members. Even if I could have one ninth of his time available to me directly, I couldn't scratch the surface of the budget that our subcommittee is considering. Either I must do it myself or assign the job to someone on my office staff, usually Carl Blake. I could use at least five full-time assistants on my Appropriations Committee work alone.

The men in power, however, usually don't see themselves as needing more staff. And to many other, less senior, members, the lack of committee staff just isn't a pressing concern. It doesn't relate directly to their re-election hopes. They'd much rather take the people they have on their personal staffs and direct them toward servicing their districts, performing chores for constituents. That's far more important to them and their long-term chances of becoming committee chairmen than digging into the intricacies of the federal budget or pending legislation.

The second reason the committee doesn't function properly is that it isn't an accurate reflection of the House as a whole. As long as the Democrats have been in control, the existing power structure has been dominated by the Southerners. For decades, the one-party South automatically returned Democratic congressmen who accumulated great seniority. Of the seven highest-ranking Democrats on the Appropriations Committee today, six are from the South. The South is guaranteed the chairmanship of this committee for years to come—if the Democrats continue to control Congress. Southern congressmen tend to be more hawkish and fiscally conservative, less oriented toward domestic spending measures. Subcommittees tend to be special-interest-oriented. Members who have a strong interest in the military or have large numbers of defense installations in their districts usually seek assignment to the Defense Appropriations Subcommittee. That subcommittee usually smiles on Pentagon requests.

The same thing is true with respect to the Agriculture Subcommittee; most of its members come from farm states. Each subcommittee tries to enlarge its slice of the federal budget pie. But there is no mechanism for evaluating priorities, for questioning the wisdom, say, of taking $500 million away from Defense and plugging it into HEW. We don't know how to begin to weigh questions like that.

The Democratic leadership has another built-in bias that reflects itself in terms of committee assignments. Often, the more conservative Democrats will assign liberals to such "liberal" committees as Education and Labor. They know that, as long as they control the appointment of members to the Appropriations Committee, they can put on the brakes at that point. Both Democrats and Republicans have gone to great pains to screen out from the Appropriations Committee those who would spend more for domestic needs. I'm a fluke. If the Republican leadership had a second chance, they probably wouldn't appoint me to Appropriations. I'd more likely get Education and Labor.

This built-in bias also reflects itself in the unwillingness to form new committees. In the last twenty-five years this nation's problems have multiplied and grown increasingly complex. Yet the leadership has appointed only two new committees—on Science and Astronautics and on Ethics. David Pryor, a thoughtful, even-tempered Democrat from Arkansas, has tried to dramatize the problems of the elderly and feels that Congress should appoint a committee to consider these problems in detail. The chances that it will are almost non-existent. The favorite argument used by the leadership to thwart Pryor's request is lack of space to house a new committee. (So Pryor sought private donations, rented a trailer and parked it at a gas station a few blocks from the Capitol, where volunteers continue work on the problems of the elderly.)

But that's not the only reason for their reluctance to appoint a new committee. Existing committee chairmen don't want to dilute their own power. They had to spend all those years waiting to climb the ladder. They're loath to create competing ladders. This is especially true in Pryor's case. He's only been here for four terms and is still in his thirties. Few senior members, who've been waiting in line for years, would want to grant a charter to a new committee and give the prerogatives of a chairman to so young a member.

Shortly after eight this evening I took Meredith to the members' dining room. No sooner had we begun to eat than two bells rang, indicating that a vote was about to start in the chamber upstairs. Ed Patten passed our table and patted me on the shoulder. He paused, looked down at me and in his best Perth Amboy drawl asked, "Didja hear those bells?"

"The trouble is," I replied, "that I'm beginning to hear them all the time."

"Wait until you're my age," Patten said. He glanced around the room at other members finishing their dinner. "All right," he shouted, "everybody out of the pool." Moving to the next table, he spotted a crony, Jim Delaney of New York. "That means you, Delaney," he said. "You may be a big shot upstairs in the Rules Committee, but you're just another one of us down here."

After Ed had left, I told Meredith for the hundredth time how much I enjoy Patten. Then I excused myself and hurried to the floor. Waiting for the vote on final passage, I struck up a conversation with Chuck Whalen. In 1970, Chuck won the highest percentage of votes of any Republican in Ohio. Typically, he's in the doghouse with the GOP establishment. They resent his liberalism and his independent approach toward the Nixon Administration. He's apt to face strong opposition in a primary next year.

A former supporter has told him, in fact, that it's no longer a question of "mending fences"; it's a question of "building" them. So Chuck said he was considering running as an independent. He can accept the prospect of losing his seat in a hard-fought general election, but he can't tolerate the thought of being defeated in "a narrow little primary by a bunch of nuts." I said I knew his feelings exactly.

VII. OCTOBER

Friday, October 1. There was a press conference at ten o'clock this morning in the Armed Services Committee Room of the Rayburn Building. Its purpose was to present a petition that 122 House members and nine senators signed—within the last twenty-four hours—condemning the one-candidate presidential "election" in South Vietnam. Bob Leggett, a Democrat from California, circulated the petition on the floor yesterday afternoon. He and I served as bipartisan sponsors of the press conference. After his initial statement we switched places in front of the microphones. I read the joint statement, emphasized the number of congressmen who had signed it and concluded by mentioning "the disgust and outrage members feel about the fact that the American government has chosen to bankroll and sanction these meaningless elections."

Returning to my office, I asked Kathleen Sadler to hold all calls while Carl Blake, Dave Brunell and I discussed the office staff situation. Betsy Boyce, my legislative assistant for the past nine months, has decided to join the staff of the Wednesday Club, a liberal Republican study group. We agreed to offer the job to Lisa Finkelstein, who had been my legislative assistant several years ago. As we broke up, it was clear that we had just finished one of those occasional meetings that later come to be recognized as important turning points. In one sense, our drive for re-election began today.

In midafternoon I drove to Lew Griffith's office in McLean to sign some legal papers pertaining to the house in Flint. Lew said the divorce proceeding has moved to the final step and that the judge in Fairfax County, Virginia, received all the papers this morning. He would probably sign the final decree before the day was over.

Later this overcast, depressing afternoon, I drove to Georgetown on an errand. Meredith went with me. About four-thirty I called the office to touch base. Kathleen told me that she had just talked to Lew Griffith's secretary, who said the divorce papers had been signed. I paused a moment, then moved on to another subject. When I hung up the telephone, I felt no clear emotion. Meredith was standing at the scarf counter. She looked tired and thin. I walked over and took her arm. As we moved toward the door, I repeated what Kathleen had said. We looked at each other for a long moment and then continued walking.

Saturday, October 2. When I arrived in McLean this morning, Donny was waiting outside wearing a raincoat, tennis shoes and a plastic crash helmet. Cathy and Laurie soon appeared with suitcases containing their overnight clothes. Early this afternoon we went to a movie. I had asked Meredith to come to the apartment after the movie was over so she and the children could get acquainted and we could all go to dinner. She was hesitant, but finally I persuaded her to come. In due course she arrived and I made the introductions.

Things proceeded much more smoothly than I had dared hope. Meredith was gentle, warm and friendly, and soon both Cathy and Laurie were talking easily with her. Donny, however, was far less open. He was wary, a bit standoffish, and Meredith just let him play it that way. She doesn't want to force a relationship with the children or seem like a "parent figure" to them. She hopes that eventually she can be a friend.

As we were getting into the car, Meredith offered Cathy the front seat. She declined, nicely, and we were off, the three kids in the back. The ride was happy and full of banter. After a super Mexican dinner in Arlington, we drove to Georgetown and parked. Strolling down Wisconsin Avenue, Laurie ran ahead and jumped up to touch the edges of some awnings. Meredith likes to do that herself, so she followed in Laurie's path.

We bought some ice cream cones and were walking back to the car when Cathy offered Meredith a lick of hers. Once back at the apartment we sat on the floor watching TV. At one point, without being obvious about it, Meredith walked into the living room so the kids and I could be by ourselves in the den. A few minutes later Laurie looked around and realized Meredith was absent. In her thoughtful, eight-year-old way she said, "I'm going to go out and invite Meredith to come in with us." She did and that was her way of expressing what Cathy had expressed with the lick of her ice cream cone.

About an hour before bedtime Donny became very hostile toward Meredith and me. He rubbed her hair very roughly and half kicked her in the shins. A few minutes earlier I had threatened the kids with a spanking if they didn't stop roughhousing. Now Donny was saying that *he* just might spank me, that *he* was really the boss. Both Meredith and I could sense his turmoil. He was struggling with some very difficult three-year-old emotions. I hugged and kissed him and told him that I didn't really want to fight.

Leaving Cathy in charge, I drove Meredith home. Earlier, I had wondered what it would be like for her to see me as a father with my children. Would I seem "different" to her? Would she feel less connected to me? I confided these fears. She turned and said she loved seeing me as a father and she thought the kids were beautiful. She told me not to worry, and I hurried back to the apartment. The kids were already in their pajamas. I tucked them into bed, and soon they were all asleep.

Sunday, October 3. I woke up first this morning and made orange juice and English muffins. Cathy and Laurie were sleeping on folding cots in the hall. I sat beside them one at a time and stroked their hair until their eyes opened. Donny wandered out of my bedroom wearing his pajamas, rubbing the sleep from his eyes. I steered him to a beanbag chair and in a few minutes he and his sisters were roughhousing again.

The time had come for me to tell the kids about the divorce. I wasn't sure how best to do it. We drove to the playground at Haines Point, a favorite haunt of ours. The sun was shining; the breeze was fresh and clean. We worked our way around the play-ground: first the small slides; then the swings; finally the circular spinning toy which the kids sit inside while I push.

Ten, twenty, thirty minutes passed and I was still searching for the right words. The children were scampering every which way; laughing, enjoying themselves. I forced myself to begin by calling Cathy and Laurie. I asked them to come sit down for a minute; I wanted to talk to them. While Donny continued to play, they walked to the picnic table.

I began slowly by saying, "As you know, I have been living away from home for more than a year and a half—"

Suddenly Donny arrived, puffing mightily. "I got to go wee-wee, Dad," he said. I asked if he could wait awhile or did he have to go this minute? "Right this minute," Donny replied, grinning mischie-vously.

He and I found a nearby tree. We pulled down his pants and he let fly. He was chuckling, hollering something to his sisters. I was trying to regather my thoughts. Once back at the table, I sat across from Cathy and Laurie. As they knew, their mother and I had agreed to seek a divorce and the process had taken many months. A few days ago the judge had signed the papers, which meant that—

Cathy interrupted and asked, "You're divorced already, aren't you?"

"That's what I was coming to," I said. "The divorce has now hap-pened." I paused, looked each of them in the eye and then con-tinued. "Divorce is a legal thing. It doesn't mean that I stop caring about Mother or what she's going to do in the future. I still feel the same way about everyone. That hasn't changed at all."

There was another pause. With no visible change of mood, Laurie ran off to play with Donny. Cathy and I got up and walked around for a while together. Neither of us said anything. Eventually we all loaded ourselves into the car and drove to McLean. Once we reached the house, Laurie and Donny disappeared through the front door without saying a word. Cathy and I walked up together, each of us carrying a suitcase. At the front steps she turned to face me. We kissed each other twice, the second time hard. I managed to say that I hoped she could keep her heart and feelings together. We hugged each other for a long minute. She said, "I love you, Dad." I replied, "I love you too."

She stood there smiling, but her eyes were as wet as mine. The ride back to Washington was especially quiet.

Monday, October 4. Just before noon today I stopped at the House bank on the first floor of the Capitol and cashed a $50 check. I asked what my balance was then and the cashier said $380. I've been trying to keep a cushion in my checking account, but the cushion is so thin that I worry about nickels and dimes. I don't see the situation changing any time soon. In fact it may get worse before it gets better. I'm not complaining. It's a fact of life. Most people's income situation is worse than mine.

Under the terms of the financial settlement agreement, I send Nancy a monthly check for $1460—$800 for alimony and $660 for child support. I have $1335 to budget for my own expenses. From that I pay $270 for rent, $200 for groceries and meals out and about $80 for gasoline, telephone and electricity. Then there are the other costs—clothes, laundry and entertainment—found in anyone's personal budget. I have an upcoming payment to make on a life insurance policy. I have two bank notes which fall due periodically and I reduce the principal and pay interest on them. I'm also trying to establish a college fund for the children. Every time I go to the district, I wind up paying the bills for countless lunches and dinners. Kathleen needed a check from me this morning for $158 to reimburse her for purchasing recent plane tickets to Michigan. I'm not a high-liver. I don't spend a lot of money on clothes or entertainment or liquor. Still, I tend to run out of funds by the end of the month.

About twelve-thirty this afternoon, I was over on the floor to answer a quorum call when I spotted John Rooney, the testy, powerful little Appropriations Subcommittee chairman from New York. We were in the R's; I had just answered my name. His name was approaching and he was coughing and trying to catch his breath so he could respond. I waited until he had finished coughing and answered his name. Then I patted him on the arm and said good-naturedly, "John, you ought to do something about that cough."

He looked at me in the way that a Marine drill instructor might stare at a recruit. He paused, then asked, "Did Ron Dellums give you that suit?'"

"Yeah," I replied. "Dellums had this suit last month, but the styles have changed since then, so he gave it to me."

"Well," Rooney said, "apparently he gave one to O'Konski too."

As I left the floor, I happened to bump into Al O'Konski. He was wearing slightly belled pants and a brown tweed jacket belted in the back. It was a carbon copy of mine. With a grin on my face, I told him what Rooney had said. O'Konski replied, very seriously, "Well, I think we ought to take that as a compliment."

Several hours later, waiting for another vote, I ran into O'Konski again, standing against the brass rail in the rear of the chamber. We talked about the redistricting situation in Wisconsin. In redrawing the lines to comply with recent population shifts, the legislators had to carve up one district. They decided to go to work on O'Konski's. He has been the lone wolf here among Wisconsin Republicans for the past twenty-nine years. Clearly, the legislators took that into account. All the other Republican districts, he said, were fully protected. In some cases they were made even more Republican. This was especially true in Bill Steiger's case. Steiger, a team player, now will be virtually impossible to beat. O'Konski, who votes his own mind, has been placed in jeopardy. He just might decide not to run again.

The most important issue on the floor this afternoon was a bill to disapprove the President's order postponing the scheduled pay raise for federal employees. I was really on the fence about this. On the one hand, I didn't want to treat federal employees any differently than other workers. I would have preferred to wait until the ground rules for Phase Two were clarified and we could treat everyone the same way. On the other hand, the Democratic leadership was forcing the issue to determine whether or not the House would support the President's economic game plan.

So this vote was an important test of Nixon's efforts to move the economy in the right direction. Carl Blake and Dave Brunell thought

I ought to support the President this time. Federal workers, they maintained, were pretty well taken care of already and this vote would have an important psychological impact. It would allow the President's plan to unfold and gain momentum. I'd still retain the option, they said, of voting against parts of the plan at some later date. I tended to agree with them and decided to vote with the Administration.

Tom Railsback, however, had decided to vote against the Administration—perhaps because his Illinois district contains a large number of federal employees. Jerry Ford walked over to try to lobby him. I was sitting next to Tom. I told Jerry my mind was still open; I wanted to hear his arguments. The clerk was calling the roll and fast approaching the R's. When his name was called, Railsback didn't reply. (Later he chose to walk down and quietly vote aye in the well of the House.) Then it was my turn. I voted against the disapproval resolution. A number of Republicans, surprised to hear me vote no, turned around in their seats. Ford was still standing there and I remember hoping that none of them thought Jerry had succeeded in pressuring me to vote his way. The resolution was defeated by a margin of thirty-three votes.

Leaving the chamber, I walked downstairs to the barbershop on the main floor of the Capitol. My shoes looked pretty tacky; they needed a shine. The shoeshine man had disappeared for a moment, so I took off my shoes and left them there and walked to the men's room across the hall. As I was washing my hands I noticed ten or twelve visitors who seemed to be from India. They were carrying cameras. One fellow noticed that I was in my stocking feet; then they all noticed. They followed me out into the corridor again and it seemed as if they were wondering whether they should take off their shoes too.

At seven o'clock this evening Meredith and I drove to the Kennedy Center to attend a reception, dinner and concert in honor of some visiting French parliamentarians. We parked and made our way up to the South Opera Lounge. We entered the room only to find that most of the guests were already seated at four large round tables. Meredith sat beside Fisher Howe of Johns Hopkins University. I found a place between the French interpreter and Mrs. Francis Wilcox, wife of the university's dean. Mrs. Wilcox identified herself as a conservative Republican, her husband as a liberal Republican. They no longer discuss politics, she said. Fortunately, I was still able to order a martini on the rocks. Mrs. Wilcox went down much easier with the martini.

The concert tonight featured the Philadelphia Symphony Orchestra conducted by Eugene Ormandy. As we walked from the dinner to the Opera Hall, we crossed paths with Henry Kissinger. He looked as if he'd gained a few pounds since the Bilderberg Conference last April—apparently the Chinese cooking. I introduced him to Meredith and chatted with him about the French parliamentarians. Then we parted ways in the crowd.

Tuesday, October 5. At eight o'clock this evening Meredith and I drove to the French Embassy on Belmont Road, N.W., to attend a reception and buffet dinner in honor of the parliamentarians. Making small talk at receptions isn't my idea of fun. I dislike the standard cocktail party environment and if I can avoid attending one I will do so every time. Tonight's affair, however, was interesting and enjoyable. The parliamentarians had just emerged from spending an hour with Henry Kissinger. One Frenchman said, "He is the President. Yes?" The other Frenchmen agreed.

After dinner we were chatting with Madame Lucet, wife of the ambassador, in a small room just off the covered balcony. Ambassador Charles Lucet walked over to join our conversation. He was carrying a scotch and water and I could tell from his general demeanor that he had had two or three drinks. Madame Lucet was drinking ice water. She took one look at her husband and, before he realized what was happening, exchanged her glass of water for his glass of scotch. A look of complete astonishment flickered across his face; he reached out his hand for the scotch again, but his wife just wasn't going to let him have that glass. She continued chatting with us as if nothing had happened at all.

Wednesday, October 6. I read in today's Washington *Post* that Joseph Karth, a Democrat from Minnesota, has taken the late John

Watt's place on the Ways and Means Committee. Karth has a marginal district that includes St. Paul, and the Republicans have made a real effort to wrest that seat away from him. Several years ago I campaigned for the Republican who was then opposing him—unsuccessfully, as it turned out. He was probably selected for Ways and Means to strengthen his position in the district. Committee assignments are often handed out for that reason.

My own committee assignment came about in an even more circuitous way. Late on election night in 1966, after the returns were in, I telephoned Minority Leader Jerry Ford to ask his help in winning assignment to the Education and Labor Committee. He was surprised by the call but was pleasant and said he would carefully consider my request.

After the ninetieth Congress convened early in 1967, the jockeying for committee assignments became intense. Some fifty-five freshmen Republicans were competing for a small number of choice assignments. Marv Esch, a first-term Republican from Ann Arbor, also wanted Education and Labor. The leadership said that only one of us could join that committee and that we should settle it between ourselves. Neither of us wished to defer to the other. I suggested flipping a coin. He declined. The impasse continued for several days. Finally, I decided to seek another assignment.

At that time, Chuck Chamberlain was planning to leave the Armed Services Committee and move up to a highly prized seat on the Ways and Means Committee. He suggested that I try for the seat he would vacate on Armed Services. Under the circumstances, it seemed the best alternative and my assignment there was tentatively arranged. Then fate intervened. Lurleen Wallace was elected governor of Alabama. Her inauguration took place on the same day that House Democrats were caucusing to fill a Democratic vacancy on the Ways and Means Committee. The leading candidate was Omar Burleson from Texas. Historically, Texas has always had a member on the Ways and Means Committee to "protect" the oil depletion allowance. This ensured the flow of vast sums of campaign money from oil interests to the Democratic Party.

While Burleson had the votes to win the vacancy, he was nonetheless being vigorously contested by Jack Gilbert, a liberal from

New York. Finally, it was time to vote. The members of the Alabama delegation still had not returned from Mrs. Wallace's inauguration. Their plane had been delayed. In their absence, Gilbert won an upset victory. Suddenly, the meaning of Burleson's loss was clear. The Democrats had failed to place a defender of the oil depletion allowance on the committee. The Republican leadership sensed a chance to upstage the Democrats. Why not put a Republican oil man on Ways and Means and divert campaign contributions from oil interests into the Republican war chest?

By coincidence, the Republicans had a bona fide Texas oil man in their midst—freshman George Bush from Houston. He seemed the perfect choice. First, however, some problems had to be resolved. Chamberlain had a claim on the Republican vacancy; he'd have to agree to step aside for Bush and remain on Armed Services. Then, too, it was virtually without precedent for a freshman to be placed on Ways and Means. The politicking behind the Bush appointment would be obvious and potentially difficult to explain.

The leadership found ways to skin the cat all around. Ford asked Chamberlain to defer to Bush for the sake of the party. Reluctantly, Chamberlain agreed—after winning assurances that he would receive the next vacancy on Ways and Means (which he did). There was one remaining vacancy on the Appropriations Committee. Because Chamberlain had relinquished his claim to Ways and Means, Michigan had "something coming" in return; it went after the Appropriations Committee vacancy—and won. Then the question became: who in our delegation would receive this prized assignment?

Chamberlain could have taken it, but he was in line for Ways and Means and preferred to keep his ranking on Armed Services until he got it. One by one, other senior Michigan Republicans chose to by-pass Appropriations. That left in contention only the six Michigan freshmen, and everyone had tentative or sure committee assignments. Guy Vander Jagt wanted the slot, but Ford and Cederberg leaned toward giving it to me. At twenty-eight, I would become the youngest member ever assigned to Appropriations and that would help draw attention away from Bush's appointment to Ways and Means. My appointment would "enfranchise" freshmen Republicans by placing them on virtually all the House committees—a

genuinely progressive step on the part of the leadership. Furthermore, it was thought that this prestigious assignment would
strengthen my re-election chances in a predominantly Democratic
"swing" district and keep that district in the Republican column.

The final coincidence was the most ironic. I had earned an undergraduate degree in economics and an MBA in finance and I had
spent three years in finance with IBM. My work there had centered
on appropriations requests and I had had the chance to help devise
the system·IBM uses to justify its capital investments. By education
and training, I was a logical choice for Appropriations. But as Senator Frank Church remarked the other day, "What does logic have
to do with the Congress?" My background had little influence on the
decision. It was the inauguration of Lurleen Wallace that put me on
the Appropriations Committee.

At eleven-thirty this morning, as I took my seat in a meeting of
the full Appropriations Committee, I happened to glance at John
Rhodes, a Republican from Arizona, and realized that somehow he
looked "different" today. Suddenly it dawned on me that he was
letting his hair grow out. My expression must have reflected my
thoughts because he smiled back at me knowingly. Rhodes's switch
away from a crew cut is significant. He's the chairman of the
House Republican Policy Committee.

Near the end of the afternoon—a long, hectic afternoon—Dave
Brunell caught up with me and said he wanted to talk about scheduling, about decisions that will have to be made over the next three
months. When he said that, it tightened my stomach into a hard
knot. I was tempted to reply. "I don't want to talk about scheduling
decisions. Now or ever again. Period." But of course I didn't. I told
him this had been one of those days. I wasn't in the right frame of
mind just now to deal with questions of commitments to travel all
over the map for the next ninety days.

Dave understood that perfectly. And having said it, I, too, realized
that probably within the hour Dave and I would sit down and wade
through those scheduling decisions. Which is precisely what we did.

Thursday, October 7. I had breakfast at my apartment this morning with Alain Terrenoire, one of the visiting French parliamen-

tarians. We were talking about our respective futures in politics and he said he thought that I was far less ambitious today than I was two years ago, when we first met in the exchange program. I explained that my life had undergone substantial changes, that I was reordering my priorities.

"Well," he asked, "do you still want to be President?"

"Yes and no," I replied. "Yes, if someone came to me tomorrow and asked, 'Would you serve as President to try to get the country moving in a new direction?' But no if that meant turning into a politician like Nixon."

We talked about Congress, the toll that it took in personal terms and the frustrations of not being able to do things that needed to be done. After breakfast, as we were driving on Constitution Avenue, I noticed that all the flags were flying at half staff. I wondered aloud who had died.

"Well," Alain said in his droll way, "your illusion. It signifies the death of your illusion to be President."

I learned this afternoon that the organizers of tomorrow's voter registration rally in Boston are short on cash. They won't be able to reimburse me for the cost of the trip or for plane tickets to the last few rallies I've attended. Those bills are still outstanding and I'll have to write a personal check to cover them as soon as possible. I wouldn't mind doing that if I had sufficient funds in my bank account; it gets a little hairy when the money's not there to spend. In any case, I'm still planning to make the rally in Boston tomorrow. Kathleen has offered to pay for the ticket with her American Express card. That will give me time to scramble around and try to come up with the eighty-eight dollars it will cost to fly there and return.

What makes my financial situation even more worrisome is a letter I received this morning from Roger Perry, a classmate at the Harvard Business School. Three years ago each of us purchased a one-eighth interest in a combination Stuckey candy store and gas station in Lathrop, Missouri. My share cost $10,000—$7500 of which I borrowed from Perry. Since then he has carried that $7500 note and I've been paying interest on it ranging from seven to ten per cent each year.

The store has yet to show a profit. While it's near the break-even point today, a series of earlier reversals created losses of $30,000. No dividends have been paid to the owners of the store. Perry has been feeling the pinch of the continuing recession. He said in his letter that he could no longer afford to act as my banker on the $7500 note and he asked me to pay all—or at least part—of it by November 27. I have only two options: sell the one-eighth interest and pay off the note in full, losing my own $2500 in the process, or try to raise sufficient capital to give Perry a partial payment and refinance the balance. The first decision I had to make was whether or not it was wise for me to stay in the Stuckey store. If it starts making money, it can help send the kids to college later. I need some sound, long-term investments for that purpose. After pushing numbers around for an hour and a half, I decided to try to hang on. I'll have to scrimp to raise enough cash to reduce that note significantly over the next seven weeks.

Friday, October 8. Meredith and I flew to Boston this morning to attend the voter registration rally at Government Center. My first reaction was dismay at the size of the crowd. Government Center Plaza can accommodate about 75,000 people. A crowd of 2000 doesn't occupy much space and tends to look smaller than it is. This crowd was 2000 at the most. The organizing efforts had failed.

Senator Muskie was speaking when we arrived and he was doing better in terms of what he said and how he said it than he had at the first registration rally in Rhode Island several months ago. Still, he didn't generate much in the way of crowd response. When he left the microphone McCloskey took his place. Pete gave a straightforward, very low-key address about the war in Vietnam and the country's priorities and stepped down to a good round of applause. Then it was Senator George McGovern's turn. He stirred the crowd when he urged "amnesty for people who have refused induction into the Vietnam war"; the rest of his speech didn't excite anyone and that's McGovern's biggest problem. He doesn't seem to get any better. He goes along at a steady pace without ever triggering the kind of response he's going to need if he expects his campaign to move anywhere.

I had looked forward to this rally for a long time. I wanted to say where I thought the country was and what the McCloskey challenge meant. Then, too, the idea of returning to Boston just did something for me. I had those feelings moving around inside but I hadn't taken the time to outline any remarks. I'd figured I could do that later. Suddenly the master of ceremonies turned to me and said, "We're going to change the format. As soon as McGovern finishes, I want to introduce you and have you go on and speak." That meant I had less than two minutes to outline my speech.

I talked about how much Boston and Massachusetts had given the country in terms of political leadership. I said the things that John and Robert Kennedy might have done were things we still had to do. Young people had to effect a renaissance in government. I finished with an appeal for Pete's New Hampshire campaign. If we could stop the war one day sooner, I said, then we would have succeeded no matter how that election turned out. When I walked off the stage one old woman grabbed my arms and thanked me for mentioning Robert Kennedy. She had tears in her eyes.

At the end of the rally Meredith and I rode the subway into Cambridge. We had arranged to meet Al Lowenstein for dinner at Chez Dreyfuss. Between bites Al told us a story about the 1968 Democratic convention in Chicago. During the final stages of that convention, delegates seeking an alternative to Hubert Humphrey took a head count and concluded that they had the votes to put Ted Kennedy over the top. But no one wanted to nominate him without getting a green light from the Kennedy family. Stephen Smith was acting as spokesman for the family and he was holed up somewhere, unavailable. Some delegates approached Al and asked him to nominate Ted anyway. Al replied that he was already pledged as a McCarthy delegate; he was required to support Gene on the first ballot. Then, too, he wasn't sure that Ted would be willing to run.

Al decided to find out if he could be released from his commitment to McCarthy. If that happened, he'd be in a position to consider the practical matter of nominating Ted. The McCarthy camp insisted that he remain loyal to Gene. Still, there was enough time for someone to make a nominating speech. "There was the time, the moment, the mood," Al said. "Everything had come together in exactly the right way. That convention was prepared to nominate Kennedy." Unless Ted's name was offered, Humphrey was the certain nominee.

Finally Al sensed it had come to the question of nominating Kennedy himself—the New York delegation had previously reserved the right to make a nomination if it chose to—and taking the responsibility for putting in motion the wave of events that would inevitably follow. He had five minutes to decide one way or the other. He walked into a men's room to try to weigh the issues alone. At the end of that five minutes he still had not reached a decision. Then, in the hallway outside, he bumped into Charles Evers, brother of Medgar Evers, the slain civil rights leader in Mississippi. Evers had heard rumors that Al might nominate Ted. He grabbed Al by the jacket, looked him in the eye and asked, "You're not going to do that to that family for a third time, are you?"

Evers' question had an enormous impact on Al's thinking at that moment. As he was moving onto the floor a woman delegate, one of the early "Dump Johnson" people, approached him and asked if he was planning to nominate Ted. When Al replied that he wasn't, she flew into an hysterical rage. She beat on his chest and yelled that he was abandoning the country. Having come so far and fought so hard, he couldn't abandon the challenge now. He was the only one who could nominate Ted. Al looked at her and blurted "Who elected Al Lowenstein to play God?" Then he rushed off by himself. He did not place Kennedy's name in nomination. What might have been did not occur.

This story, as Al told it tonight, illustrates the kinds of decisions politicians are sometimes called upon to make. You have to make judgments under pressure—judgments whose results can be very far-reaching—and you don't feel equipped to make them because you don't know enough. Yet you must make them. And you do the best you can under the circumstances.

Monday, October 11. This was Columbus Day; the House was not in session, so Meredith and I drove to Georgetown to do some errands this morning. Because I was thinking about the trip I had to make to Flint, I felt off stride. Georgetown's noise and congestion didn't help calm my nerves. Meredith was up-tight too. We were in our own separate emotional compartments. As we walked along Wisconsin Avenue I began talking—my way of trying to reach her —without even thinking about how my words might be interpreted. I was depressed, I said; I felt that we were "just going through the motions."

Suddenly Meredith stopped and burst into tears: long, shaking sobs. I wanted desperately to take my words back. I hadn't intended to hurt her; I hadn't realized how fragile those feelings were just then. I stood beside her, patted her gently and said how very sorry I was. Finally, without looking up, she began talking. My "going through the motions" comment had been just too much; it was unfair, so untrue. I struggled to explain that I hadn't meant it in a deep sense at all—only in terms of how we were spending our morning together: running little errands in Georgetown.

Back in the car, we talked about our respective abilities to sense and respond to each other's needs. She said she felt that too often I failed to sense her mood, to understand her inner feelings. She was right about that. But, I said, she had to *help* me understand those moods. Meredith tends to deal with emotional problems internally and she has enormous strength in this respect. Whenever things are hardest for her, she deals with them silently, in her own way, and soon—with the passage of time—she works things out. We talked a long time and she promised she'd try harder to express her thoughts. That's not going to be easy. She's private, she keeps a lot to herself, and she doesn't let too many people near her.

Soon it was time to go. I packed an overnight bag and said a difficult good-by.

Less than thirty minutes remained before my flight. I whipped by the Longworth Building and met Dave Brunell on the corner. He briefed me in two minutes about the meeting in Flint tonight and handed me a packet of pertinent facts and figures. Then I raced to the airport. Arriving with five minutes to spare, I called Meredith to say good-by again.

Now I'm at the Durant Hotel in Flint, and it's late. I've just written my parents a letter telling them that the divorce is final.

Knowing their feelings about divorce, I found it a painfully difficult letter to write.

Tuesday, October 12. I returned to Washington this morning and dashed to the Capitol to vote on an amendment to exempt women from the military draft. As I reached the House and hurried to the floor, I found my way blocked by one of the doorkeepers. He was helping Bill McCulloch, a Republican from Ohio, climb the stairs and enter the chamber. Now seventy, Bill is the ranking Republican on the House Judiciary Committee. He's one of the most able and decent men in the Congress, a long-time fighter for equal rights. Within the last two years his health has failed and he has undergone major surgery twice. Although he has recovered to the point where he can get around slowly with the help of aides and a cane, he apparently goes from lucid moments to times when he is not sure where he is. He is much more stooped over now and his hair is very white. At times he seems to be fading away before our eyes.

Some months ago his wife and daughter publicly announced his retirement at the end of this term. Ohio representatives, who must lose one seat in Congress next year because of reapportionment, breathed a collective sigh of relief. They assumed they could use his district as their "carving district" and protect all other incumbents. Then McCulloch indicated he did intend to run again. He hadn't authorized his wife and daughter to make that earlier statement. I don't see how he can handle the strains of another campaign, his fourteenth. Poor guy. He's caught in the web. He's lived with the hope that someday the Republicans will capture Congress and he can become chairman of the Judiciary Committee. He just can't relinquish that dream.

There are so many old men in Congress that we actually have a lot of emergency medical gear just to keep them alive. We have our own ambulance parked behind the Capitol, ready to go at a moment's notice. In the cloakrooms, just out of sight of the galleries, we have stretchers and oxygen tanks. Doctors are always on duty whenever the House is in session and they can rush to the floor in less than sixty seconds. Sometimes they have to. On one occasion, I saw a senior member have a seizure on the floor. Unable to

breathe, he slumped down in his seat and his face turned white.
The doctors arrived in time to revive him and get him to a hospital.

Wednesday, October 13. The mail this morning included a nice
letter from my former kindergarten teacher—with a twenty-dollar
contribution to the McCloskey campaign. I wanted to mention this
to Pete and about noon I spotted him on the House floor talking to
Peggy Heckler from Massachusetts. Pete was saying that Senator Ed
Brooke had asked him to keep a low profile in the state in order to
avoid stirring up conservative Republicans who might retaliate
against Brooke. Peggy thought Brooke was right. This bothered me.
The Massachusetts primary is one of our best chances to offer a constructive alternative to Nixon's policies, and I resented the suggestion that Brooke's self-interest should make Pete back away.

I was mad and I let it show. While I like Brooke, I challenged
his record in the Senate and said I felt that he had led few fights of
conscience there. Peggy disputed me. Her voice rising, she went on,
"That's the trouble with you, Don. You're always starting fights."
That remark really got to me, so I replied, "How could that be
worse than never starting any fights?"

Peggy's own behavior here has been very cautious. She avoids
political risks by seldom speaking out on controversial issues. While
she's liberal in private conversation and often courageous in votes on
the floor, her voice is usually absent from the public debate. What's
so frustrating about this is that she is an able, forceful speaker capable of enormous leadership on the issues. I think she's just as
gifted as Bella Abzug. But Bella is prepared to fire away and let the
chips fall where they may. Peggy wins about seventy per cent of the
vote in her district every time, but she worries so much about losing
the next election that she makes little use of her mandate. What does
victory mean if you don't try to do something with the mandate?

We weren't shouting at each other, but we were speaking in a
louder than normal tone, and we *were* intense about it. A vote was
in progress on the floor and, in a nice way, Pete said, "I hate to see
my friends arguing." So Peggy and I ended our discussion. Later I
talked to McCloskey alone. He said he's willing to lie low in Massachusetts for the time being, but he plans a strong push there in the

months to come. He went on to say that he simply can't stomach the Nixon people any more. If the challenge fails, he's through with this kind of politics. He didn't elaborate.

Late this afternoon my mother called from Flint. She was very upset. My forty-three-year-old uncle is in the intensive care ward at Owosso Memorial Hospital with another heart attack. And, to add to that, she had heard at church today that I had gotten married again. I assured her I hadn't done that and promised to let her know in advance if and when I did. During our conversation I tried to kid her and said, "Well, thanks for calling to find out what I wanted for a wedding gift." There was a long silence at the other end. "Mother," I continued, "don't lose your sense of humor." Finally she began to chuckle, and we ended on a good note.

Thursday, October 14. The main topic of discussion at the Michigan Republican delegation breakfast this morning was the busing controversy. This is one of those issues that can kill politicians. It's absolutely fatal for a guy who miscalculates. Most of my own GOP colleagues are fairly conservative anyway, so it isn't hard for them to oppose busing. And they're delighted by the dilemma the state's Democrats now face.

Several days ago Minnesota Senator Walter Mondale suggested taking some Senate investigators to Warren, Michigan, to look into the busing dispute there. Michigan Democrats squelched that idea. Most of the more "liberal" Democratic members from Michigan are scrambling to find a "safe" position on the issue. The last thing they want is a federal investigation that would stir up more public outrage. What was so distressing to me was the rationale my Republican colleagues at this morning's breakfast used to support their stand. They were saying that busing is expensive, that it adds to traffic congestion and air pollution, that drug pushers can get on the buses—quickie justifications to bolster positions on the side of the issue that promises political survival. Busing can be counterproductive—in some cases it clearly is. There is a complicated set of trade-offs to consider, and the answer varies from case to case. But that's not the level at which they were considering it.

On the floor this afternoon I had a long and candid discussion with a Democratic colleague. He finds himself in a marriage that has lost its meaning. He doesn't want to hurt his wife or his children. And yet with every passing day he finds he has less and less ability to go through the motions of marriage. He doesn't find relief or satisfaction in his work or his friends. He's experiencing so much nervous tension that his health is going downhill. He's taking tranquilizers in fairly heavy doses to cope with the strain he feels inside.

He doesn't know what to do about this, he said. He seemed almost apologetic about saying these things to me, but I was touched that he felt he could talk to me. I asked him if it would be possible to patch up his marriage, move to a point where it might work again. No, he said, that probably wasn't possible. He wants to try to rock along, keep his marriage together. Any disruption of the status quo would be so unpleasant that he would rather avoid it— if possible.

"Here I am in the prime of life," he said. "I have everything that a man could want: status, a good income, a beautiful home and wonderful children. And yet I'm miserable inside. This dilemma's grinding me down." Unfortunately, there was little I could do except listen sympathetically.

Late this afternoon I flew to Detroit with Jim Sharp, the retired thirty-eight-year-old black Marine who will be taking Paul Visser's place in my district office. Between bites of airline chicken I drafted an outline for tonight's speech at the University of Michigan law school. As I was leaving the plane, State Senator Coleman Young, a black Democrat, introduced himself and asked if I was going to "do a John Lindsay." I grinned and replied that I hoped it wouldn't come to that.

Friday, October 15. At ten o'clock this morning I had a frank and friendly meeting with Don Ellis, Larry Huber, Carl Bramlet and Norm Bully, top area officials of the United Auto Workers. They're able men, strongly committed to the welfare of their workers. In 1970 they had the guts to argue for UAW ticket-splitting. Many local union officials had gotten the ball rolling by indicating their support for me. It meant defying years of tradition and scrapping the old war cry of "Make it emphatic; vote straight Democratic." It was a difficult decision for the UAW leadership, but once they had reached a judgment, they fought to make it stick. They indicated this morning that I'd probably receive the union's support again in 1972.

In my district office at noon I met Jack Hamady, an executive with a supermarket chain, and one of my most steadfast and sympathetic supporters. He had asked me to be his guest at today's luncheon of the Rotary Club. I wanted to speak with some of the local businessmen and get their opinions on the Administration's new economic program. When it was my turn to speak I thanked the businessmen for helping Paul Visser and formally introduced Jim Sharp to them. I wondered, briefly, what they would think about my having a black district office manager. I feel they will measure him on his ability alone. After lunch I got together with Harding Mott, C. S. Mott's eldest son, and Saul Seigel, president of the Flint Area Conference. We talked at length about the need to improve community problem-solving techniques and agreed that some new top-flight talent was needed. I said I'd contact the city council members to see if I could help them identify prospects for the vacant city manager's job.

Monday, October 18. In the Republican cloakroom this afternoon I spotted Dave Martin standing in front of the UPI ticker. He's a conservative from Nebraska who pretty much keeps to himself and seldom rocks the boat. He was absorbed in his reading and didn't hear me approach. The story that seemed to interest him most concerned Patsy Mink, a Democrat from Hawaii. She had just announced that she is going to enter Democratic presidential primaries in several Western states. Martin took out a felt-tipped pen, circled the story and wrote "Ha, ha" at its top. He was just about to tear off the copy and hang it from the spike.

"You know, Dave," I said, "I've always wondered who was writing those cryptic comments on wire service stories. And now I know who it is."

Martin spun around quickly. For a moment he seemed flustered;

finally he grinned. "Yeah," he said, "I guess you caught me in the act."

Later this afternoon, after the House adjourned, I sat alone in my office and tried to think about where I am at this point in my life. The job takes such an enormous toll, mentally and physically, that it's hard to maintain the pace I set in 1966 and have tried to keep ever since. As I get older I find myself doing the same things over and over again: trips to the district, constituent office hours at shopping centers, office work, speeches, the unending shuffle back and forth between the office and the House floor to answer quorum calls and vote, the endless commitments to do things and be places. I still feel enthusiastic and committed to the idea of public service, especially if I can help someone or get something done. That's a basic part of me. Knowing I'm going to bat for 500,000 people back home keeps me revved up. But the job is draining my life away. I feel I'm being used up, consumed. It's hard for me to see past the next election. I know I want to run again, but beyond that, I don't know.

Tuesday, October 19. The Washington *Post* this morning carried an article saying that House action was pending on the military procurement bill. This contained the Senate-passed Mansfield amendment to set a date for the end of U.S. participation in the Vietnam war pending the return of our prisoners. The White House, the article said, was calling the shots as to whether or not we'd get a clear-cut yes or no vote. If a preliminary head count showed the amendment would pass, Jerry Ford would use whatever tactics were necessary to keep it from coming to a direct vote. To do so, he'd need the co-operation of Speaker Carl Albert. I didn't think he'd have much trouble there.

Last June, when the Mansfield amendment first came to the floor of the House in the form of an amendment to the draft extension bill, the leadership knew in advance that they had the votes to defeat it. They allowed a direct vote. Today, the situation was different. My instincts told me the leadership would choose to play it safe.

The quorum bells rang at twelve-twenty. I walked to the Capitol and answered my name on the first roll call. Jerry Ford was talking with Brad Morse on the floor. I waited for him to finish, then asked what the leadership had decided. Within an eighth of a second I knew what the answer would be. Jerry paused and I could sense that he was trying to decide whether to give me a detailed explanation or simply to say that they were going to prevent a direct vote and that he'd tell me his reasons later.

"I hope you guys realize you'd get licked if you allowed a vote," I said, and walked to a seat at the rear of the chamber. Eddie Hébert, chairman of the Armed Services Committee, sought the Speaker's recognition. He got it immediately. He said he was seeking unanimous consent to bring the military procurement bill to the floor of the House. He was required to do this under the rules of the House. Any member could object to Hébert's request. If one did—and could persuade at least forty-four other members to stand—he could force a recorded teller vote on whether or not to consider the bill on this legislative day. But it was clear this afternoon that to force such a vote would be a waste of time.

Several members did resort to a parliamentary device to delay the proceedings temporarily. They rose and shouted, "Reserving the right to object." Under the rules, Speaker Albert had to recognize them. Using the lever of possibly objecting to the unanimous consent request, they succeeded in asking some questions and receiving the answers. I had no plans to speak on the measure myself, but as I listened to the answers being given by Hébert and Les Arends, the ranking Republican member of Armed Services, I felt my frustrations rising.

Speaker Albert was about to recognize Arends for the purpose of offering a "motion to instruct" the House conferees to the Senate-House Conference Committee. That committee's job would be to reconcile any differences between the military procurement bill that had passed the Senate and the measure that finally emerged from the House. We knew the "motion to instruct" would be phrased in such a way as to block any chance of a vote on the Mansfield amendment.

Under the rules of the Senate, amendments not directly related to the bill in question can be tacked onto it anyway. The House is much less free-wheeling. It operates under a strict rule of "germane-ness." Any amendment that doesn't pertain directly to the bill in question is considered "non-germane" and ruled out of order. By carefully drafting legislation, committee chairmen can prevent the House as a body from attaching policy amendments unrelated to the subject actually under discussion. By using such tactics, they blocked a vote on the war for nearly ten years—until this past June. While the Constitution states that only Congress can declare war, it wasn't until after we'd lost 50,000 American lives and wasted nearly $150 billion that the House got its first chance to vote directly for or against the war.

Chairmen can almost always block consideration of any bill that comes before their respective committees. When it is introduced, each piece of legislation is assigned to an appropriate "committee of jurisdiction." Bills aimed at ending the war, for example, depending on their exact language, would be referred either to Foreign Affairs or Armed Services. With Doc Morgan as chairman of Foreign Affairs; with the late Mendel Rivers, a Democrat from South Carolina, and his successor, Eddie Hébert, as chairmen of Armed Services, these bills would be doomed immediately. So while dozens of anti-war bills were introduced in the House—including several of my own—none of them had the slightest chance of emerging from their respective committees of jurisdiction.

If some miracle occurred and an anti-war bill were reported out of its committee of jurisdiction, it would then move to the Rules Committee, which is tightly controlled by eighty-two-year-old Bill Colmer, a Democrat from Mississippi. The Senate has no Rules Committee. A bill reported out to the Senate floor can be debated there for weeks—unless two thirds of the senators vote to shut off debate—with absolutely no restrictions to the amendment process. But here in the House, each piece of legislation reported out to the floor requires a specific "rule." This sets the time that will be allowed for debate and defines the scope of amendments that members can offer. Not surprisingly, the chairman has absolute control over the time allowed for debate. Usually he will assign a portion of the time to the ranking minority member of the committee —who then controls that portion. If you want to speak, you must go to the chairman or the ranking minority member and ask for time. If they refuse, you are out of luck. Typically, the chairman allocates the bulk of the time to proponents of his point of view.

A rule must accompany a bill when it goes to the floor. Without it, the bill dies on the doorstep of the Rules Committee. The make-up of the Rules Committee is conservative and this gives additional power to an arbitrary chairman. Colmer is not about to assign a rule to a bill opposing the war. At times the Speaker and others in the leadership will complain loudly about the arbitrariness of the Rules Committee with respect to a particular bill; at the same time they will urge Colmer privately to keep the bill bottled up. To remain in power, Colmer has only to please 500,000 constituents in Mississippi—so national pressures don't faze him.

There are even further roadblocks in the legislative process. One is the predisposition of the Speaker. Few bills ever come to the floor for a vote against his wishes. Speaker Albert has long supported the war, as Speaker McCormack did before him. Then, too, any bill requiring the expenditure of funds must not only clear the initiating legislative committee; it must also repeat the procedure within the Appropriations Committee. In recent years Appropriations has refused to fully fund certain authorization bills that have cleared the House. In fiscal year 1970, for example, our committee refused to appropriate some $8.5 billion that the House had "authorized" for expenditure.

Arends was ready with his motion to instruct the House conferees. He had mimeographed copies of it and a background rationale but he was unwilling to distribute them to other members in advance. To do so might give them time to find arguments against it. Lucien Nedzi of Michigan asked Arends pointedly if he would tell the chamber the exact nature of his motion. Arends, of course, refused.

This irritated me. After four or five Democrats had reserved the right to object, asked their questions and then withdrawn their reservations, I sought the Speaker's eye, reserved the right to object and was recognized. At this point I was standing in the well of the House. Arends was sitting at the Republican table fifteen yards away. I asked him if I was correct in assuming that the House would be given only one hour to debate the bill and that he, Arends, would control that debate. He nodded and said yes. Then I asked if he would distribute copies of his motion. He said he would—later. I thought it was inexcusable that the leadership would resort to parliamentary tricks to prohibit members from knowing what they were going to vote on ahead of time and then allocate only one hour to the entire debate. I couldn't stay silent when they asked unanimous consent to proceed in that manner. So I exercised my option to object.

That had little effect other than to delay the proceedings for another five minutes. Hébert moved that the House endorse the idea of sending its conferees to meet with the Senate conferees. This required the Speaker to take a yes or no vote. He asked for a voice vote and ruled it approved. I chose not to try to force a roll call. That would have succeeded only in wasting more time, antagonizing members and possibly losing votes for our side. Speaker Albert recognized Arends and gave him an hour to use as he saw fit. Arends then distributed copies of his motion. If passed, it would prohibit the House conferees from accepting any Senate amendment that was "non-germane" to the House bill. This of course included the Mansfield amendment. After reading it, I walked over to his desk and asked for time to speak. He agreed to give me two minutes. He was good-natured about it and did the same for Lou Nedzi, Bella Abzug and Chuck Whalen.

Despite the one-hour restriction, the debate was spirited. Whalen seemed very upset about the parliamentary maneuvering and the inherent dishonesty of the tactics used to thwart the majority will. "Young men are in Vietnam this minute having their guts blown out," he said, "while we in the Congress argue about germaneness." It was probably the most direct and radical statement he's made since coming to the House. But it was a good illustration of what such tactics can do to reasonable men.

During her two minutes Bella Abzug spoke with fervor against the war. Sam Steiger, a conservative Republican from Arizona, was standing in the rear of the chamber. As Bella turned to leave the well, Steiger cupped his hand to his mouth. "Right on," he yelled. "Right on. Right on." While his conservative colleagues laughed, Sam beamed at his own cleverness. One evening in 1967, during his first term in Congress, Sam appeared on the Joe Pyne TV show and talked at length about the House. Some of its members, he said, were so stupid that he wouldn't hire them to push a wheelbarrow. That remark didn't sit very well with people here and it took him nearly four years to live it down and reingratiate himself with the senior members. Today he fancies himself as the cloakroom humorist.

I had scribbled some notes on a piece of scrap paper. With some force I called on my colleagues to recognize that we didn't meet at 1600 Pennsylvania Avenue. Rather, we met in the Capitol. The reason was that we were required by the Constitution to think for ourselves and not be rubber stamps for the President. When I finished I noticed that all the applause seemed to be coming from the Democratic side. I noticed some who had supported the war when Lyndon Johnson was President.

Toward the end of the hour Arends called on Eddie Hébert, who walked down into the well. I was sitting beside McCloskey in the rear of the chamber and I was surprised to hear Hébert take note of my comment that we didn't meet at 1600 Pennsylvania Avenue. He said he agreed with "the gentleman from Michigan" on that point. Then, very shrewdly, he went on to say that the House didn't meet at the other end of the Capitol either.

Some of the older members clapped and cheered that remark. They detest the Senate and can always be counted upon to rise up indignantly any time someone suggests that the Senate is transgressing on House prerogatives, attempting to by-pass House rules or "blackmailing" the House by attaching "non-germane" amendments to bills. Hébert was manipulating that long-standing antagonism to strengthen his own position and deflect the thrust of my argument— that we were serving as rubber stamps for the President. I turned to Pete and said, "Hébert is damned clever."

When Hébert finished, the time limit expired. Speaker Albert had agreed with the Republican leadership to block a direct vote on the Mansfield amendment. Thus the first vote was labeled a "vote on the previous question." It was a parliamentary motion that would have to be defeated if we wanted to bring about a direct vote on the war. If we succeeded, Arends' amendment would be set aside and someone else—possibly Chuck Whalen—would have a chance to offer a substitute. Presumably that substitute would instruct the House conferees to accept the language of the Mansfield amendment. Then, after another hour of debate, we would be able to vote yes or no.

Because the key vote came on a parliamentary question—and not on the Mansfield amendment itself—the leadership was able to persuade and pressure additional members to support their position. If those members had been forced to vote yes or no publicly on an end to the war, many would have felt compelled to vote for the amendment. But a "previous question" vote is a parliamentary gimmick. It's often used to kill a bill the members are afraid to vote on directly. It's hard for the average citizen to understand—and easy for the congressman to explain away. Guy Vander Jagt, one of my Republican colleagues from Michigan, voted with us today in the effort to defeat "the previous question." This was the first time he had stood up against the war and I made it a point to congratulate him. He gave no sign that he wanted or welcomed my comment. Yet I appreciated the fact that he had broken with his past support of the Administration. Unfortunately there weren't enough of us. We lost that vote by a count of 215 to 192.

No sooner had the Speaker announced this result than we faced a yes or no vote on Les Arends' motion to instruct. That amendment was defeated by an identical margin of 215 to 192. The House conferees were sent to meet their Senate colleagues with no instructions at all. We were back where we started—except that the leadership of both parties had again succeeded in blocking a direct vote that could have ended the Vietnam war.

At one point this afternoon I was sitting next to Herman Schneebeli, a Republican from Pennsylvania. He's a short, bespectacled, baldish man with the look of an aging Ivy Leaguer and I've been told that he roomed with Nelson Rockefeller at Dartmouth College in the 1920s. When he first came to the House fourteen years ago Schneebeli earned a reputation as a progressive member. In recent years he has become more conservative. As we were finishing the roll call he turned to me and asked, very matter-of-factly, "What are we taking up next, the coffee bill or the Alaskan natives bill?"

His question really bothered me. It seemed so very typical of the way the House operates. Having deliberately avoided a vote on the war—which will sentence any number of Asians and Americans to death—we would move along without even batting an eye and ask ourselves, "What comes next, the coffee bill or the Alaskan natives bill?" And when Schneebeli topped that by praising Nixon's progress in ending the war, I had to challenge him. We exchanged some sharp words until we realized that there was simply no point in discussing the issue further. Both of us backed away.

At the end of the vote I bumped into Hébert in the well of the House. He was in high spirits. His side had won; the tension of the moment had passed. Despite our frequent disagreements, members of the House are usually courteous to one another. I took this opportunity to tell him I thought his remarks this afternoon had been tough and effective and that he was a worthy adversary. He chuckled and accepted my comment graciously. He tries very hard to win, he said.

Wednesday, October 20. During lunch today the bells kept ringing for quorum calls and votes. As I was waiting for one of those votes on the floor of the House, I spotted Otto Passman and asked him when he thought the foreign aid bill would come over from the Senate. His reply was intended to catch the ear of Eddie Hébert and draw him into the conversation. Which is what it did.

Hébert is a tall, broad-faced man with an engaging smile. His glasses are very thick, but failing eyesight doesn't seem to slow him down at all. I nodded hello and as a follow-through to yesterday's conversation told him that he had been a tough competitor on the military procurement bill. He smiled and indicated a willingness to talk.

When he's engaged in a fight on the floor, Hébert was saying in his slight Louisiana drawl, it's no holds barred. He'd "use a hatchet or anything else I had to chop another guy to pieces in order to win an argument." Then he added, "By the same token, when it's all over, I'll be the first guy to go down and invite the other member to come back into the cloakroom with me and have a 'do.'" As an illustration, he told me about himself and a former member of the Armed Services Committee. Over the years they'd prided themselves on their reputations as "tough sons of bitches" when it came to considering legislation before the committee. Some years ago industrialist Henry J. Kaiser was heavily involved in defense contracts. Armed Services was holding a hearing on one of those contracts and Kaiser was scheduled to testify.

The night before, Kaiser and one of his aides invited Hébert and this other member out for an evening on the town. They stayed out half the night, carousing and having "one helluva time." At three o'clock in the morning they were still drinking together and Hébert sensed that Kaiser was sizing him up, figuring that "this guy Hébert must be a real pushover." Next morning, Hébert continued, the hearing room was packed. When Kaiser appeared, Hébert "just cut him to ribbons. I've never been more brutal with anyone in my life," he said, "as I was with him under those circumstances. Finally, we took a break. Kaiser came over to me and said, 'Well, Mr. Hébert, I thought we were friends.'

"We are friends," Hébert replied. "The only reason this has happened, Mr. Kaiser, is that my wife and secretary came to the hearing today. And last night, when I got home so late, they wanted to know who I'd been out with. I told them I'd been out with you. And my wife said to me, 'That's the trouble with you, Ed, you're getting soft.' So they're here today and I thought I'd just take this opportunity to show them that I'm really not soft at all."

Hébert laughed as he told me the story. He had really taught Henry Kaiser a lesson in how the House works. He had also given me a new insight into his own personality. I gained a new respect for his shrewdness and honesty.

As Hébert and I were talking, Ed Patten sat down next to me. In his jocular way he leaned across me and asked Hébert, "Hey, Ed, what do you do with your old suits?"

"With the way you vote, Ed," Hébert replied, "you wouldn't even get my socks." Patten had voted against Hébert in yesterday's "previous question" battle. Hébert remembered that.

We voted twice during the lunch hour on bills affecting Alaskan natives and then on a bill to provide survivors' benefits for members of the armed services. I saw John Rhodes from Arizona and told him that I had noticed in committee the other day that he was letting his hair grow out. A short, affable fellow, John resembles comedian George Gobel. "Yeah," he replied, "there aren't many of us left with crew cuts here."

We paused and tried to figure out who those members are. All are Republicans—"Vinegar Bend" Mizell from North Carolina, Ed Derwinski from Illinois, John Hunt from New Jersey, and Walter Powell from Ohio. A few minutes later I saw Powell and repeated my conversation with Rhodes. "Well," he said, "it may be that we'll end up with one guy in the House wearing a crew cut. But I can assure you there will be at least one and that one will be me."

Late this afternoon Paul Visser called from Flint. He had heard rumors that Arthur Summerfield might finance a primary challenge against me next year. During the Eisenhower Administration, Summerfield served as Postmaster General. He was chairman of the Republican National Committee as well, and in effect served as Ike's chief political operative. He's told me many times about his role in deciding that Dick Nixon should go on TV and make his Checkers speech. That's the type of tactical maneuver Summerfield would recommend. His philosophy is that you always find ways to turn minuses into pluses. If something in a political game plan goes haywire, his instinct is to ask, "Well, how can I turn this to my advantage?" He's crafty and forceful and when it comes to playing political games to achieve specific tactical objectives, he's as clever and deadly as anyone I know.

Summerfield has always been a conservative Republican. As he's gotten older, he's become even more conservative. We've been pleasant and straightforward with one another but our relationship has never been close. About a year and a half ago he sailed his yacht up the Potomac into Washington and invited me to meet him on board. This was during the time that Charlie Goodell was giving Nixon so much grief in the Senate. In a friendly, fatherly way—yet with forged steel in every word—Summerfield told me that Goodell was killing himself and that I should be careful I didn't do the same thing. Following Goodell's lead would ruin my own political future.

In order to set myself apart from Goodell—in order to spike the

Administration's growing concern about me—I should make a speech on the floor of the House attacking Goodell for what he was doing. That, he said, would move me back into the good graces of the Administration types and smooth my own road ahead. My refusal to do this, I was later told, dumfounded him. When he adds to that my divorce, my association with McCloskey, and my anti-Nixon posture, Summerfield apparently concludes I've lost my mind. If he were younger, he might run against me himself. As it is, he may try to persuade a friend or relative to oppose me.

Thursday, October 21. I received an invitation to appear on the "Today" show next Monday morning to argue in favor of the U.S. "two China" policy at the United Nations. John Rarick, a Democrat from Louisiana, will be arguing against it. For some advice on what to say, I put in a call to Ambassador George Bush at the U. S. Mission to the U.N. in New York. An aide said that at the moment he was unavailable; he was involved in a debate about a shooting into the Soviet delegation's apartment building. He'd return my call as soon as he was free.

Finding some time on my hands, I wrote Les Arends to thank him for his courtesy Tuesday in granting me two minutes to speak on his motion to instruct. Then I wrote Chuck Whalen a longer letter to say that I thought his voice had become one of "the strongest and clearest on our side of the aisle." I told him his leadership was an inspiration to me and wished him the best for the period ahead.

Late this afternoon Bush returned my call. Elected in 1966 to the Seventh District seats in our respective states, George and I soon became close friends. Our voting records differed. Mine was more liberal. His reflected the more conservative make-up of his Houston district. But we were always kidding each other on the floor. George had a habit of walking up behind me quietly and using his toe to catch my foot in mid-stride and make me trip over myself. I would return the favor every chance I got. At one point I flew to Houston to speak at a fund-raising breakfast for him. Another time he came to Flint to speak at a fund-raiser for me. Just before Christmas 1969 he secretly collected the worst pictures of me that my staff could find. He wrote hilarious captions for them, pasted them into a scrapbook and presented it to me at a meeting of the 8-66 Club. I show it only to close friends.

Early in 1970 George stopped by my office in the Longworth Building to talk about the approaching campaign. He was involved in a tough Senate race with Democrat Lloyd Bentsen. I told him some of the problems I was facing in my Republican primary. I said I was having a hard time raising funds. Although I didn't want to admit it, the cash situation at the time was critical. George said he wanted to help. He took out his checkbook and began writing. I was reluctant to accept any money from him. I knew he'd need it for his own race and said so. He brushed that off airily. "Life has been pretty good to Barb and me," he said. "I can afford to help and I want to." When we'd finished talking, he laid the check on my desk and left. I glanced at it and saw that it was for five hundred dollars. I was overwhelmed. That money was vital to our success in the primary. The feeling it represented meant an awful lot more to me.

He seemed warm and good-natured on the phone this afternoon. Both of us tend to use our hands while speaking; he kidded me about "watching the karate chops." I kidded him in return and warned him to be careful of "that guy from Zambezi." Then we got into the nuts and bolts of the "two China" policy. He gave me key points supporting that policy as well as the arguments of those who opposed it. The outcome next week in the U.N. will be very close, he said. He thinks the odds in favor of the U.S. position have improved. He explained the procedural situation to me. The first vote—on the important question motion—will tell the story, he said.

Friday, October 22. The House was not in session today, but after lunch I drove to the office to catch up on my paperwork. About three o'clock a Vietnam veteran named Jim Dehlin came by to see me. He lost both legs in a mine explosion last December 23, and since his return to the U.S. and his admittance to Valley Forge Army Hospital in Pennsylvania, he's been experiencing incredible harassment. He even received a letter of reprimand from his commanding officer. It concerned petty things: the length of his hair, the shape of his mustache, the fact that he once returned to his quarters in his wheel chair ten minutes late.

Jim's hair, it occurred to me, was shorter than Les Arends' hair—
and Arends is the ranking Republican on the Armed Services Committee. After listening to Jim's story and reading that letter of
reprimand, Brunell and I were furious. That the Army should take a
man's legs and then harass him over the length of his hair irritated
the hell out of me. No wonder the Army's destroying itself. With
crap like that, it deserves its fate. There will be fireworks in this case
before its over.

Shortly after eight this evening FCC Commissioner Nick Johnson
and his date arrived at my apartment for dinner. Tall, smiling, with
black curly hair, Nick and I shared a Junior Chamber of Commerce
award in 1967 and have been friends ever since. Relaxing over Mai
Tais, we talked at length about life in the Congress and on the
FCC, about our prospective future careers and our personal lives.
Nick's been separated from his wife for the past sixteen months and
has an apartment downtown.

Both Nick and I face the necessity of having to produce incomes
of at least forty thousand dollars to meet our alimony and child support costs as well as pay our minimum living expenses. As a result,
we are prevented from taking leisure time to do other things we
might want to do. Both of us mused about how nice it would be to
spend several months traveling through Europe. As a practical matter, it's impossible. We must "sell" virtually all our time and energy.
After Nick and his date, Hildegarde, left, Meredith teased me about
how much I had eaten. I replied somewhat self-consciously that I
could afford to since I had been "slimming up."

"That's the problem," she said, laughing. "You need to start slimming down."

Monday, October 25. Shortly after six o'clock this morning Meredith
and I drove to the NBC Studios on Nebraska Avenue. Dave Brunell
met us there at six forty-five. We walked into the cafeteria, ordered
coffee and sweet rolls and joined John Rarick from Louisiana,
Molly Sharp of the "Today" show and Bill Monroe, the NBC interviewer. Molly then walked us to the studio—on the way she asked
how things were going in my office with "Brunell at the helm."
Dave laughed and corrected her: "You mean with Brunell in the

bilges." She also motioned toward Meredith and quietly asked me, "What does that lovely girl have to do with your life?"

"Just about everything," I replied.

We arrived at the studio and were ushered inside. The NBC people outfitted us with microphones and a make-up man daubed powder on each of our faces to take the shine away. The "Today" show had already begun. Bill said we'd be on from seven-fourteen to seven twenty-five. We waited and on cue we were introduced. Bill asked me one question; then he turned to Rarick. There were three or four more exchanges and, toward the end of the segment, I answered one question raised by Frank McGee in New York.

The Riegle-Rarick debate centered on the question of whether or not the U.S. was right in supporting a "two China" policy. Later this afternoon, all of that seemed academic. The vote took place in the United Nations and the U.S. suffered defeat. World events are moving in such a way today that the U.S. is no longer in a position to call the shots. Had we proposed that "two China" policy in the U.N. last year, we might have been successful. The fact that we waited so long meant we were destined to lose despite the last-minute arm twisting. Increasingly, other countries are reacting to world realities rather than waiting and letting those realities overtake them. Eight hundred million Chinese is a big reality.

Tuesday, October 26. The Republican Conference met in the House chamber this morning to discuss the education bill and designate Chuck Mosher as the ranking Republican member on the Science and Astronautics Committee. Chuck is a tall, friendly former newspaper editor from Oberlin, Ohio, who's serving his sixth term in the House. He was one of the first Republicans to oppose the war in Vietnam. Because I have such a high regard for him, I made a special effort to remain for the vote.

While I was waiting at the rail in the rear of the House, Don Clausen approached me and asked what was happening. When I told him he took me aside and tried to give me some friendly advice. Clausen is a good-natured California Republican. He started the Congressional Flying Club and, with his strong, square face and solid build, looks every inch the athlete he once was.

"I like you personally, Don," he began, "for a couple of reasons." He paused to let me digest that. "And one is because your first name is the same as mine."

I found that an interesting reason for liking someone. He didn't tell me what the second reason was.

In recent months, Clausen said, he felt that I had alienated many Republicans in the House. In that situation, I could not be effective in pushing the things I cared about most. "Remember when you were the bright star?" he asked. "You had quite a following here." He said he thought I had an excellent mind. But, like a punch-drunk fighter, I had been "swinging wild." I had also been swinging too much.

"You can't swing all the time," he said. "You have to learn how to box. When you finally throw the big punch, you know it's going to do the job." His point was that I ought to use a different strategy in trying to make things happen here. "A bird has to build a nest before it produces an egg," he said. He thought I ought to do more home-work, prepare my groundwork better, before I came forward with a basic thrust. He told me he has several specific goals. One is to shatter Democratic control of the House. A second is to break up the federal bureaucracy and a third is to "revitalize" the federal sys-tem of government. I said I could agree with those objectives and suggested there was another goal worthy of his consideration—an end to the war in Vietnam. "That's history," Clausen said, and brushed it aside.

There is no limit to what a man can accomplish in Congress, he said, if he doesn't care who gets the credit for it. If the two of us could spend more time together, he could elaborate on that point. There were lots of ways to make things happen, to bring about changes in policy. For him, the best way to do that is behind the scenes in a non-public way.

I don't know whether he's been able to accomplish very much. Clearly, however, he thinks he has. At some point I'll take him up on his offer and go talk with him. My feeling is that my chances of accomplishing very much using his strategy would be minimal. What probably happens is that you end up riding developments as they occur, thinking you're responsible for making them happen when that's not the case at all.

There was a mix-up in the scheduling of House business today. The Rules Committee didn't grant a "rule" to the Higher Education Act. As a result, it couldn't be brought to the floor for a vote. Several members used the time to vent their spleens against the United Nations for its decision to seat Red China. Then, at one o'clock, the House adjourned for the day.

Later this afternoon I received a call from a man named Fred Gale who has a radio show in New York City. We talked for fifteen minutes about the vote in the U.N. and the reaction in Congress. We also talked about Nixon's record and the McCloskey campaign. It's an odd feeling to have an off-the-cuff conversation with someone you can't see and to realize that perhaps a million people may be listening on the radio.

Wednesday, October 27. I talked to Carl Blake this morning and we agreed that sometime next month he'll fly to Flint and spend about ten days concentrating on the problems of the auto industry.

The GM installations in my district comprise one of the most massive economic concentrations anywhere. GM pays out over $800 million in wages each year in my district alone; payments to area suppliers run the total to well over $1 billion. It's often said that if the national economy gets the sniffles and auto sales drop, the state of Michigan catches cold and Flint suffers double pneumonia. Unlike other large corporations, General Motors over the years has not sought major contracts or subsidies from the federal government. Their reluctance, I think, stems from the operating ethic that dominates the company. They wish to have the latitude to run the company their own way; they drive themselves to achieve top job performance and take pride in the results. Many GM managers feel the federal government ought to improve its own internal efficiency before it criticizes private industry.

My association with GM's management has tended to be at arm's length. In Washington, GM lobbyists have concentrated on the Executive Branch and those members of Congress who serve on committees directly concerned with auto industry legislation. Members of the Appropriations Committee seldom see industry lobbyists. Some GM people in Flint have wondered why I wasn't more conversant with their problems. Ironically, I've often wondered why GM people seldom contacted me. This communications gap really hit home the last time I talked with Bob Breeden. I was angry with myself for not knowing some of the facts he mentioned. I realized I needed to establish a regular means of staying better informed on the industry's problems. Carl Blake's trip to Flint will be a first step in establishing a flow of information.

Later, in the Republican cloakroom, I talked to Gene Snyder from Kentucky. A tall, reticent member with a droll sense of humor, he's one of the few Republicans who has voted consistently to end the war in Vietnam. In view of his Southern constituency, that's been a tough position to defend. He's very much his own man and although we're not particularly close I have a deep respect for him. We talked about the vote in the United Nations and I pointed out that I had supported the Administration on the China issue and had appeared on the "Today" show to say so.

"Well," Snyder replied in his easygoing way, "even a blind hog finds an acorn once in a while."

I chuckled and said that was a pretty good remark. "If you liked that one," he said, "let me give you another. And this is one we use out in Kentucky. Even a stopped clock is right twice a day."

VIII. NOVEMBER

Monday, November 1. Early this afternoon two women from the Flint chapter of an organization called Save Our Schools came by the office to oppose school busing and to lobby for the school prayer amendment proposed by Chalmers Wylie. Frances Lascowski and Jessie Brenhaltz both had fire in their eyes and when I closed my office door we got down to brass tacks immediately. They come from the same East Side neighborhood where I spent the first nineteen years of my life. Their children are attending Lowell Junior High, which is my alma mater.

With the most intense feeling, they listed their objections to school busing. The buses are expensive and unsafe. They add to traffic congestion. Kids are being denied the right to participate in after-school activities. The schools they have to attend are too far from their homes; what would happen in an emergency? It is hard for parents to belong to PTAs. The local communities should manage the schools, they said, without any interference from the federal government. Neither woman mentioned race. In fact, they said they believed in integrated schools—but not in cross-town busing. It's hard to describe their apprehension, outrage and fury. They were so upset that they couldn't even sit still.

I listened attentively and told them I had doubts that massive busing is the answer to the problem of equal education. But it isn't enough just to be "against" busing. We have to find a better answer and support it as an alternative. From there we moved on to discuss the school prayer amendment. They seemed convinced that the lack of prayer in public schools is largely responsible for the country's declining moral values. Earlier, they said, they had waged a successful campaign to place an American flag in every classroom in the area to stimulate patriotism. I explained my misgivings about the prayer amendment and my belief that voluntary prayer was absolutely protected under the First Amendment to the Constitution. No uniform prayer, I said, could possibly be written to suit all viewpoints and I am opposed to any government involvement in proscribing religious practices.

The two problems, I went on, are connected. Frances and Jessie are trying to apply a basic principle in the school prayer amendment. But they oppose that principle when it comes to the question of busing. What it all boils down to is the role of the federal government and the degree to which it should involve itself in local disputes. With the school prayer amendment, Frances and Jessie are inviting the government into the schools. With busing, they are telling the government to stay out. We debated those issues separately and then together for nearly two hours. We agreed on some points, disagreed on others, but wound up with a better understanding of each other's points of view. I was glad they had come. We parted on friendly terms.

A key vote came today on a matter related to busing, the $1.5 billion Emergency School Desegregation Act. It was written to provide funds for school districts that are shouldering extraordinarily heavy financial burdens as a result of integration. The general impression was that in some instances the bill would funnel money to school districts forced to implement court-ordered busing plans. Actually, only a small portion of the funds in the bill could have been used that way.

The measure had the Administration's backing. Nonetheless, most members felt they had to vote against it. They didn't want to be tainted by a possible inference that they supported busing. Even Les Arends, the Republican whip, was opposing the bill. I chided him, saying I thought he was supposed to support the Administration. I pointed out that Tom Railsback, who is also from Illinois, was voting with the Administration this time. And I said that I was too.

"Yeah," Arends replied, "you guys will vote right on these little horseshit things so that on the big ones you can be wrong." The bill was defeated by a vote of 222 to 135.

At the end of the day's agenda, Speaker Albert had attached the controversial coffee bill. For reasons that weren't entirely clear to me, H. R. Gross was angry about this and he was determined to block consideration of the measure. Gross can be deadly on parliamentary maneuvers. This was "suspension day" on the floor of the House—all bills came up under "suspension of the rules," a situation that allows no amendments and requires a two-thirds vote for passage. With ten "suspension" items still remaining, Gross knew he could force ten roll-call votes. Each manual roll call takes thirty-five minutes to complete. We would spend five or six hours on roll calls alone. Add two or three quorum calls at thirty minutes each and it was clear that Gross could delay action on the coffee bill until very late this evening. And every minute we spent in session after seven o'clock, the harder it would be for the Speaker to insist on continuing.

Jim Delaney, a Democrat from New York, was so angry about this that late this afternoon he offered a motion to adjourn. It was defeated by more than two hundred votes but it used up more time and showed the increasing displeasure of the membership. Finally the Speaker surrendered. He pulled the coffee bill from the agenda. The last items on the schedule passed quickly on voice votes. The chamber emptied like a bathtub when the plug is pulled.

Tuesday, November 2. There were some minor fireworks on the floor of the House today. Wayne Hays was absent yesterday and missed eight roll-call votes. He was furious about that. He asked for a quorum call at seven minutes past twelve and later offered a motion to adjourn. That necessitated a roll-call vote just to keep the session going. If a member is striving to maintain a ninety per cent attendance record, he can afford to miss only one vote in ten. By missing eight votes in one day, a member would have to be present for the next seventy-two in a row to earn an over-all average of ninety per cent. A day like the one Hays had yesterday can kill your voting percentage for the entire year.

During the quorum call I spotted Charlie Mosher and told him that I had been happy to vote for him the other day as ranking Republican member on the Science and Astronautics Committee. He thanked me graciously and said that he was equally pleased that fourteen of the sixty-four members present in the Republican Conference had decided to vote against him. That meant that he had accomplished something during his years in the House—and stepped on some toes along the way. "Otherwise," he said, "I would have felt that I was harmless here."

As I was leaving the floor I bumped into the two SOS women from Flint who grilled me yesterday about my stands on school busing and the prayer amendment. They pounced on me for yesterday's vote in favor of the Emergency School Desegregation Act. I took them aside and tried to explain that the money in the bill would have gone only to assist school districts that were desegregating voluntarily or were under court order to do so; that it would have provided financial relief only in those cases. I called my legislative assistant, Lisa Finkelstein, and asked her to bring them a copy of the bill so they could understand exactly what was involved. Then I escorted them up to the gallery and seated them in the section reserved for members' guests.

Late this afternoon, walking out of the Speaker's lobby on my way back to the Longworth Building, I spotted Ed Patten in the doorway. He was wearing a wide red, blue and green tie that hung down below his waist. From a distance I yelled, "Hey, Ed, is that your tongue hanging out or are you wearing a new tie?"

He stopped, looked at it and replied, "This tie is phosphorescent. It glows in the dark."

Just then Tom Steed from Oklahoma walked by and in a deadpan way said to Patten, "I worry about you when I see what you are carrying." And he was looking directly at Patten's stomach.

Patten returned his glance. "Well," he said, "I'm not as fulla shit as some of the guys around here."

Thursday, November 4. The main topics of conversation at this morning's Michigan Republican delegation breakfast were fairly predictable: campaign spending reform, redistricting and the continuing hassle over school busing. At one point Ed Hutchinson said he wished things could be like they used to be. Race wouldn't matter, he said, and we could live without "having to pay attention to the color of a man's skin."

There was a momentary pause as all of us considered that. I was about to respond, but Jim Harvey spoke first. "Ed," he said, "with all due respect, I have to disagree with you on that. Things weren't all right and they hadn't been for a hundred years. If we were born black—those of us here in this room—we'd have been leading the fight against discrimination. We wouldn't have stood for it.

"And I think people's attitudes are changing on this," Harvey went on. "The city of Saginaw passed an open housing ordinance with sixty per cent of the vote. What people won't accept is 'instant integration.' But they will accept and are accepting gradual integration."

Hutchinson had spilled something on his jacket and tie. I noticed him dip his napkin in a glass of water and begin rubbing the spots. He worked on them for at least five minutes. Finally I said that I had a couple of suits at home that needed to go to the cleaners; maybe I should bring them in for him to do instead. He looked up agreeably and then went back to cleaning his tie. As we were leaving the breakfast I continued my little joke and asked Ed if he could also clean suedes. If so, I had a leather jacket that I'd be happy to give him. He looked at his tie once more. He seemed satisfied.

During today's first quorum call I talked to John Hunt, a Republican from New Jersey. A former police officer with a very deep voice, John presents his views forcefully and, for emphasis, wears a tie clip in the shape of a .38-caliber police special. Because he was wearing an orange shirt, I asked him if he were mixed up on the calendar. Today was November 4; Halloween had already passed. No, he said, not at all. The shirt only signified that he was an Orangeman from New Jersey. A friend had given him the shirt along with the orange and brown striped tie he wore.

Bella Abzug had asked to speak to me earlier, so when I saw her on the floor I walked over and sat down next to her. Several seconds passed before I realized that she was having an argument with John Seiberling from Ohio. John had just voted for an amendment to allow colleges to maintain student quotas based on sex. It was designed to allow all-male colleges to remain that way. Bella was furious. She said she'd remember John's vote; that she detested people who practiced discrimination based on sex. In his polite, soft-spoken way, John tried to placate her. He had no success. Finally, shaking his head, he just walked away.

The issue of sex discrimination is a relatively new one here and the women concerned with it have had to fight some "in-House" battles. About three years ago, for instance, Charlotte Reid and Leonor Sullivan approached the House Gym Committee and asked that certain time periods be established for them to use the facilities, especially the swimming pool. Previously, the pool was reserved for men only and they swam without suits. But it was quickly agreed that the pool would be available to women on Monday, Tuesday and Friday mornings. If the men wanted to swim at that time, they would have to wear bathing suits.

Similarly, about three years ago, the women got quite upset about the fact that male members were about to reduce funds for the beauty shop in the House Office Building. They organized for battle. Not only did they reverse the decision; they succeeded in promoting an *expansion* of beauty shop services.

Both Bella Abzug and Shirley Chisholm were elected in 1970, and they brought a new kind of female militancy to the House. Shirley Chisholm immediately challenged the system by refusing to accept assignment to the Agriculture Committee—she insisted that agriculture was irrelevant to the concerns of her big-city district. She "won": the feminist Ms. Chisholm was shifted to Veterans' Affairs.

Meredith and I ate lunch today in the members' dining room. We found a table and were studying the menus when the lady who normally seats guests walked over and asked: "Do you have a congressman joining you?"

"What?" I replied.

"Will a congressman be joining you?"

I looked at her and smiled. "I am the congressman."

The House had convened at noon and would remain in session for the next fourteen hours to consider the Higher Education Act of

1971. As the debate droned on into the evening, the mood of the House got uglier. Tempers frayed. Members missed scheduled flights. The service in the members' dining room deteriorated as a skeleton kitchen crew struggled to feed everyone. Cigar and cigarette smoke curled around the chamber. Some members read the evening papers, listening with one ear to the debate. As the evening wore on, the old brass spittoons in the rear of the chamber overflowed with candy wrappers, soggy cigarette butts and other assorted refuse. Newspapers were scattered across empty seats. House employees positioned in front of the Speaker's chair struggled to stay alert.

At one point I walked into the Republican cloakroom for a Coke. John Byrnes from Wisconsin was playing gin rummy with Harold Collier from Illinois. Collier had removed his coat, revealing a bright yellow shirt. John Rhodes, Bob Michel, Bill Harsha and Glenn Davis kibitzed from the sidelines. Fred Schwengel was fast asleep on a leather couch, resembling a cadaver. Brownie Reid stood alone at the food counter sipping a glass of milk. The crowd in the gallery was slim: some congressional staff members, the more dogged representatives of the press, half a dozen anxious and dressed-up dates waiting for the session to end, weary doorkeepers leaning against the wall for support. As the final vote neared, I saw HEW Secretary Elliot Richardson enter the gallery with a covey of aides.

The Higher Education Act was only an excuse to vent all the emotion of the busing issue. For many Southerners, this was the long-awaited day of reckoning; the busing issue had "come home to roost" in the North. For many Northern liberals, it was a moment of deep agony. Gut feelings for human rights were pulling in one direction; practical reservations about the value of wholesale busing were tugging in the other. Those reservations ran the gamut from honest concerns about its net pluses and minuses to the raw fear of aroused anti-busing sentiment. And there were dozens of self-serving politicians of both parties who were delighted to ride the anti-busing wave for all it was worth, knowing that they were socking away thousands of backlash votes.

The debate itself was angry and discourteous, often dark and mean. There were shouts of "Vote! Vote!" as members attempted to speak. When amendments to ban busing were put to a voice vote, the anti-busing forces shook the chamber with their thunderous, savage "Ayes." O. C. Fisher, a Democrat from Texas, angrily declared that "the American people are sick and tired of being kicked around." He referred to busing as someone's "pet whim."

Ron Dellums, a black from California, stood before the Southerners and in a strong voice said that he realized "the history of bigotry and racism in the South. I would suggest," he continued, "that we be as concerned and fervent about saving the children in this country as many in this Congress are about saving their jobs." Jack Edwards from Alabama, a normally gracious member, replied bitterly. Referring to busing in the North and, specifically, in Michigan, he bellowed, "Let's hold their feet to the fire until we stop this busing foolishness. I'm going to vote against this Michigan amendment [to delay busing in the state]. It is interesting to see them squirm now. Where were they when we needed them so badly over the years we have been trying to stop busing?"

The normally reticent Jim Corman, a Democrat from California, even brought the President into the debate. He challenged Nixon's "view of morality" and his alleged efforts to "pack the Supreme Court with people opposed to civil rights." President Johnson, Corman said, urged the elimination of racial discrimination because it is immoral. "President Nixon has consistently told the American people that our government will do only that which is required by the courts. Those who suffer racial discrimination will be denied executive action and moral leadership."

Shirley Chisholm, a black first-termer from New York, stepped into the well with fire in her eyes. Her words rang through the chamber; she stabbed her finger accusingly at Jerry Ford. She charged "sham and hypocrisy." "Racism is so inherent in the bloodstream of this country," she said, "that you cannot see beyond a particular limit. You are only concerned when whites are affected. I say to the members: Where were you when the black children were being bused right past the white schools in the community? Come out from behind your mask. Forget they are white children. Forget they are black children. Just remember one thing. They are America's children."

The key votes came on a series of amendments—most of them re-

corded teller votes. Many had been drawn deliberately in such a
way as to maximize their symbolic impact and they were poor ex-
cuses for legislation. Some made a meaningful yes or no vote almost impossible. A few seemed blatantly unconstitutional. Others,
although poorly drafted, seemed reasonable in principle. One or two
were an even mixture of these good and bad features.

Bill Broomfield from Michigan offered an amendment to delay
the implementation of all court-ordered busing plans until the full
appeals process has been completed in the courts. This amendment
caused me the greatest agony. I supported its over-all aim, yet at the
same time I was troubled to have to support a measure that seemed
to interfere with the judicial process. Additionally, his amendment
was bound to delight the hard-core segregationists. They would
support anything to delay integration. The thought of being sand-
wiched in with them upset me enormously.

That's the problem with so much legislation here. Often, you're
unsatisfied with a yes or no vote. Sometimes you'd like to vote
"sixty per cent yes and forty per cent no." And sometimes you'd like
to vote "neither." But on recorded teller votes it all comes down to a
red or green printed card on which you write your name, your state
and the number of your district. It's either yes or no.

The teller lines began to move, with members depositing their
cards in the wooden boxes at the rear of the chamber. Weighing
everything as best I could, I netted out about 52–48 in favor of voting aye. Tom Railsback and Jim Harvey, close friends and good
lawyers, told me they were voting aye. But Peggy Heckler agonized and voted no. Pete McCloskey arrived late. He's a constitutional lawyer and when he heard that this amendment might interfere with the judicial process, that was enough for him. He reached
for a red card, scribbled his name and marched on up the aisle to
vote no.

That moved me to 51–49. About ten minutes of the twelve-min-
ute voting period had ticked away as I stood in the well weighing
everything again. It was a nagging, confused swirl. I didn't want to
interfere with the judicial process. Yet I did think appeals should be
heard before court-ordered busing plans were implemented, particularly in de facto cases. Somehow, I thought, we've got to give the

kids in run-down ghetto schools a truly equal educational opportunity. And we've got to do it now—not several years from now.

But how? As a practical matter, I'm not convinced that massive
busing is the way to produce equal education. Citizen faith in government has been stretched to the breaking point. Would people
accept wholesale busing at this time and under these circumstances?
I seriously doubted it. Would it drive the country toward an Agnew
or a Wallace? I feared it would.

Many of my Southern colleagues were standing near the aye box
to laugh at and savor the pain of liberals moving in their direction.
This made me reluctant to vote for the amendment. And yet I knew
that I was going to vote later against banning federal funds for
busing. I knew that I'd vote against the constitutional amendment
opposing busing—because we need flexibility to handle different
areas of the country in different ways. Both positions would be dan-
gerous politically. Perhaps a vote for the Broomfield amendment
was the best way to let my constituents know that I had honest reservations about the wisdom of wholesale busing.

Finally I asked myself how I'd vote if I were voting secretly; if it
were just a private exercise in a room by myself. I decided that
I'd probably vote aye but that I would want several hours to
think about it further. The House was tense and noisy. My head
was aching. I couldn't be sure I was right and it was tearing me
apart.

Most members had already voted. Finally I knew that I couldn't
wait any longer. I pulled out a green card, wrote my name on it
and dropped it in the box. I continued walking, first out of the
chamber and then out of the Capitol. I felt awful. The Broomfield
amendment passed by a vote of 235 to 125. The fact that my
vote didn't affect the outcome one way or the other provided no
consolation at all.

Later in the evening we deliberated the controversial amendment
to ban the use of federal funds to pay for school busing. With
school districts under mandatory court order to bus, I thought the
federal government should provide financial help. Pontiac, Michigan,
for example, had been forced to lay off some policemen and teachers
to pay for court-ordered busing. That meant a red card for me—a

vote against the ban. Only two of us in the Michigan delegation voted that way. As I was walking up the aisle to cast my vote on a third amendment, Ed Patten called out to me. "Hey, Riegle," he said, "drop this in the box for me, willya?" I took his card and looked at it—a misprint that was blank on both sides. He smiled broadly as I laughed.

Finally, at two o'clock in the morning, the chair announced we were ready to vote. The announcement was greeted with a chorus of hurrahs, rebel yells and general bedlam. With the restrictive busing amendments attached, the bill was certain to pass. I sat down next to Flo Dwyer, a Republican from New Jersey. A long-time liberal, she has a keen grasp of the issues. She also has a wry sense of humor. As I sank into my chair she turned and flashed a weary smile. "Happy New Year," she said.

Friday, November 5. I woke up at six-thirty and as I groped my way into the shower I could hardly keep my eyes open. Nonetheless, at seven twenty-five I was on a plane to Detroit. The physical therapist in the Capitol had loaned me his special heating pad to soothe the pain in my chest. I'd packed the pad in my suitcase. It weighed a ton. As I walked between terminals to catch the plane for Flint, that suitcase almost pulled my arm out of its socket. I began feeling pains in my chest again. Christ, I thought, the heating pad was making the situation worse. I should have left it behind.

At noon I met with a delegation of area physicians. They recited their complaints about existing health insurance plans and the mountains of red tape with which they had to deal. I noted their complaints and described the kind of health care legislation I thought the Ways and Means Committee might recommend. A young, dark-haired surgeon interrupted to say that he might have to leave. He was scheduled to operate on a thirty-four-year-old mother of four children for a "non-specific brain tumor." He explained how tough it was to find the tumor itself. "Sometimes you have to go through the good stuff to find the bad stuff," he said. I looked at his small hands and simply couldn't imagine that within the hour they would be at work inside someone's brain.

After a speech at Powers Catholic High School and a stop at the district office downtown, I drove to see a long-time supporter named Joe Megdell. We talked for an hour and a half about the war, the GOP in Michigan and my own political future. He said he wanted to help me financially. Unfortunately, however, he'd suffered some recent reverses in business. He said he was a new member of the "ex-millionaires club." Lack of funds is something I understand very well.

Saturday, November 6. This was Senator Griffin's birthday; twelve Republican senators and four Cabinet members were flying to Michigan to speak for him at a series of dinner "salutes" around the state. At four forty-five this afternoon I waited at Bishop Airport to welcome Pennsylvania Senator Hugh Scott, who was to be the featured speaker at our get-together in Flint.

At the dinner this evening were some 250 Republicans who had paid fifty dollars each for admission. I spoke for about three minutes. Then it was Scott's turn. He praised Griffin generously and made several nice references to me. Then he delivered some heartfelt remarks about what a congressman really should be. He said a congressman has to be independent and make his own best judgments. "His job," Scott added, "is not to weigh the mail but to weigh the evidence." He stressed the personal agonies such judgments often impose on decent and reasonable men. He said good people can and do come out on different sides of the same issue.

Later, on the plane to Detroit, I told Scott how pleased I'd been to hear him say what he thought a congressman should be. His remarks might ease some of my problems with that audience. "I hope so, Don," he said. "That's why I did it." I was disarmed and flattered by his thoughtfulness. We talked about the Nixon Administration and the outlook for 1972. Scott was instrumental in setting up General Eisenhower's state-by-state campaign in 1952; then he served a successful term as Republican national chairman. The White House people today, he said, seldom ask him for advice. They consult him only on specific legislation. We agreed that the party has made no progress in building a majority base and that our chances of winning control of Congress next year are minimal.

Shortly after midnight we switched planes in Detroit and I had a chance to talk to Illinois Senator Charles Percy all the way to Washington. He told me about the time the Administration asked him to undertake a nine-nation trip to sound out the possibility of a new peace initiative in Vietnam. He accepted the assignment with pride and seriousness and, once back, organized his findings carefully. In due course he was called to the White House to consult with Nixon. No sooner had he begun to outline his findings, however, than he sensed that Nixon was preoccupied; the President kept checking his watch. Sensing that he was not getting through, Percy rose to leave and said that he'd prepare a written report. Nixon stopped him, urged him to stay and sit down again. Whereupon for the next forty-five minutes they discussed . . . politics in Illinois.

Sunday, November 7. In the papers this morning I was interested to read the reviews of Lyndon Johnson's new book, *The Vantage Point: Perspectives of the Presidency 1963–1969.* Reviewers seemed to feel the book is so homogenized that the real Johnson doesn't emerge. That's too bad. With the monumental exception of Vietnam, Johnson's presidency looks better to me every day. Had he been able to outgrow his deal-cutting reflexes and his passion for manipulation, he might have become a truly great President. It's unfortunate but not surprising, I thought, that in this book he continues to disguise himself.

As I read those reviews, I couldn't help remembering my own experiences with LBJ. Early in 1967 the Foreign Operations Subcommittee began digging into the Vietnam war. We pursued it from every conceivable angle. It wasn't long before we became aware that this was not appreciated by Johnson and his aides. I never criticized Johnson personally or suggested that his motives were evil, but I did make speeches critical of his policies. And LBJ was the kind of man who took criticism personally. He got very angry about me.

One evening there was a White House reception for all members of Congress. I was standing in the center hallway talking to Charlie McGuire, then a staff assistant to the National Security Council. The President stepped out of an elevator and walked up behind me. Without excusing himself, he barged right in and asked McGuire about some White House business. After a minute or so he paused; that gave Charlie an opportunity. "Mr. President," Charlie said, "you know Congressman Riegle here?"

The President grunted, ignored me and continued his monologue.

I was taken aback. This was not a casual thing; it was a rebuff, an overt snub on his part. Then I noticed something very interesting. While the President was facing McGuire and speaking directly to him, he was looking at me out of the corner of his eye, measuring me to make sure I had caught his rebuff, trying to sense my reaction.

After he finished and walked away, I asked Charlie, "Does he always operate that way?"

"Well, yeah," Charlie said. "That's sort of the way Lyndon Johnson operates some of the time. When you're around him awhile, you get used to that."

Not long afterward I went to the White House for a bill-signing ceremony on one of the foreign aid measures that our subcommittee had considered. All of us received ceremonial pens. As the President gave us those pens individually, a White House photographer took pictures. Later a picture of me with the President was sent to my office. I, in turn, sent the picture to my friend Bess Abell, social secretary at the White House, and asked if the President would be kind enough to autograph it for me. She submitted my request. The President roared back and said something to the effect that I was getting under his skin and that he'd be damned if he'd autograph the picture.

Bess didn't want to take no for an answer. She went back and asked him to reconsider. A week or so later I received the picture in the mail. It was inscribed: "To Donald Riegle—who I hope will think better of me with age—Lyndon B. Johnson."

I thought about that inscription for some time afterward. I wondered what he meant. He could have been saying, "If you were older and smarter you wouldn't be disagreeing with me." Or, in a very sensitive way, he could have been saying that he hoped with the passage of time I'd view him more sympathetically. Finally I decided that the second interpretation was probably correct, that the inscription was a plea to be understood and not to be judged too harshly. Having reached that conclusion, I felt badly about it. After all, in 1967 Johnson had taken the almost unprecedented step of asking me—a freshman congressman and a Republican as well—to represent him at the inauguration of Brazilian President Arturo de Costa e Silva. I had been greatly honored by that. Then, too, my working relationships with most White House aides had been excellent—much better, in fact, than my relationships with the Nixon people today.

So the inscription on that picture just remained in my head. I felt troubled about it, vaguely uneasy. As Johnson entered his last month in office, I approached McGuire and asked if he could arrange a personal meeting with the President. Charlie scheduled that appointment on January 19, 1969, LBJ's last day in office. I was ushered into the Oval Room late that afternoon. We shook hands and I sat in the chair beside the President's desk. It seemed that his entire desk was covered with telephones. In fact, there was a telephone bank with thirty-five or forty extensions that he could play like a piano.

I told the President that I'd asked to see him because of the inscription, and I reminded him of the incident at the White House reception several months earlier. Johnson chuckled out loud. Clearly, he remembered it with relish. I went on to describe how I felt about him personally and said that my disagreement over Vietnam didn't carry over onto the personal side at all.

We talked for ten or fifteen minutes. I was so intensely involved in trying to make my point that, when I finished, everything else seemed anticlimactic. I believe he said he thought I'd have a long career in politics, but I'm not really sure about that. I remember being impressed again by how tall he was, particularly when he stood up behind his desk. He looked solemn, very old that day. I sensed that deep emotions were churning inside of him, that he was not leaving office happily.

Monday, November 8. I ate breakfast at my desk this morning and spent two hours drafting a reply to letters from constituents asking about the U.N. decision to seat Communist China. There were many phone calls and interruptions. I wanted to get to the men's room but never found time. At lunch I noticed that my hands were shaking.

The prayer amendment came up in the House for a vote this afternoon. John Buchanan, a Republican from Alabama who is also a Baptist preacher, took the floor to argue in favor of it. He gave a ringing, sermonlike speech; his sentences grew longer and longer and turned into paragraphs. Instinctively, I found myself breathing harder to compensate for him. He seemed to have no need at all to stop and take a breath.

During the debate I wrote what for me was a long speech setting forth my position. I felt clear in my head and heart on the decision to oppose the amendment. I only hoped that my constituents would be able to follow my reasoning.

This was one of those rare votes on which a "no" would inevitably cost the member support at home in the next election. I heard Bill McCulloch's voice as he voted "no"; I felt a flash of admiration for him. Bill Steiger, Wilbur Mills and Speaker Carl Albert also voted "no." When the ballots were counted, the prayer amendment had received 242 votes, twenty-eight votes short of the required two-thirds majority. One hundred and sixty-two members had accepted the risk and voted "no." At moments like that I'm proud to serve in the House.

Tuesday, November 9. In the men's room this morning I found myself standing next to Dan Flood from Pennsylvania. I noted we'd probably be voting on the black lung benefits bill today. That's an issue with direct bearing on the people in his district. He smiled, twitched his wax mustache and gave me a capsule history of hardcoal mining there. All his high school classmates, he said, had gone into the mines and all of them were dead today as a result of black lung disease. He shook his head sadly and said there was no cure.

When he graduated from Harvard in 1924, some 66,000 miners worked underground in his district. Today there are only 1600. The coal companies came in and mined the coal and took the profits. Then they went away. "They left us nothing," Flood remarked; "no schools, no hospitals, no libraries." In recent years, he continued, his district's major export has been high school graduates. There is little opportunity at home any more and the district's population has dwindled by 100,000 or more. Small industries are just starting to grow up and are trying to stem the outflow of people. He doesn't know whether they are going to be successful.

Wednesday, November 10. During today's session I dropped the community school bill that Senator Church and I are cosponsoring into the hopper of the House, thereby formally introducing it. I wanted to insert some accompanying remarks into the Congressional Record, so I went up to ask the Acting Speaker, Dick Bolling from Missouri, if he would be presiding when the roll call that was presently under way ended. I needed to be recognized for a unanimous consent request to insert those remarks in the record.

"No," Bolling replied; the Speaker would return soon. "I came up here to talk to the Speaker," Bolling continued, shrugging, "and he handed me the gavel and left." Albert did resume his chair several minutes later. He recognized me and I was able to get the necessary consent.

Later this afternoon Bill Natcher walked over to where I was sitting and took a small piece of paper from his pocket. Referring to that paper, he said he planned to recommend to his District of Columbia Subcommittee that it increase the budget for community schools from $241,000 to $482,000. I knew how difficult it was to find the money and I thanked him with feeling.

Action on the floor today centered around the Continuing Resolution, a temporary measure to fund all federal agencies whose fiscal year 1972 appropriations bills have not yet passed the Congress and been signed into law by the President. Both the defense and foreign aid bills were in this category. Under the rules, the Continuing Resolution itself was subject to amendment. At one point John Seiberling, a soft-spoken liberal from Ohio who is serving his first term here, offered an amendment that would fund the Defense Department for only five more days, until November 15. His intent was to strike out money for the war in Vietnam. But, whether by accident or design, his proposal would have shut down the entire Department of Defense.

Finally his amendment was put to a voice vote. It was shouted down overwhelmingly. Not sensing that he had placed himself in a potentially embarassing position, Seiberling requested a recorded teller vote. He expected at least twenty anti-war liberals to stand with him and force that vote. To his surprise, many conservatives also rose because they sensed, correctly, that most liberals would oppose the amendment as being too extreme. Those conservatives saw a chance to punish Seiberling, embarrass him with his own amendment. They couldn't let it pass.

Tellers with clerks were ordered and virtually the entire membership walked down the nay aisle. Most of the hawkish members stood around chuckling as various "liberals," myself included, lined up to oppose the amendment. When Pete McCloskey voted no, they gave him loud applause. Toward the end of the voting period, most members had cast their ballots and remained in the chamber. Eddie Hébert, the stalwart of the military-industrial complex, filled out a green aye card as a joke and walked halfway down the empty aisle to where Seiberling stood by the ballot box. All eyes were fastened on him. He advanced a few steps, then paused, generating a wave of appreciative laughter. After a few more minutes of this, Hébert finally turned away smiling, ending the joke and triggering more applause.

Seiberling's amendment lost by a vote of 356 to 10. Then five members stood in the well and sought recognition to vote "present." One of them was Father Bob Drinan, a Democrat from Massachusetts, and when he cast his ballot he was met with an ugly burst of catcalls, hoots and boos. Cedie Cederberg stood beside me, holding his pipe, his lips twitching, and said, "They ought to have yellow cards for those who want to vote present."

"If that's the way you feel," I said, "why don't you drop in a bill to that effect?" Cederberg turned away.

Then John Dow, a Democrat from New York, offered an amendment to strike out funds for the foreign aid bill. On October 29 the Senate had rejected the aid bill. The House, Dow said, should follow the Senate's lead. This triggered a long and spirited debate. Even Otto Passman rose to oppose Dow's amendment.

For twenty-five years Otto has made a great show of declaring himself an unrelenting opponent of foreign aid. Yet as chairman of the Foreign Operations Subcommittee he has been charged with responsibility for bringing the foreign aid appropriations bill to the floor of the House. Thus on final passage, he has invariably voted for that bill. And so while Otto has kept insisting that he is a mortal enemy of foreign aid, many members haven't believed him. They've known that he strongly supports parts of the foreign aid bills— particularly the military assistance grants to South Korea (or, as he calls it, "South Kor-rear") and Taiwan. By leading today's defense of foreign aid in the Continuing Resolution debate, Otto was exposing himself to a frontal attack from anyone mean enough to launch one.

As Otto spoke I saw Wayne Hays walk into the well and offer a preferential motion, a privileged parliamentary maneuver that would give him the chance to make a five-minute speech. As Hays began, I observed his tight smile and narrowed eyes and I sensed that, like a coiled snake, he was about to strike. He ripped into the Agency for International Development. "AID is the most ineffective and inefficient do-nothing organization in the U. S. Government," he said. He recounted how Calvin Coolidge once was asked how many people worked in the White House. And Coolidge had replied, "About half of them." If someone asked Hays about AID, he'd have to say "almost none of them. They want to stay on the payroll in their easy chairs. Do not tempt me too far," Hays added, "or I will name names."

He did that anyway. AID Adminstrator John Hannah, Hays went on, "would surely be unemployed if he did not have that job, because Michigan State got rid of him." He also ripped into Otto Passman, labeling him "a proponent of foreign aid legislation." It might have stopped at that if Otto hadn't asked Hays to yield.

Never a friend of Otto's, Hays replied acidly, "I yield to the gentleman from Louisiana, the 'father' of foreign aid."

When Otto gets excited on the floor, he begins to twitch, jerking his arms, head and neck in abrupt motions. Many members mimic these mannerisms privately in the cloakrooms. Watching Otto perform in the well, Wendell Wyatt from Oregon turned to me and remarked, "Otto is the only man I know who wears out a suit from the inside."

Otto was now in the awkward position of having to argue against the amendment and at the same time to try "to set the record straight." He presented his case effectively and was just concluding when H. R. Gross from Iowa, an unremitting foe of foreign aid, decided to get into the act. Gross, who had done his homework, remarked in his resonant voice that he was "somewhat surprised that the gentleman from Louisiana would plump for this Continuing Resolution." Gross then proceeded to quote from several of Otto's past criticisms of AID and foreign aid generally.

Otto fidgeted nervously at the microphone by the Democratic desk. He asked Gross to yield several times. Gross refused to yield. Finally he did—to John Ashbrook from Ohio. Ashbrook yielded to Hays. And Hays, with clever sarcasm, suggested that "we hold the gentleman from Louisiana guilty of being the father of foreign aid under the Negotiable Instruments Act; if you cannot find the maker, then you hold the endorser." The chamber rocked with laughter.

Hays yielded to Gross who, in turn, yielded to Otto. Once again Otto defended himself. Gross, a master of deadpan humor, concluded by advising Passman, "I just wish you would get right with your maker on this subject and vote against it just once."

A few minutes later Doc Hall, a Republican from Missouri, offered a substitute amendment that would cut out economic assistance but retain military assistance. I took the opportunity to speak against both the Dow amendment and the Hall substitute. What I really wanted to do was defend John Hannah and Otto Passman and take a light swipe at Hays. Finally, both amendments were defeated by voice votes. Otto walked over to the Republican side of the chamber to thank those of us who had spoken in his behalf. "I felt just like the groom at a shotgun wedding," he said, "standing beside a pregnant bride I'd never slept with."

Thursday, November 11. There was a full Appropriations Committee meeting this morning to consider the $71 billion military spending bill. Defense Subcommittee Chairman George Mahon presented the measure to the full committee. He had written a 135-page report and he highlighted its major items. He proceeded informally, at one point skipping from page 33 to 72 in one jump.

"You're going pretty fast," Ed Patten remarked. Mahon gently replied that there were some things in the skipped pages that might be "hard to understand."

After some discussion, it was time to offer amendments. Eddie Boland from Massachusetts offered one to cut off funds next June 1 for the U.S. effort in Vietnam—pending the safe return of all POWs. After a brief but spirited debate, that proposal was put to a vote. It lost, 31 to 15. Then I rose to offer an amendment that would have allowed the Pentagon to spend only ninety-five per cent of the funds it received from the Congress this fiscal year. This five per cent cut would have saved some $3.5 billion. My suggestion met little support in the full committee, but I had expected that. It was a necessary preliminary to offering it on the floor. There I could get a recorded teller vote that would put every member on the record for or against a cut in military spending. With the elections only one year away, I should pick up some votes.

I noticed that Patten had taken two new pencils from the table in front of him and placed them in his breast pocket. "A little graft," he explained softly.

Finally George Andrews from Alabama rose to offer an amendment adding funds to start procurement of an additional nuclear frigate for the Navy. For a member of the Defense Subcommittee to propose an additional item without Chairman Mahon's prior concurrence was unusual indeed. Mahon listened quietly. John Rhodes from Arizona, Bill Minshall from Ohio and Bob Sikes from Florida stood up to say that they supported Andrews. Glenn Davis, a Republican from Wisconsin, opposed the amendment, however. He could support the additional frigate on its merits, he explained, but not under these circumstances. The subcommittee had decided earlier in executive session to delete the frigate; somehow, word of that decision had leaked out. Admiral Hyman Rickover had telephoned all the members of the subcommittee and urged them to reverse themselves. Davis had resented—and resisted—this back-door pressure. So had Mahon.

"There are many trees in the forest," Mahon said. "The sturdy oak bends a little in the wind, but maintains its position. But there are weaker trees than the oak in the forest." He went on to make the case against the frigate at this time and criticized the tactics that had been used in an effort to steam-roller the committee. When it came to a vote, Andrews lost badly but gracefully.

As we set to adjourn the meeting, Andrews was assigned the task of moving formally that the full committee report out the military spending bill to the floor of the House. "This weeping willow from Alabama," Andrews rumbled in his gravel voice, "moves that the sturdy oak from Texas"—there was a roar of laughter—"seek a rule waiving points of order and report the bill to the floor." Afterward Andrews sent Mahon a note. "I didn't get a frigate," he wrote, "but I got something close to it."

I stepped into the men's room next door. Ed Patten was leaning over the sink with his face close to the mirror. I asked him what he was doing.

"I'm losing my hair," he said, "and I'm only fifty-nine."

I told him his hair looked fine to me; it was just his imagination.

Ed bent down into the sink, put his mouth under the faucet and swallowed for several seconds. Then he took a mouthful, rinsed the water around and spit it out. Just then Tom Steed stepped out of one of the stalls and approached the sink. Patten's eyes widened in mock astonishment. "Say," he roared, "aren't you Congressman Steed? Can I have your autograph?"

After dinner this evening I really felt weary. It has been an exhausting week and I found myself wishing that I didn't have to fly to the district in the morning. I told Meredith that I felt like a Christmas ornament—something breakable that would shatter if it were dropped.

"Don't worry," she said, smiling warmly, "I'll hang you on my strongest branch."

My apartment is cold tonight. I called my landlord and asked him to please turn up the heat. He promised to do it tomorrow.

Friday, November 12. On the plane to Michigan this morning I drafted a statement on school busing. I finished it later in my room at the Durant Hotel. Seven handwritten pages; for better or worse, they expressed exactly how I feel. Together with remarks on the economy and the auto industry, the busing statement was going to comprise the thrust of my luncheon speech to the Flint Rotary Club. On my way down into the lobby I was still editing my notes.

One hundred twenty-five Rotarians attended the luncheon today; every seat was filled and I noticed that Jim Sharp's was the only black face there. I nibbled at the breaded veal patty and the piece of apple pie, then spoke for about forty minutes and seemed to be connecting. The applause I received was encouraging. Dave Brunell rated the performance as a 9.5 on the 10 scale. I can only hope he's right.

Early this afternoon I sat in on a round-table discussion about the needs of senior citizens in the Model Cities area. Then I met with a group concerned about a local urban renewal project. It was an infuriating bureaucratic mess: a tortoise-paced project already seven years old that has shown no concern for the problems it has created for area citizens. I made it clear to Jim Sharp and Nancy West of my district staff that they would have to dig into this one. "Ram a red-hot poker through the pipe," I told them "and clean it out now."

Back at the district office, I met with a delegation from Save Our Schools. Two of the women in that delegation were the ones who had visited me in Washington. I took off my coat, rolled up my shirt sleeves and for the next fifteen minutes outlined my feelings about school busing. Mrs. Louise Davis, the attractive, dark-haired president of SOS, said she wanted the press to leave. She was adamant. I told the newsmen at the meeting that, under the circumstances, they had better leave.

The attorney for SOS is John Sopt, a conservative Republican who challenged me in the 1970 primary. Although he opposed school busing, he also opposed racial segregation. He was a constructive bridge-builder in the discussion and I appreciated his help. Jim Sharp's presence was a moderating influence, too. I could sense that he was upset and knew he was weighing the pros and cons of entering the conversation himself. He decided to hold back.

All but one in the delegation favored *voluntary* busing of poor youngsters to better schools. I kept asking them, "What can we be

for that can provide equal education and integration *without* wholesale busing?" They asked me to support a discharge petition for a
constitutional amendment prohibiting school busing. I said I
couldn't do that. When we finished, I felt that most of the group understood and could accept my position. I was irked but not surprised
to hear that Mrs. Davis had later remarked to a newsman that I was
ignoring the will of the people. A little raw meat for her constituency.

At the Durant Hotel, I asked for a room with twin beds so Dave
and I could talk further. We had waited all day to find time to go to
the bathroom, so it was a question of who would get the john first.
Reluctantly, I told Dave to go ahead.

Monday, November 15. There were six roll calls on the House floor
this afternoon. Members who'd been absent last Thursday and had
missed the five roll calls then were demanding recorded votes to
build up their percentages. At one point I passed John Erlenborn,
Republican from Illinois, talking to Bob Michel. They were discussing Bill Springer's "announcement." When I walked back to ask
what announcement, they told me he had decided not to seek re-
election in 1972.

Springer is the ranking Republican on the Interstate and Foreign
Committee and, at sixty-two, seems to be in good health. It's almost
without precedent to see ranking members like Springer and, last
month, Charlie Jonas of North Carolina retire of their own free will.
I remarked to Michel that apparently Bill had decided to leave while
he could still walk out under his own power. Bob agreed; Springer
had told him that he didn't want to "hang around and become another Bill McCulloch."

The departure of Springer and Jonas will have an impact on
senior members. Many have bought retirement homes in Florida or
the Caribbean. Increasingly, they must be weighing the choice of
leaving alive like Springer and Jonas—or dead like John Watts. In
the last five years I've seen the pressures increase enormously:
longer sessions, recorded teller votes, the lowering of the voting
age, a new public awareness of the issues, powerful citizen lobbies,
an erosion of the traditional House veneration of senior members,

the aggressive efforts of the McCloskeys, Whalens and Abzugs who refuse to play by the old rules. As Cedie Cederberg remarked to me in the Republican cloakroom one day, "It's not as much fun here as it used to be."

Late this afternoon I was standing in the chamber when the clerk called the roll. In response to his name, Ed Patten stood in the well and raised his ham-sized fist, giving a big thumbs-up sign. The clerk saw it and duly noted, "Patten votes aye." Later I stopped him and asked, "What's the matter? Lost your voice?"

"That's the new signal," Ed replied, smiling broadly. "It means, Up your ass." And he flashed it once again. Then he became serious. He said he hoped we'd adjourn early so he could watch the Monday night pro football game on TV.

Tuesday, November 16. I ate lunch today at the Republican round table in the members' dining room in the Capitol. The table, which seats ten, is the equivalent of the potbellied stove in the old country store—a center for gossip, story-swapping and serious conversation. I took a vacant chair between Pete Biester of Pennsylvania and Dave Dennis of Indiana. They were discussing the Defense appropriations bill and the pending Boland amendment which would cut off funds for the war in Vietnam after next June 1. Dennis was strongly opposed to it and said his conscience wouldn't let him support it.

Biester left the table, and Burt Talcott from California took his place. "How in health are ya?" he asked. Bill Harsha, Bill Steiger and Dan Kuykendall sat down and then Fred Schwengel joined us. As I finished my salad, I asked Dave Dennis what had surprised him the most about Congress since he came here in 1969. He paused for a minute or so, then replied that it was probably the fact that Republican minorities on House committees so seldom offer clear alternatives to Democratic initiatives. Steiger said that wasn't altogether true: Republicans on the Education and Labor Committee frequently offer legislative alternatives. Dennis conceded that sole exception.

I suggested that perhaps it is due to the fact that Democrats have controlled the Congress for thirty-six of the last forty years and thus have dominated all the committees over that period. The Republicans have been reduced to permanent minority status; they have been co-opted by the system and decided they have more to gain by working with the Democrats than by opposing them. Dennis reflected on that and said he tended to agree.

When I first came to Congress, I ate lunch often at the Republican round table. It was a chance to get to know my colleagues better and to be tuned in to the general thrust of events. I seldom grab that chance any more. Usually, if I have time for a sit-down lunch, I'll share it with Meredith. Otherwise I'll order a hot dog on the run in the Republican cloakroom. I find that I have less and less in common with many of my Republican colleagues. We tend to want to talk about very different things. A quorum call interrupted today's conversation. I paid my bill, left a tip and headed for the floor.

In the Republican cloakroom, Charlie Gubser had the needle out for me. He said he'd heard that Shirley Chisholm, a black Democrat from New York, had asked me to be her vice presidential running mate. I replied that I'd rather run with her than with Richard Nixon. Gubser laughed heartily. He probably thought I was kidding.

Later this afternoon I ran into McCloskey and took a seat beside him in the chamber of the House. "I find myself somewhere between dismay and despair," he said. It wasn't the New Hampshire primary— he still feels optimistic about that. It was just that financial problems are weighing on him heavily. He'd met with Norton Simon this morning and spelled out his predicament in detail. He'll be $60,000 in the red by the end of November unless new funds are forthcoming. I noticed at that moment that Pete's breath was awful and I told him so. He said he thought it must be the cheese he'd eaten at lunch. I sent a page for a roll of Life Savers and gave them to Pete with instructions to eat them all.

Before leaving my office I called Cathy in McLean to arrange to have dinner together tomorrow. I suggested she might want to ask a friend to join us. She replied that she'd rather just eat enough for the friend and not have to bring her along.

Wednesday, November 17. In the Longworth Building this morning I struck up a conversation with Roy Taylor, a Democrat from North Carolina. As we hurried toward the subway to the Capitol, he observed that "good legs are as important to a congressman as a good brain." Charlie Gubser and Ferdie St. Germain joined us in the subway car for the twenty-second ride.

"Behaving yourself, Riegle?" Gubser asked.

"Trying to."

"It comes easier as you get older," Taylor said.

There was a pause. Then Gubser remarked, "Common Cause ran a newspaper ad in my district saying what a son of a bitch I am and it was signed by six hundred people."

I couldn't resist the opportunity. "I'm surprised that only six hundred have figured it out," I said.

"There wasn't room for any more names in the ad," Gubser said.

Off the subway, up the escalator, into the elevator, up to the second floor of the Capitol, we moved toward the floor of the House. Otis Pike, a tall, handsome Democrat from Long Island, caught up with us and remarked to Gubser: "You must have done something bad to someone. That's the only time I ever see you smile."

During the debate on the Defense appropriations bill, one of the pages pointed out that John Lennon and his wife, Yoko Ono, were sitting in the visitors' gallery. McCloskey was seeking time to speak on the Boland end-the-war amendment. I had decided to wait and speak for my own amendment to limit Pentagon spending which was due up next. But as a member of the Appropriations Committee, I could seek recognition to speak for five minutes and be recognized ahead of the other members.

Dan Rostenkowski, a Democrat from Illinois, was acting speaker at the time. When he recognized me, I announced my support for the Boland amendment, then yielded to McCloskey, who used my allotted time. On the floor, I asked Jim Harvey if he could support my amendment today. "Mel Laird is a friend of mine," Jim replied

with obvious sincerity. "He was real upset with me when I supported the Mansfield amendment. I just can't support your amendment." I understand his dilemma and appreciate his candor.

The debate continued. Doc Long from Maryland gave what I
thought was a pretty pathetic argument in support of Boland's
amendment. He said, "A lot of this opposition [to the amendment]
comes from those who want the President to get full credit for getting
us out of Vietnam. I have had to take my share of the responsibility
and the blame. Now I want to be able to take some of the credit.
I want to be able to tell my constituents that I had something to
do with getting us out of Vietnam." Many members groaned; I
wanted to throw up.

Acting on the spur of the moment, I decided to walk up to the
visitors' gallery, meet John and Yoko and let them know that
some of us in the Congress appreciate his music. They were just
rising to leave. I introduced myself to John who, in turn, introduced
me to Yoko. She was wearing a black beret that accentuated the
unique structure of her face. We walked down the stairs together.
John said they'd enjoyed the debate, but he wondered why more
Republicans hadn't spoken. We parted at the second-floor landing.
As spectators crowded in around them, I hurried to the floor. Many
members were already standing and the chamber was noisy. Finally
George Mahon moved to limit debate. Each member who still
wanted to speak would receive forty-five seconds.

When the time had expired, Rostenkowski assigned Mahon and
me as tellers and told us to monitor the nay votes. Hurriedly, I
scribbled my name on a green aye card and left it in the box at
the other side of the chamber. Then I walked to the teller position
at the rear. First I had to verify that the ballot box was empty
and then that members voting no passed by in a single file and
handed their red cards to the official counter, who then dropped
them in the box.

I watched my colleagues walk past. They included virtually all of
the Southern Democrats—with some courageous exceptions—and
most Republicans. It was the first time I had seen the members who
would continue the war pass in front of me one by one. Jim
Harvey seemed to be looking the other way as he gave the counter

his card. Finally Mahon asked me to announce the results; it was time for "tellers in the negative to report." I announced 238. The Boland amendment had been defeated rather decisively.

My own amendment was the next order of business on the floor. I gathered my papers and hurried down to the well. Rostenkowski looked directly at me. "For what purpose," he asked, "does the gentleman from Michigan seek recognition?"

"I have an amendment at the desk."

The clerk read my amendment and I began to speak. But Rostenkowski interrupted, saying, "The gentleman will suspend, the House is not in order."

There was a pause, then he continued. "The gentleman from Michigan is recognized for five minutes." He banged the gavel repeatedly. The House, still buzzing over the vote on the Boland amendment, slowly quieted down. As I started again, I noticed that the chamber was full. Probably half of my time had elapsed before I hit my stride, yet by the end of my five minutes I thought I'd made my point. I knew that I would lose. My strategy was to obtain a recorded teller vote—to put every member on the record for or against a five per cent cut in military spending. That's the kind of vote a new-priorities challenger can use effectively against an incumbent in 1972. No sooner had I finished than several senior members rose to seek recognition. First Frank Bow and then George Mahon spoke against my amendment, but graciously. Then Silvio Conte, a Republican from Massachusetts, had to get in a dig or two. He said he thought my amendment was "ill planned, ill conceived and ill timed."

That ended formal debate. The chair called for a vote. I requested tellers with clerks and the chair ordered them. This time I was assigned as a teller on the aye ballot box. I took my post and watched those who had supported my amendment file past. Fifteen of the 74 were Republicans, McCloskey, Chuck Whalen and Brownie Reid among them. I thanked each one as he passed by. The amendment was defeated 307 to 74.

Thursday, November 18. Bill McLaughlin, our Republican state chairman, attended this morning's breakfast of the Michigan Republican delegation. Chuck Chamberlain asked him how much of the party's $1.575 million budget in 1972 would be allocated for the twelve incumbent Republican members. "None," McLaughlin replied; we'd be better off trying to raise our own funds. This really irritated me and I asked him how he planned to split that budget. He said that $675,000 is going to retire the debt on Lenore Romney's unsuccessful 1970 Senate campaign; $650,000 is going to the Griffin race and the remaining $250,000 is needed to run the state central organization.

I registered a strong objection and argued that some money ought to go into the congressional races. I also made it clear that I didn't see where state central operations and activities meant one helluva lot in the Seventh District. McLaughlin bristled, but at least he knows how I feel about this. Significantly, he pointed out that the party itself is receiving fewer and fewer contributions. Most contributions are going directly to individual candidates. One automobile company, for example, has sharply reduced its contributions to the GOP and in 1970, instead, made direct contributions to some ninety different candidates in the state. The company, McLaughlin explained, felt that it would get more for its money this way. It would have "more direct leverage."

I saw Chuck Teague today, the conservative Republican from California who's always kidding me. He was most deferential. "Mr. President" this, he said, and "Mr. President" that. At one point he said he wanted me to name him ambassador to Ecuador. He repeated the word very slowly: "Ec-ua-dor." I think he liked its sound. I told him to consider the appointment definite.

Friday, November 19. Someone told me today that Spiro Agnew has just made a really contemptible remark about Pete McCloskey. Apparently Agnew said that Pete was selling his art collection to pay for his campaign and that he'd even been forced to sell "his favorite painting—Benedict Arnold crossing the Delaware." The more I thought about that remark the madder it made me feel. I told Meredith I was going to nail Agnew on the floor of the House.

Meredith disagreed; she felt that I ought to let it go by. There was nothing to be gained, she said, from making an angry reply. I thought about that and realized she was right. I shouldn't waste my time or energy on Agnew. I'll spend an extra weekend in New Hampshire instead.

Saturday, November 20. Meredith and I went to an early showing of *The French Connection* tonight. A few seats away, I spotted Lowell Weicker from Connecticut and thought to myself, "There's a guy who came to the House after I did and he's already moved on up to the Senate." Waiting for the movie to start, I started counting other House colleagues who've moved up to the Senate: eleven that I could name. Four more have become governors and several have moved into key positions in the Administration. I'm beginning to feel like an old-timer here.

Sunday, November 21. I read in the Washington *Post* this morning that a security guard at the McDonald's hamburger stand four blocks from the apartment was shot and killed during a robbery last night. Where, I wondered, were all the police who normally trip all over themselves writing traffic tickets on Capitol Hill? Did the guard have a family? How many other lives did that tragedy touch? Meredith lives in this neighborhood too; I worry about her safety.

After breakfast I picked up the children in McLean. The weather was changing, growing colder again, and that would chase us inside. We drove to the playground at Haines Point. The wind was cutting in off the Potomac but the kids still ran like animals just released from the zoo.

After watching *The Adventures of Sinbad* at a theater in Falls Church, we drove to the Tysons Corner shopping center to do some pre-Christmas window shopping. In one area there were several bird cages and tropical plants and we stopped to watch the birds. I tried imitating a bird whistle and actually got one of the birds to answer me. We had whistled back and forth for a minute or so when I happened to look through the huge cage to the other side. I noticed that the bird was actually a middle-aged man. He was whistling just as earnestly as I was. He hadn't seen me yet; I slipped away quietly.

Monday, November 22. Some new Gallup Poll figures came out today and they're encouraging. Nationally, McCloskey won 13 per cent of Republican voters. He gleaned 23 per cent of the independents and 33 per cent of the Democrats. Given his minimal public exposure, this is an excellent showing. In the key independent voter category, Nixon won only 54 per cent of the vote. If Pete could confront Nixon on TV, he'd win the major primaries. I'm convinced of that.

Tuesday, November 23. The House was not in session today because of the Thanksgiving recess. I spent time in the office, answering mail and making some scheduling decisions with Dave. Learning that McCloskey was upstairs on the fifth floor, I walked up to see him. Jules Witcover of the Los Angeles *Times* was due for an interview, so I stayed to listen.

Witcover asked for Pete's reaction to Agnew's "Benedict Arnold" remark. Pete replied that no single statement better illustrated his reasons for challenging Nixon. That "they" would link a Republican dissenter with an infamous traitor had only steeled Pete in his determination to run—not because of personal anger at the insult to himself, but rather because of what it revealed of the Administration's operating principles.

To what extent, Witcover asked, had campaigning in New Hampshire diverted Pete from performing his duties as a congressman? Pete replied that he insisted on being present for all crucial votes and that he was devoting mainly recess periods and personal time to the effort in that state. As we talked about some of those crucial votes, Pete admitted his frustrations. The Congress, he said, had voted to set a date for ending the war in Vietnam. Then it had reversed itself and refused to cut off funds for the war after that date had passed. "That's tantamount to saying we're assholes," McCloskey went on, "and we are."

Thursday, November 25. Late this morning Meredith and I started cooking a Thanksgiving dinner. We'd bought a fresh turkey yesterday—and everything to go with it. I have an aversion to raw meat and by-passed the kitchen until the naked bird was stuffed and in the oven. I kept poking my nose into the kitchen trying to help, but Meredith was deep into her cooking and gently but firmly steered me out of the kitchen. I got the message, settled myself in front of the TV, and watched the Kansas City Chiefs get the message from the Detroit Lions.

Friday, November 26. I flew into Flint early this morning, held a brief press conference and then visited the regional headquarters of the UAW and the offices of UAW Local 581. At one o'clock I met with Ed Freer, regional director of public relations for General Motors. Over the next hour and a half Ed made his feelings on the issues very clear. At one point we were talking about a bill that had been before the House several months earlier. He wanted to cite something specific in that legislation. He pressed his intercom button and asked his secretary to "bring in the Don Riegle file." That surprised me—a "Don Riegle file." She brought in a manila folder. Ed sorted through it until he found the material on the bill in question. I wondered what else was in that file. I came away with a deeper appreciation of the pressures Bob Breeden has been feeling from his fellow executives because of his support of me.

Our good friends and supporters had been invited to a sneak preview open house at the new district office this afternoon and evening. The party was a huge success. The Breedens came; so did the Blackmons and dozens more.

Late this evening Dale Hicks, a college classmate of mine, asked if we could talk privately. We found a small office and closed the door. Dale is thirty-six, sensible and refreshingly open. He explained that his business interests, building and real estate, are prospering nicely now. Within a matter of months he wants to take a leave from his firm and work for a year without pay on my Washington staff. I am deeply touched by his offer—and the obvious faith it represents. I thanked him warmly and said I would look forward to his being part of our operation. As we continued talking, the conversation turned to our respective personal situations. Married at a young age, Dale recently went through a difficult divorce. That experience had put him in touch with himself. "You know, Don," he said, "I was never twenty-five. I've been thirty-six years old for the past fifteen years." I knew exactly what he meant.

Saturday, November 27. After spending all day at the "public" opening of my new district office, my right hand was red and sore from greeting people for seven straight hours and I wasn't sure I could smile again even if I wanted to. My dad and I left the office and walked to my room at the Durant Hotel. Another twenty minutes, I knew, and I would have to leave for my plane. Dad seemed somewhat depressed. We talked about Mother's health —she has a very bad cold—his job and my personal situation. We finished our conversation sooner than I would have liked, but planes tend to leave on time and I had one to catch.

Once in my seat on the aircraft, I talked to a young girl who reminded me of Cathy. When I asked her age, she replied, "Seventeen, soon to be eighteen."

"Oh, you'll be able to vote in 1972."

"Yes," she replied, "vote and drink."

I thought about that and said, "Voting may drive you to drink." She laughed wisely.

Monday, November 29. The debate on legislation to reform the financing of election campaigns was under way on the floor this afternoon. At one point Joe Skubitz, a Republican from Kansas, turned to me and remarked, "We may be so liberal about this that we'll remove ourselves from office." He thought about that for a moment, then said, "I don't mean 'liberal'; I mean 'fair.' "

Tuesday, November 30. Floor debate continued today on the campaign financing bill. I listened attentively; this is one of the most important problems the nation has to face and solve.

The issues in the debate were very complicated and there were more members on the floor than is normally the case this early in the week. They realized, of course, that meaningful reform legislation could spell defeat for vulnerable incumbents. The self-protective mood of the House made it very clear that substantive reforms simply weren't going to pass.

The House was willing to approve an amendment sponsored by Bertram Podell, a Democrat from New York, which set a $50,000 limit on the amount a candidate could spend for media and advertising. On the surface, such a measure appeared to be a distinct plus. It would prevent wealthy men or wealthy "interests" from "buying a congressional seat." The catch, of course, was that most challengers would need to spend considerably more than $50,000 in any one campaign in order to offset an incumbent's built-in advantages. The amendment was "stacked" in favor of the incumbents. Such reforms always receive enthusiastic support on the floor.

John Dent, a short, mustachioed Democrat from Pennsylvania, sought recognition to speak in favor of Podell's amendment. "Perhaps the time has come," he said, "when we should do a little peddling of ourselves among our people. What truth is there in an election when one spends the money to hire a John Wayne or somebody to represent him on the air? I am sure if I had to go on TV, I would have to hire somebody because I would never be elected on my looks.

"All my campaigning is done with little items. There is a matchbook now and then and maybe a little pen and pencil, little insignificant things. I try to go to every wedding, every christening, every funeral. I cannot walk down the street without someone saying hello and even little kids calling me Johnny. I remember when the governor came to town and they let me ride in the car with him and everybody was hollering 'Johnny' and he said, 'Don't they know my name is George?'" The chamber rocked with laughter. "So if you're going to represent your people, don't represent them through a shadow man. Represent them yourself and you will not need these enormous sums of money."

At another point this afternoon we had a recorded teller vote on an amendment that would compel congressional candidates to file their campaign contribution records with the U. S. District Courts. I favored the idea and walked into the well of the House to get a green card. Torbett Macdonald, a Democrat from Massachusetts, was also picking up a card when he was stopped by Harold Donohue, a short, solemn-faced man who's serving his twenty-sixth year in the House. Donohue said he had qualms about the amendment but he was reluctant to vote no. If he did, he'd have to explain why Macdonald, his friend and colleague from Massachusetts, had voted the other way.

Macdonald conceded that he didn't think the amendment was "worth a damn," but inasmuch as he had been involved in the "reform" movement, he didn't want to cast any "anti-reform" votes. He shot a furtive glance at the reporters in the press gallery above the Speaker's chair. He was trapped, he told Donohue. The press coverage on this bill was too heavy. It wasn't worth it to have to try to explain a no vote. He'd vote aye, unhappily, and save himself a fight that he didn't need.

As I stood in the aye line waiting for it to move, Wendell Wyatt from Oregon remarked to me that Wayne Hays had just "taken advantage of a senile old man."

"Quit complaining, Wyatt," I said. "You had it coming."

He smiled at my attempted humor, then explained what had happened. An elderly member had entered the chamber late. Hays had collared him and asked, "You don't want to file more reports, do you?"

The old-timer, Wyatt said, answered no. Whereupon Hays handed him a red card and aimed him up the nay aisle.

After the vote I stopped in the men's room to comb my hair. Former member Pat Jennings—now Clerk of the House—was sitting in the raised wooden chair waiting for a shoeshine. Spark Matsunaga, a Democrat from Hawaii, stopped to admire Jennings' brown, ankle-high boots. He said he thought he'd buy a pair himself.

Jennings replied that they were comfortable, but warned that his trouser cuff sometimes got caught on the top of the boot. "You'll find that you have to shake your pant leg," he went on, "just like shaking out that last drop." That brought laughter from around the room.

In the Speaker's lobby this evening, I noticed that W. R. Poage from Texas, the chairman of the Agriculture Committee, was decked out in a tuxedo. Obviously he was planning to attend a formal dinner after the vote on final passage. Cederberg was walking past. Stopping in front of Poage, he fingered the Texan's lapel admiringly. "Farm prices," he said, smiling, "must be up to a hundred per cent of parity." Later, as we walked into the House chamber, I asked Cedie if he knew where Poage was going tonight.

"Probably to a fertilizer convention," Cedie said.

By this time the roll call was under way for the vote on final passage. Spotting some of his cronies, Cederberg vented his spleen on the issue of "reform." "I've been here twenty years," he said, "and I've seen a lot of reform bills, and I haven't seen any reform come out of here yet."

Dick Poff, a Republican from Virginia, looked at Cederberg and said with an air of resignation, "All it's done has been to complicate our lives."

The Campaign Financing Act of 1971 passed the House by a lopsided margin of 373 to 23.

As I was leaving the Capitol, I saw Ed Patten moving through one of the revolving doors. Parked by the steps was a long Cadillac sedan and Patten peeled off to enter it. I was surprised to see that he had such an expensive car, so I yelled to him, "You're livin' pretty high, Patten."

He turned, smiled very broadly and shouted back to me, "These are my golden years."

IX. DECEMBER

Thursday, December 2. Because I was scheduled to speak at a luncheon of the National Association of Community School Directors in Miami today, I had to leave from National Airport at ten o'clock this morning. I didn't want to be away from the floor this afternoon —and have to miss three roll-call votes—but the community school concept is just beginning to gather nationwide momentum. I felt it was important for me to help in any way I could.

I was "up" for the speech, and when I finished, I received a standing ovation. That came as a nice surprise.

My plane was due to leave at two-thirty. We arrived at the airport with four minutes to spare. The temperature in Miami was 76 today. I felt it against my face for a total of probably three minutes. That's what I'd call a "quickie vacation" in the Florida sun.

Late this afternoon Speaker Albert brought to the floor the conference report on the bill to protect wild horses. I wondered if someone would demand a roll-call vote. I turned to Ed Patten and asked him if he knew whether there'd be a vote. He thought for a second and then replied, "On wild horses there ought to be a few nays"—and he rolled his eyes.

Friday, December 3. The Foreign Operations Subcommittee met at eleven o'clock this morning for the first time since Charlotte Reid left the House and took up her post at the FCC. My new seat is just to the left of Garner Shriver's, indicating that I now rank second in seniority on the Republican side. I'm glad to be sitting next to Garner; we often kid back and forth and share rolls of Life Savers. Unfortunately, we still have no foreign aid authorization bill. It's bogged down in conference over the Mansfield amendment. In an effort to end that stalemate, the leadership is moving forward with a foreign aid appropriations bill—despite the lack of authorizing legislation.

Subcommittee Chairman Otto Passman was talking about the tentative "markup" of the bill, settling on specific dollar amounts for each category of activity. He was recommending a cut of some $1.5 billion in the $4.3 billion request. This would produce a final figure of $2.8 billion and that would be the lowest total in the twenty-five years of the AID program. One of the categories Passman mentioned was a "grabbag" group called "American schools and hospitals abroad." In recent years, more and more diverse projects have been added to that group, largely as a result of intensive lobbying. This year the subcommittee seemed determined to cut down on these private projects.

Passman began describing the proliferation of foreign hospitals seeking U.S. funds. "One of these hospitals," he said, "even offered me a free male operation. I told them, at my age, I'd already worn it off." A few minutes later a subcommittee member suggested reopening the discussion on the amount of funding for migration and refugee assistance—shortly after we'd already settled on a final figure. Otto brushed off that request. "We've buried it," he said, "and put flowers on the grave. Let's not dig it up now."

After an hour of heated discussion Shriver leaned over to me and sighed wearily, "I think I've been in here too long."

Saturday, December 4. Late yesterday afternoon I flew to Chicago to speak to the Emergency Conference of New Voters—the wind-up session in our yearlong series of voter registration rallies. The auditorium on the Loyola University campus was packed. The rally was a success and I was enthused by the sense of commitment those young people displayed.

Early this evening I returned to Washington. I stopped by the office and found Kathleen there. She noted how tired I looked and urged me to go home to bed.

"You're going to wind up like one of Otto Passman's suits," she said: "worn out from the inside."

Monday, December 6. Chairman George Mahon gaveled to order this morning's meeting of the full Appropriations Committee. Before introducing Otto Passman to present the foreign aid bill, he remarked, "This is a splendid bill, one which the archest enemy of foreign aid can embrace"—there were smiles of appreciation around the room—"and we will now hear the usual low-key presentation from Mr. Passman. The gentleman from Monroe, Louisiana, is recognized."

There was a buzz of conversation on the Republican side of the room as Otto rose to speak. "Here we go," one member remarked. Another grinned and said, "I wish I had a tape recorder." Otto spoke for about an hour. In his colorful yet thorough way he explained each category in the complicated bill. At the end of his presentation the committee adopted an amendment suspending aid to India and Pakistan until the end of the South Asia war. Then we took a voice vote and passed the bill itself. It wasn't unanimous. Several Republicans preserved the option to speak and vote against the bill when it came to the floor.

Tuesday, December 7. Leaving the Longworth Building for a quorum call this afternoon, I passed Ron Dellums in the hall. An ex-Marine with an M.A. in social work, Dellums is a real activist in the Black Caucus. On the floor he cuts a striking figure—tall and erect in tailored Edwardian suits. Because I was running late, I had decided to drive to the Capitol and I offered Ron a lift. As we neared the car I asked him about the political situation in California. Congressional redistricting, he said, is still up in the air. He wants to run again and thinks a second victory in the Berkeley area would make an important point. But he was less clear about his long-range plans. He found it difficult to imagine himself as a career member of Congress. "This place makes a total robot out of you," he said. I told him I was struggling with the same feelings.

Wednesday, December 8. Shortly after noon today I received a telephone call from my daughter Cathy. She'd come to Washington with her junior high school class to visit the Library of Congress. I was tickled to hear her voice and told her that I'd see her soon. In the Library's lobby, Cathy ran over and threw her arms around me. She introduced me to her teacher and several of her classmates. I suggested that they stop at the Capitol when they left the library. They agreed and so at two-fifteen I met them on the steps and took them to see the rotunda, the old spiral staircase, Statuary Hall and the House gallery.

No sooner had they been seated in the gallery than the teller bells rang for a vote on an amendment to bring the U.S. contribution to the United Nations back to where it was last year. I took Cathy to the floor, filled out a green card and walked toward the aye line. Bella Abzug was standing there and as soon as we had cast our ballots I introduced her to Cathy. I said that Cathy hadn't decided yet whether or not to run for Congress. Bella beamed and said that Cathy looked like her dad; she complimented her on her firm handshake and urged her to run for office at school. Cathy, who's a little shy, gave Bella her warmest smile.

A few minutes later we excused ourselves and returned to the gallery to lead the other students out of the Capitol. Cathy and I held hands on the way. Once outside, we said our good-bys. As the group moved away Cathy suddenly hugged me. "Will I see you this weekend?" she asked. I said yes and then I couldn't manage any more words. She waved at me as she ran to catch up with her classmates. I felt the damp air against my face and I was very sad. I walked outside the Capitol and sat by myself for a while.

The House remained in session very late tonight to vote on a bill entitled the Strategic Storable Agricultural Commodities Act of 1971. About eleven o'clock Keith Sebelius from Kansas took the floor and made a passionate speech in favor of doubling the amount of wheat the government intended to buy next year. On and on he spoke, pleading for the interests of the wheat farmers in the Midwest. "And when you go into a restaurant," he said, "if you don't eat the rolls, at least mess them up."

Sam Steiger from Arizona was standing behind the back rail wearing his cowboy boots. Every thirty seconds or so he made loud clucking noises just like a mother hen. Clearly, he felt that Sebelius needed the accompaniment of some barnyard sounds.

At eleven-twelve, "Vinegar Bend" Mizell from North Carolina, a former pitcher for the Pittsburgh Pirates, sought the Speaker's eye and was recognized for a five-minute speech. He began by saying he wouldn't need *all* the time. That was greeted by loud applause. He waited for the chamber to quiet down again, then said, "I think the last time I got that much applause was when I was knocked out of the box in Cincinnati." That brought down the House.

Thursday, December 9. The House considered the Tax Reform Act on the floor this afternoon and the maneuvering over this bill provided me with more insight into the way Nixon functions than anything in recent memory. The issue of greatest controversy was an amendment attached to the bill by Senate Democrats that would have given citizens an opportunity to allocate one dollar of their federal taxes to help finance presidential campaigns.

The cost of these campaigns has skyrocketed almost out of sight. Nixon plans to spend between $20 million and $30 million for his re-election effort. Given the absence of significant numbers of small contributors, most of this money—as well as the funds raised on behalf of the Democratic candidate—must come from a limited circle of wealthy individuals and special-interest groups. These "fat cats" are often rewarded with ambassadorships or prestigious positions in the new Administration. Maurice Stans, for example, was Nixon's chief fund raiser in the 1968 campaign. Today he's Secretary of Commerce. The special interests that contribute to a successful campaign also expect consideration. All too often, they get it.

Last March 11, Agriculture Secretary Clifford Hardin said there would be no change in the government's established price support for milk, which was then $4.66 per 100 pounds. On March 23, Nixon met with a dozen representatives of the dairy industry. Two days later the Administration reversed itself and increased the price support by 27 cents for every 100 pounds of milk. Later it was discovered that the political-action arm of the Milk Producers Association had collected $322,500 for Nixon's re-election campaign. Eighty-five thousand of it was "contributed" the week before the increase in the federal subsidy; the rest was given after the announcement was made—funneled through dummy organizations such as the Supporters of the American Dream Committee.

This sort of chicanery has flourished on a bipartisan basis for years. In this instance, however, its practical effects are especially unfortunate. The *Wall Street Journal* quoted one economist as saying, "It could cost consumers hundreds of millions of dollars."

The Senate-passed amendment we considered this afternoon—while conceived primarily to rescue the Democratic Party from a financial plight—was a sound piece of legislation. It would have enabled both parties to finance presidential campaigns without having to sell their souls to the highest bidder. But Nixon seemed determined to defeat the amendment. With the prior assurance of all the 1972 contributions he could possibly use, he simply didn't need the tax checkoff money. His deeper concern, however, was to block the Democrats, to cripple their campaign financially. He had the edge and he intended to keep it.

Knowing that Nixon would pull out all stops in an effort to kill the amendment, Senate Democrats cleverly waited until they could attach it to a major piece of legislation, a bill so vital to Nixon that it would be "veto-proof." They chose the Tax Reform Act, a measure that was absolutely essential for the nation's economic recovery. A veto of the bill would plunge the country into a tailspin. Nixon realized this. Nonetheless, he said he would veto the *entire* measure if the dollar checkoff amendment were attached to it. At first his promise was greeted here with disbelief and astonishment. Would he really sabotage the nation's economic recovery by vetoing this bill? It was clear that he would.

Nixon's announcement triggered major shock waves in the business community. I had indicated my support for the tax checkoff plan. Suddenly I began receiving calls from auto industry executives. Repeal of the seven per cent auto excise tax—part of the Tax Reform Act—was essential, they told me. A presidential veto of the act would cause immediate chaos. They pleaded with me to oppose the dollar checkoff amendment because it was "threatening" the entire act. In their desperation, they weren't persuaded by the fact that it was Nixon who was threatening the act—with his veto.

Under the same sorts of pressures from the business community, Ways and Means Committee Chairman Wilbur Mills finally decided to yield. He modified the checkoff amendment so it wouldn't take effect until after the 1972 election. This would protect Nixon— and remove the threat of a veto. When Mills gave way, the Democrats lost; many of them felt they had been betrayed.

Friday, December 10. We convened at ten o'clock this morning, hoping to pass the Tax Reform Act by late afternoon. At one point I noticed Phil Ruppe from Michigan standing by the news ticker in the Republican cloakroom. "We must be close to adjournment," he said with a grin. "The stock market is going up."

Toward the end of the debate John Rousselot from California rose to offer a motion to recommit the act to committee. John's a conservative purist on all economic matters and he opposes any new grant of regulatory power to the President. When a member offers a motion to recommit, he must "qualify"; the Speaker routinely asks him if he is opposed to the bill. The member then responds, equally routinely, "I am." When Speaker Albert put that question to Rousselot today, John replied in a strong voice, "I *definitely* am."

Albert smiled and said, "Then the gentleman *definitely* qualifies."

A few minutes later it was time to vote on final passage. We passed the bill, giving the President the power to continue to regulate the economy. I supported the measure, but with reluctance and misgivings. I'm not sold on the concept of massive governmental involvement in the control of the private sector of the economy. Federal bureaucracy is seldom the answer to anything. My preference is to pass carefully written laws that prevent abuses in the private sector but leave the private sector free to produce and do its job. Nonetheless, with the economy in difficult straits today, I felt compelled to support Nixon's Phase Two initiatives. They seemed to me the only practical option available.

Leaving the floor, I walked down the long steps outside the Capitol. I passed a young Democrat who came to Congress in 1970 and asked him how he liked the place.

"Shit, it's a nut house," he said. Then he sighed resignedly, "But it's all right, I guess."

Monday, December 13. Early this afternoon I was standing at the sink in the men's room off the House floor when I noticed a tall, gaunt man with a scar on the right side of his neck. He was staring straight ahead, seemingly lost in thought. It was John Dowdy, a Democrat from Texas, who is presently on trial in federal court in Baltimore. He's charged with taking a $25,000 bribe in 1965 to block a government investigation of a construction company that was allegedly swindling homeowners in Washington, D.C. A member of the House for the past nineteen years, Dowdy may be sent to prison. He takes the stand in his own defense tomorrow. He seems very alone. Few members speak to him or even notice him.

Several hours later I saw Charlie Gubser from California getting his shoes shined. "Gubser," I said, "you ought to show a little generosity and give a decent tip today. After all, it's the Christmas season." The shoeshine man and I exchanged winks.

Gubser laughed self-consciously and fished in his pocket. In the hallway outside he caught up with me. "You put me on the spot," he said. "I had to give the man a dollar. Now I won't be able to contribute to McCloskey's campaign." He walked away, chuckling to himself.

This was "District of Columbia Day" in the House and most of the speeches on the floor concerned bills affecting Washington, D.C. Most—but not all. At one point Clarence Miller, an Ohio Republican, was recognized for a five-minute address. "Mr. Speaker," he began, "today we should take note of America's great accomplishments and in so doing renew our faith and confidence in ourselves as individuals and as a nation. The U.S. has consistently been a world leader in the production of eggs. According to the Department of

Agriculture, total U.S. egg production in 1968 was over 69 million eggs."

Miller regularly calls our attention to such easily overlooked facts, and the Congressional Record brims with his pithy observations.

Tuesday, December 14. Al Lowenstein was in town this morning and arrived at my office shortly before ten-thirty. He confided that he has decided to run for Congress again in 1972. Progressive Democrats, he said, will have a chance to elect enough new members to control the Democratic caucus. They could elect a new Speaker and eliminate the seniority system. That prospect appeals to him.

We talked about McCloskey's challenge and the outlook in Pete's congressional district. The New Hampshire primary is March 7. The filing date for congressional candidates in California is March 10. Depending on what happens in New Hampshire, Pete will have three days to decide whether or not to seek re-election to the House. While we were discussing this, my office door swung open and McCloskey himself appeared. He greeted us warmly, then slumped down on a black leather couch. The conversation turned to campaign finances. Al said he had a thousand-dollar royalty check coming from a publisher and wanted to contribute it to McCloskey's campaign. Pete sat upright on the couch, leaned forward and emphatically gave Al the finger. Al ignored the gesture and said he really wanted to help. "No," McCloskey insisted. Al and I looked at each other. We knew that Pete was serious. He had made up his mind. We didn't try to argue the point.

On the floor this afternoon, I spotted Bill Hungate, a thoughtful, prematurely graying Democrat from Missouri who has just announced his resignation as chairman of the House District Judiciary Subcommittee. For any chairman to resign voluntarily is almost unprecedented, so I stopped him to ask the circumstances. Despite his best efforts, he replied, lobbyists from collection agencies, small loan companies and other businesses were succeeding in their efforts to influence legislation before his subcommittee. Invited to testify publicly, these lobbyists have declined and chosen to keep pressing their efforts behind the scenes. Apparently, staff members of the

House District Committee and its subcommittees have been going along with that.

As far as Hungate knows, Chairman John McMillan of the House District Committee doesn't seem to object to this practice and hasn't disciplined or warned the staffers. On occasion, McMillan has even called Hungate's Judiciary Subcommittee into session himself to consider measures affecting these local firms. Hungate never learned about this until after the fact. He told me he thought a major scandal might erupt over the way the legislation is being developed. He felt powerless to stop these end-run plays; he couldn't function effectively. Under the circumstances, he said, his only real alternative was to resign.

One of the prevailing myths about the House is that many congressmen and their staff members spend time accepting money, gifts or the favors of call girls from omnipresent lobbyists in return for their help with special-interest legislation. It *may* happen occasionally but certainly not to the extent that some people believe. Because I'm on the Appropriations Committee, whose duties are general, I don't see as many lobbyists as I would if I belonged to a specialized committee like Public Works or Post Office and Civil Service. No one has ever approached me to suggest a bribe of any sort. That could be because the people who might try such a thing feel I'm so powerless here that it wouldn't be worth the effort. I'd like to think it's because they know I'd throw them out of the office. I *have* heard rumors about kickback-type situations involving members of committees that handle big contracts, but I've seldom seen them substantiated. In fact, I know of only one or two instances of that happening during my time in office.

The one incident that I recall most vividly actually occurred before I came to Congress. In 1965, as a casewriter at the Harvard Business School, I was doing a study of how the Post Office Department and Congress agreed on increases in postal rates for different classes of mail. I flew to Washington to conduct my interviews. At the time, Post Office and Civil Service was probably the most corruption-prone committee in the House. There was a direct relationship between its decisions and the amount of money that a mail-order company, for example, would have to pay to send its

packages. Lobbyists swarmed all over the members of that committee. The favorite ploy they used to reward sympathetic members
was to hold phony testimonial dinners. A sponsoring organization
might come in and buy a hundred tickets at fifty dollars each and
maybe only two or three ticket holders would actually attend the
event. Funds spent for the rest of the tickets would go to the
"deserving" member. It was all a charade, a devious way to funnel
money to a member who would be expected to show his appreciation
for this largesse by favoring the sponsors' legislative proposals.

One afternoon the late Joe Pool, a Democrat from Texas and a
member of the committee, invited me to attend a testimonial dinner
that was being given for him that night at a Washington hotel. I
had nothing better to do, so I went along. There was Pool in a
rather small room with about two dozen people including the
lobbyists who had underwritten the affair. Sales of the bogus tickets
probably produced five or ten thousand dollars for Pool. Later, those
same lobbyists appeared before the committee. They asked for help
in keeping the rate structure low and the government subsidy high.
I don't know how Pool reacted, but the whole situation was a disgrace.

Lobbyists here range from the inept and pitiful to the really
powerful. Some national trade associations put out an awful lot of
material which suggests to their members across the country that
terrific things are being done. In reality, the Washington end of the
operation may have no influence at all. Other organizations—the
road builders' group, for example, and most of the larger unions—
get in there and shoulder for position. They do their homework.
They know what they want and how to get it. They reward compliant
members with campaign contributions and votes at election time.
That's really the best currency in this town.

Wednesday, December 15. On the floor this afternoon, I asked Jerry
Ford if he would be willing to come to Flint sometime in February
to speak at a fund-raising affair for me. He said that, although his
schedule was busy, he was willing to do it. He'd try to confirm a
mutually agreeable date by the end of the week. Given my disagreements with the White House, Jerry could have declined. The

fact that he said he'd come without hemming or hawing about it says a lot about him.

Waiting to vote on the conference report on the Defense appropriations bill, I struck up a conversation with Fletcher Thompson, a Republican from Atlanta. I asked what his happiness level was today compared to what it had been before his election to Congress in 1966. "It's much, much lower," he said. "If all I wanted was happiness, I would have been better off staying in the Georgia State Senate, practicing law on the side, golfing once a week with my friends and enjoying my family. You know, we don't have friends any more—only acquaintances. We're on the run all the time and there's always something more to do."

Fletch went on to say that he's having trouble sleeping at night. "I can't turn my mind off," he explained. "I'll be thinking of something and try to force it out of my mind—and something else pops in." The only thing that helps him, he said, is taking a hot bath. He's aged in the five years that he's served in the House. I can see it around his eyes. He's on the verge of declaring a Senate candidacy in 1972. That means the pace will get worse.

Thursday, December 16. Early this afternoon, New York Democrat John Dow rose and addressed a question to the majority leader. "There seem to be rumors floating around about why we are or are not adjourning," he said. "I believe it has to do with the foreign aid bills which are now in conference with the Senate. I wondered if our distinguished leader could clarify the situation and tell us just what it is that is the crux of this difficulty?"

"The gentleman pays me an unusual compliment," Hale Boggs replied, "when he refers to the idea that I can clarify this situation. What specific rumors does the gentleman refer to?"

"I did not ask what the rumors were, really," Dow said. "I asked what is the crux of the difficulty in the conference between the House and The Other Body."

Like a schoolteacher lecturing an errant pupil, Boggs proceeded to tell him. "The gentleman will recall that we passed the foreign aid assistance authorization and The Other Body passed two foreign aid bills. We passed a regular foreign assistance appropriation. The

Other Body has not approved the regular appropriation bill. Yesterday we passed a continuing resolution to carry on the functions of the Agency [AID]. The Other Body is now debating that continuing resolution. They will continue to debate it for some time. We have no way to adjourn this Congress unless both bodies are ready and willing to adjourn. We have completed the work of the House. That is the best answer I can give."

Before Dow could reply, Abe Kazen, a Democrat from Texas, jumped to his feet and asked the question that was on everyone's mind. "Well," he cried, "can we go home?"

Friday, December 17. The House went into session today just long enough to pass an adjournment resolution by voice vote. Barring a special session, we'll be in recess until January 18. In this first half of the 92nd Congress, we had 151 quorum calls and 319 recorded votes. I was present for 122—or 80.7 per cent—of the quorum calls and 272—or 84.5 per cent—of the votes. With my trips to the district and other speaking engagements, I feel pretty good about this attendance record. Still, I hope to do better next session.

Late this afternoon, I boarded a plane for Flint.

Saturday, December 18. Dave Brunell and I had breakfast this morning in the coffee shop of the Durant Hotel in Flint and laid out an agenda for my eight o'clock meeting with the "kitchen cabinet." When we arrived at my district office, the staff was already there. So were such "cabinet" members as Bob Breeden, Bob Williams, Al Blackmon, Jack Milhouse and Paul Visser.

Would I support Nixon? Some wanted to know. How about Griffin and local Republican candidates? The questions came one after the other. I answered them as well as I could. Then Dave began discussing our financial situation. Thus far in 1971, we have spent $10,000 on unreimbursed plane trips to Flint, newsletters and questionnaires and other office expenses. We have raised about $4000 in contributions. We still owe $6000, most of it to printing companies. Dave emphasized the fact that we had received no help from the local or state party organizations since 1970. We wanted to try to pay our bills by the end of the month, he said, and start 1972 with a clean slate. Al Blackmon asked if he could tell potential contributors that any funds they gave would go to pay our own bills and not be funneled into the McCloskey campaign. We said he could count on that.

When we finished our pitch, the room was still for what seemed like an eternity. I'm not sure what I expected. Without the help of these men, we wouldn't be able to raise very much. Bob Breeden spoke first. He said he would take the responsibility to raise a thousand dollars. Blackmon said that he would too. Joe Shomsky and Chuck Duryea made similar commitments. Bob Williams and Roosevelt Ridgeway, a black electrical contractor, followed suit immediately. One, two, three, four, five, six. It happened so quickly that it took me a minute to comprehend what these commitments represented in terms of individual faith. Awkwardly, I stammered my thanks.

Minutes later the meeting broke up. Breeden was the last to leave and as he pulled on his topcoat I thanked him again. He said that he wouldn't have volunteered to raise the money unless he believed in me. We shook hands firmly and I told him that he was one of the few people I really love. "You know I feel the same way," he said.

Tuesday, December 21. In a withering blast, seventy-four-year-old Senator Margaret Chase Smith of Maine attacked the poor attendance records of her colleagues today. "The Senate," she said in a speech, "is a club of prima donnas intensely self-oriented; ninety-nine kings and one queen dedicated to their own personal accommodation." She went on to suggest that any senator who missed forty per cent of the roll calls in that body ought to be expelled.

That was strong medicine and it brought to mind a brainstorm I had nearly three years ago: Stop paying each member of Congress a fixed salary and institute instead a merit pay plan based on job performance. Effective, hard-working members would receive more; lazy ineffective ones would receive less. An independent pay board would establish individual salaries by evaluating a member's committee work, service to his district, positions on controversial issues and attendance record.

That idea nearly frightened Blake and Brunell to death. They felt that even the suggestion of such a plan would so infuriate my colleagues that life in the House would become impossible. The idea would get nowhere, they said. Why stir up a hornet's nest? They were right, of course, so I kept the notion to myself. But I still like the idea.

Wednesday, December 22. The mail this morning brought a note from Jerry Ford saying that he would come to Flint to speak on my behalf on any of three dates in February. In a gracious way, he indicated that he had never received travel expenses for the last such trip he'd made to Flint, back in 1966. I called his office and said we'd see to it that the old bill was paid immediately.

At noon I picked up the children so we could celebrate an early Christmas together. Once we arrived at my apartment, they dashed into the living room and let out yells of surprise. Hanging there were three piñatas: a multicolored rooster for Cathy, a blue and lavender lion for Laurie and a bull with big horns for little Donny. Laurie and Donny wanted to dig out the toys and candy immediately. Cathy preferred to leave her piñata hanging intact for the time being. All three children carefully sized up the presents under the Christmas tree.

Early this evening we went out for a pizza dinner. We came back to the apartment at ten and, after some laughing and joking, Cathy and Laurie finally went to sleep. Donny hopped into bed with me. He bounced around my bed and then he lay silent for a moment. Suddenly he looked up and said: "Why did you and Mom get a divorce?"

It came like a lightning bolt. What could I say that a three-and-a-half-year-old would understand? Finally I replied that it was a long story. I wasn't sure he'd understand until he was older. There were many reasons. . . .

"But why, Dad, why?"

"Because it seemed like the right thing to do."

I hated those words as soon as I had spoken them. The truth

was that I didn't really know how to answer him. Perhaps he
sensed that, because he didn't ask again. We talked about other
things for a while and soon he quieted and I thought he'd fallen
asleep. Then, without a word, he lifted my hand to his face and
kissed it.

Friday, December 24. Meredith and I were walking in Georgetown
this afternoon when I felt someone punch me lightly on the arm.
It was Don Rumsfeld, a former colleague in the House who later
became a top White House insider. He was wearing an old leather
jacket and had two of his children with him. After exchanging
clichés about the difficulties of last-minute Christmas shopping, we
wished each other a merry Christmas and went our separate ways.

Early this evening I received a call from Lowenstein. He'd had
lunch with Charlie Goodell and had just spoken to McCloskey
by phone. He was convinced that Pete could raise campaign funds
in New York, but he worried that Pete might not follow through on
the idea. He felt that I should call Pete myself, stress the urgency
of such an effort and volunteer to co-ordinate it.

After we'd finished our conversation, I thought how very ironic
it was that I'd talked to both Rumsfeld and Lowenstein in the last
few hours. Rumsfeld first introduced me to Al, in 1968. Their
friendship dated back to the early fifties, when they wrestled against
each other in college. When Rumsfeld left the House to head the
Office of Economic Opportunity, hand-picked for the job by Richard
Nixon, Lowenstein passed the word among the agency's constituen-
cies that Don could be trusted to do what was right. That helped buy
him a critical "grace" period. As the months passed, however, the
Nixon Administration began to dismember OEO. Rumsfeld was
perceived as the man who had been chosen to destroy the agency.
Lowenstein found that his own credibility had been damaged.
Nonetheless, he stood by Don.

They remained close friends until the fall of 1970 when Al
sought re-election to Congress. His challenger was a Republican
named Norman Lent whose forces depicted Al as a radical revolu-
tionary—the sort of man who would incite students to riot and
march under the Viet Cong flag. It was such a vicious campaign

that Pete and I allowed Al to use our names in ads refuting those charges.

As the campaign's tempo increased, the vilification of Lowenstein became even more extreme. Polls showed that Lowenstein and Lent were running neck and neck. If the charges made against Al could be exposed once and for all as a pack of lies, the tide would swing in his favor. Al turned to Rumsfeld, explained the situation and asked if he would be willing to say that Lowenstein was not a bomb-throwing traitor. Rumsfeld said that he would.

Rumsfeld was approached by a Long Island newspaper for an interview. He vouched for Al's character and loyalty to his country. The story enraged local Republican leaders. They asked the White House to force Rumsfeld to withdraw his statement. Al was sure that Don would stand firm. But hours later, Lent's forces made public a letter from Don. It endorsed Lent's candidacy. As far as Al was concerned, the fact that Don hadn't told him about the endorsement in advance was even worse than the letter itself.

Forty-eight hours before the election, the Fair Campaign Practices Committee agreed to evaluate the literature that Lent's supporters were using. Al called me in Flint around noon. He asked if I would fly to New York and appear at the hearing as a character witness. Thirty minutes later, I was en route to the airport. Upon arrival in New York, I was ushered into the hearing room and seated next to Lowenstein. Lent sat across the table. He seemed startled when he heard me called "Don." Perhaps he thought I was Rumsfeld.

When I was introduced, I vouched for Al's character and stated emphatically that the brochures spread out on the table were wholly inaccurate. Even Lent disavowed the worst of them. But the damage had been done. Lent won the election by some 9000 votes. Last January, when the 92nd Congress was sworn in, I shook hands with Lent. We haven't spoken to each other since.

Saturday, December 25. I talked with the children by phone this morning. Donny said Santa Claus had left many good things. Cathy and Laurie said they were sharing an electric baseball game. They seemed excited and it was obvious from their conversation that Nancy had done a great job making their Christmas full and happy. I know it wasn't easy.

Monday, December 27. Statistics published today indicate that some three million young people under the age of twenty-one have already registered to vote. In states where they registered by party, 55 per cent claimed to be Democrats, 24 per cent Independents and only 21 per cent Republicans. Republicans tend to register first; as the volume of registrations increases, the cumulative GOP percentage will probably drop.

Tuesday, December 28. Along with twenty-nine House Democrats, I signed a telegram today urging Nixon to stop the intensified bombing of North Vietnam and concentrate instead on negotiations in Paris. The telegram was not a perfect vehicle to express my opposition to what's been going on, but it was the only one presently available.

In the Longworth Building I bumped into McCloskey. I mentioned my conversation with Lowenstein about fund raising in New York and told Pete that I was at his disposal. Then I noticed a rip in the front of his shirt. I pointed to it and asked, "A bullet hole?"

"No," he grinned. "That's what happens when you pack by rolling all your gear together. My razor took a nick out of the shirt."

Wednesday, December 29. Ohio Republican John Ashbrook announced that he was a candidate for the presidency today. A forty-three-year-old Harvard graduate who has spent eleven years in the House, he is an articulate conservative. During his press conference, he referred critically to Attorney General John Mitchell's remark about this Administration's civil rights policies—"Watch what we do, not what we say." That's the heart of Ashbrook's challenge and, in a sense, of McCloskey's challenge too. Neither man, one a conservative and the other a liberal, feels he can trust Nixon. The hallmark of this Administration is a pattern of seeming deception and constant effort to disguise true intentions. During the war between India and Pakistan, for example, the

Administration proclaimed a policy of evenhanded neutrality. The minutes of White House meetings, revealed by columnist Jack Anderson, showed that the U.S. really favored Pakistan. The lack of any clear moral purpose—either in terms of national goals or in the operating principles of the men at the top—is spoiling public faith in government. Ashbrook senses this. So does McCloskey. What the press has missed thus far is that their separate challenges spring from the same soil of disillusionment.

Friday, December 31. The headline over the lead story in this morning's Washington *Post* was DOWDY CONVICTED IN BRIBE CASE. After fourteen hours of deliberation, a jury in Baltimore had found the Texas congressman guilty of bribery, conspiracy and perjury. He faces a maximum penalty of forty years in prison and a fine of $40,000. The last member convicted of a crime while in office was Thomas Lane from Massachusetts, who was found guilty of tax evasion fifteen years ago. Dowdy's was a depressing case in every respect—from the crime he committed to the personal tragedy of a broken man.

Meredith has the flu today, so I went grocery shopping for a New Year's Eve celebration. When midnight came we listened to the noises in the distance. I raised a window and shook some old sleigh bells but we couldn't really get in the spirit of the thing. Meredith wondered aloud if we'd see the year 2000. It seems very distant, but at the speed our lives are moving, it may get here next month.

X. JANUARY

Saturday, January 1, 1972. J. Edgar Hoover is seventy-seven today—seven years over the mandatory retirement age for federal employees. He stays on as director of the FBI in violation of the spirit of the law. Both Johnson and Nixon have winked and looked the other way in signing executive waivers allowing him to circumvent the law. It's no wonder that so many people don't respect the law. They see our top officials disregarding it themselves.

Tuesday, January 4. Carl Blake's wife Marge gave birth to a six-pound, ten-ounce son yesterday. Carl is bursting with pride.

He and I first met in 1961 at IBM soon after I joined the company. He was working in manufacturing-engineering. As fellow MBAs we developed a close working relationship and, soon, a friendship as well. At IBM, we collaborated on developing a new technique for evaluating capital investment alternatives; after months of effort it was officially adopted for use, first by our division of the corporation and then by IBM itself. Since 1967, Carl has shared administrative assistant's duties with Dave Brunell. He manages the Washington office operations and is responsible for the preparation of my committee staff work.

Wednesday, January 5. The morning mail included a letter from the commanding officer at Valley Forge Army Hospital in Pennsylvania. It was in response to my inquiry about the harassment of double amputee Jim Dehlin because of the length of his hair. The colonel said that he had ordered the letter of reprimand removed from Dehlin's file. He was investigating further and would be back in touch.

John Byrnes from Wisconsin, the ranking Republican on the Ways and Means Committee, announced today that he will not seek re-election. After twenty-five years in the House, he wants to finish his "productive years" in the "private sector." His decision to retire is highly significant. It reflects his obvious belief that we Republicans will not win control of the House in the foreseeable future.

Thursday, January 6. Dave and I talked with Al Toffel this morning about the status of the McCloskey campaign. It seems certain, Toffel said, that the campaign will make it through the New Hampshire primary. Fund raising has increased to a point where it's just about covering monthly costs. The $40,000 deficit has held steady for some time. As far as the campaign's day-to-day operations are concerned, Pete himself is still the number one problem. His unwillingness to delegate responsibility is hampering everyone. As a former corporate manager, Toffel has found ways to work around the interference. Steadily and skillfully, he has more or less battled Pete to a draw. But it's still a constant struggle. A lesser man would have quit months ago.

Toffel expressed concern about John Ashbrook's challenge. It's splitting the anti-Nixon vote and making it harder for Pete to attract news coverage. If Ashbrook outpolls Pete, he said, Nixon will turn even more to the right. And that will be the exact antithesis of what McCloskey has sought to accomplish. Unless Pete clobbers Ashbrook, we lose all the way around. But even if he does whip Ashbrook, it's clear to us that Pete's not going to be nominated or elected President in 1972. Even if he scores well in New Hampshire, it doesn't seem likely that he will ever have the resources necessary for a sustained challenge.

As our meeting broke up, Toffel confided that he had $5000

squirreled away to spend on media in New Hampshire. I didn't
have the heart to remind him of the $322,500 from the dairy
lobby that the Nixon people will probably use for media themselves.

Friday, January 7. Some weeks ago, Meredith and I decided that
we would be married in the middle of January. Today we drove
to Easton, Maryland, to apply for the marriage license. We want
the wedding to be in nearby Oxford, a picturesque village on
Chesapeake Bay. Once in Easton, we found the courthouse and,
finally, the office of the clerk of the court. An elderly woman
asked if she could help us. I told her why we'd come and she
gave me the license application. When I completed it, she looked up
and said, "That'll be one dollar." I remarked that this was one of
the few bargains left for one dollar. "No," she replied without
smiling, "it'll cost you three dollars more when you pick up the
license next week."

At the Methodist Church in Oxford, I introduced myself to the
Reverend Kyle Smith, a pleasant, soft-spoken man of about forty-
five, and talked to him about our plans. I said we want to be married
by the House chaplain away from Washington, D.C., and that
just the two of us will be present for the ceremony. He graciously
agreed to our plan.

Saturday, January 8. Over dinner this evening, Meredith, Dave and
I talked about the book that will come from this diary. I said I
was somewhat apprehensive about the reaction it will draw from
colleagues and constituents. Dave is worried because it will be
published just before the primary filing date. He fears that material taken out of context could be used against me by an un-
scrupulous challenger. Meredith has more doubts than either Dave
or I. She's concerned about the book's possible effect on what
little private life we have left, the bitterness and anger that it may
arouse. She fears that, on balance, the book may be more harmful
than helpful to me.

I agreed that because of the book there will be bitterness in
some quarters, and some of the people who will be angry have

excellent ways of getting even. So I have the same deep and conflicting feelings about this book, but I think people have a right and a need to know what goes on in Congress, and writing about Congress from the inside is a challenge for me. My hope for this book is that it may prompt a few young people to enter politics, though it's always possible that it may send them running in the opposite direction. At any rate it's a gamble.

Sunday, January 9. In this morning's Washington *Post,* columnist Dave Broder wrote that McCloskey and McGovern are competing for the same pool of voters and volunteers in the New Hampshire primary. He noted that Pete has fewer volunteers than McGovern "but has been scoring better in personal appearances—particularly before youth groups." Nixon, he concluded, has to be considered the overwhelming favorite among Republicans. Then he added, "For those who believe in omens, the photocopying machine in Nixon headquarters kept breaking down and, last week, burst into flames."

Monday, January 10. The normal volume of mail arrived at my office this morning and I asked one of my interns to give me a breakdown on its composition. Included among the 263 pieces were 13 newspapers, 7 magazines, 40 bulletins from various groups and associations ranging from the Sport Fishing Institute to the Christian Anti-Communist Crusade, 18 advertisements, 7 invitations (a National Prayer Breakfast, a coffee in honor of orthopedic surgeons, an American Legion cocktail party), 2 bills (for air travel and Xerox machine charges), and 8 "Dear Colleague" letters asking for my support on legislative proposals that other members are sponsoring.

There were 88 cards and letters from people in my district, 27 of which set forth views on specific issues. School busing and Peace Corps funding led the list with 8 each. Only 2 letters mentioned Vietnam. There were 10 requests for information about subjects ranging from the recycling of paper to federal regulations on occupational therapy and a number of requests for help on personal problems. The mail I must act upon personally will be referred to me, but most of it will be handled by the staff. They're authorized to act in my name within specific guidelines, and they can solve many problems without my direct involvement. Once in a while, however, the system malfunctions and a letter gets sidetracked. Several weeks ago a woman wrote me wanting to buy a flag that had flown over the Capitol. Somehow her letter wound up in the pile of Christmas cards that I received. I sent her the flag last week with an apology.

The mail this morning also included a note from McCloskey. "It crosses my mind," he wrote, "that I haven't thanked you recently for standing hard and tough through the current conflict. As Oliver Wendell Holmes, Jr., once said, 'Civil strife is far more difficult than combat.' This fight we're in is well worth making and while it may be lonely today, our cause is just and it's a great deal easier to make the fight with you standing by to help. Keep the faith and thanks. Pete."

Tuesday, January 11. Together with John Murphy, a Democrat from New York, and Bob Kastenmeier, a Democrat from Wisconsin, I taped a thirty-minute show for educational TV stations in the House recording studio this afternoon. Tucked away in the basement of the Rayburn Building, the studio is furnished with attractive props. There's an ornate desk and a large, full-color photograph of the Capitol behind a make-believe window. To the viewer it appears that Congressman X has a lavish office which looks out over the Capitol. The truth may be that he is crammed into undistinguished quarters. For about twenty dollars, a member can have two one-minute color tapes of himself commenting on the issues of his choice. TV stations back home sometimes air these tapes without editing. So all that it costs a member is his time plus twenty dollars to "buy" a minute of exposure on a local newscast. It's one of the hundreds of small but vital advantages that make incumbent congressmen difficult to beat.

Late this afternoon, I called the chaplain of the House, Reverend Edward Latch, to ask if he would be able to go to Oxford,

Maryland, to perform the wedding service for Meredith and me. He agreed and we set the ceremony for Friday at noon.

Just before 7:00 P.M. I drove to the airport to begin a two-day trip to the district.

Wednesday, January 12. My wake-up call came at five-fifteen this morning, and I dressed quickly in order to get to the Buick plant gates before six o'clock. Men in work clothes were arriving in clusters of three and four, most of them carrying lunch buckets, brown bags and thermos bottles full of coffee or soup. It was cold and as I greeted them I shifted from foot to foot. In the next thirty minutes I shook about five hundred hands. There were plenty of smiles and many of the men called me by name. Four or five refused my hand and brushed right past. Still, it was a far cry from the times in the 1940s and 1950s when my dad stood at the gates. Often, his campaign cards were knocked out of his hands or were torn and discarded before the men entered the plant. There were rough shoves and ugly comments. In previous years I always stood alone at the gates. This morning a number of union officials came out to welcome me. Things have nearly come full circle, and Dad is the one who blazed the trail.

At noon I stopped at the Riegle Press, a printing company owned and operated by my grandfather, John L. Riegle. My father, chief salesman and vice president, greeted me warmly, then walked with me though the back room where the large presses were turning out school forms and legal blanks. Spotting Lawrence Bradley, I stopped to talk with him. He's worked at the press for as long as I can remember. He's a man with a warm laugh and a good sense of humor.

He seemed very down today, older and more serious. I told him again how sorry I was about his son, Bobby, who was killed in Vietnam several months ago. Bobby loved to race motorcycles and, although he was only nineteen, he'd won dozens of races in Michigan and nearby states. Being an excellent mechanic, Lawrence often accompanied his son to these weekend races and helped him keep his machine in shape. He told me that he and his wife still keep Bobby's trophies all over the house. "Every day," he said, "when I walk through the house, I think . . . about Bob." He couldn't continue. For several moments he stared at the concrete floor.

He started again, his voice soft. Bobby's birthday, he said, was the day after Christmas and Bobby had always loved to decorate the tree. He said that he and his wife hadn't been able to bring themselves to get a tree this year. He had to stop again because his shoulders were shaking. He wiped the tears away, then looked up at me and said, "It just didn't seem like Christmas this year."

This afternoon I stopped by Hurley Hospital to pay a call on a patient. As I was getting the room number from the receptionist, a conservatively dressed man, about sixty years old, walked up and said bluntly: "The President has more information than you have on foreign affairs. You should give the Administration more support on foreign affairs." Obviously, he didn't want to discuss the issue further, so I nodded and thanked him for his opinion. As he walked away, he turned and said again: "Remember, *more* support for the Administration." Just then I felt someone tap my arm. It was a young man with a blond beard who was wearing granny glasses. "And I'd like you to give *less* support to the Administration," he said.

Late this evening I visited Mother and Dad and told them I planned to marry Meredith. I had hoped for a rational conversation, but after fifteen minutes or so I picked up my coat and left the house. I couldn't listen again to what I've already heard a million times before.

Thursday, January 13. I talked at length this morning with four men representing different soft drink bottling companies in Flint. They were concerned about a recent Federal Trade Commission ruling that would threaten their exclusive area distributorships. Under this ruling, a Coca-Cola bottling firm in Detroit, for example, could move into Flint and sell large quantities of Coke at lower prices than the local bottler. By picking off the high-volume chain store outlets, distant bottlers could drive the local men out of business. This ruling would hurt the average consumer, the men around the table insisted. Although the consumer might pay ten cents less for a six-pack of Coke at a supermarket, he wouldn't be able to purchase the drink at small neighborhood stores. Distant bottlers wouldn't bother to service low-volume operations. I agreed to dig deeper into the economic consequences of the FTC ruling and to consider supporting a bill that the small bottlers' national lobby has drafted in Washington to remedy the problem.

My next stop was at the headquarters of UAW Local 599 near the Buick Foundry. The union's major interest now is a program of "30 and out"—full retirement after thirty years on the job. Its leaders also want a change in Social Security laws so that a man who retires at fifty-two will not have his monthly payments based on the lower salary he might earn after his retirement. That's what present laws require. A man's Social Security payment, the UAW leaders suggested, should be based on his ten best earning years. They noted that the congressional retirement plan calculates a member's retirement on his *three* best earning years. Why should politicians receive a better break from the government than men who work with their hands? It was a legitimate question and I agreed to try to help.

Flying back to Washington late this afternoon, I changed planes in Cleveland and walked to a flower stand in the airport lobby. I asked the pretty Korean girl there to pick out the best half dozen pink roses she had. "I'm getting married tomorrow," I said, somewhat awkwardly.

Friday, January 14. At ten o'clock this morning Meredith and I met Reverend Latch and his wife by the Capitol steps. They agreed to follow us in their car to the United Methodist Church in Oxford. As we were driving along Route 50 near Annapolis, Meredith said I looked like I hadn't shaved for a week. I reached up, felt my chin. Sure enough, with everything else I'd had on my mind, I'd forgotten to shave. When we stopped at the courthouse in Easton to pick up our marriage license, I took my shaving gear into the men's room, peeled off my coat, shirt and tie and began to lather up. As I was completing the job, an elderly man walked through the door and suddenly stopped short. I could see him in the mirror as he studied me for a moment, shook his head and went about his business. Finally, our two-car caravan arrived at the church and the Reverend Kyle Smith escorted us inside.

As we stood in the foyer, Reverend Latch examined the license and advised me on the procedure we would follow. I glanced over at Meredith. She was wearing a tailored, ivory-colored blouse and a beige, floor-length skirt with an interwoven soft cream design. We walked to the front of the church and she stood on my left as we faced Reverend Latch. He asked if we had rings. I nodded and felt my pocket for the sixteenth time. I turned and looked at Meredith again. Her face was soft and calm. Her blond hair hung just below her shoulders and in her hands were the six pink roses tied with an ivory ribbon. The moment was more beautiful than I could ever have imagined. My emotions were brimming; it was hard to breathe.

Reverend Latch told us to join our right hands and then he placed his hand over ours. He asked me to repeat after him: "I, Donald, take thee, Meredith . . ." I tried to speak but found that I couldn't. My feelings were just too great and I was on the verge of tears. Meredith touched my arm softly, smiled up at me and whispered, "I, Donald . . ." Reverend Latch leaned forward and told me to take my time.

"I, Donald, take thee, Meredith"—I could feel tears running down my cheeks—"to love and to cherish . . ." Then Reverend Latch asked Meredith to repeat the same vow. Her voice was soft but strong at the same time. I could see tears in her eyes. We were both a little shaky as we placed the rings on each other's fingers. Then Reverend Latch joined our right hands again and announced that we were husband and wife. I bent over and kissed Meredith's forehead. With a smile, Reverend Latch said, "You may now kiss the bride."

Sunday, January 16. The apartment was warm and inviting this evening when we returned from two days on the Eastern Shore. The thirty-three-year-old sentimentalist took one of the wilted rosebuds and pressed it in a book on the shelf. Neither Meredith nor I wanted the week to start.

Tuesday, January 18. The House reconvened today for the second session of the 92nd Congress. The quorum bells rang at 12:02 P.M. and for the next forty-five minutes returning members greeted each other effusively. Many were tanned from vacations in Florida or the Caribbean. Others wore sporty new suits they had purchased during the recess. The chamber buzzed with loud hellos, story-swapping and laughter and I was reminded once again how *physical* a place this is. Congressmen don't just speak to one another. They punch each other on the arm, slap each other on the knee, grab at each other's jackets and—occasionally—give each other a goose. I do these things myself unconsciously. Sometimes this habit brings unexpected results. Not long ago, for example, I was sitting next to Larry Winn, a Kansas Republican, and gave him a hard thwonk on the knee. For a moment I thought I had broken my hand. "That's all right," he smiled. "You can smack me there any time you want." In my exuberance, I had forgotten that Larry walks on an artificial leg.

During the recess, some things had changed. As chairman of the House Administration Committee, Wayne Hays had ordered the refurbishing of the Speaker's lobby. New crystal chandeliers had been installed and the old red wooden coat shelves removed. I draped my topcoat over a chair and walked into the Republican cloakroom. In a phone booth there, I tried to place a long-distance call to my district office. I couldn't get the operator. Cloakroom aides explained that the redoubtable Hays had ordered the phones rewired so no one could make long-distance calls. Apparently some members had been dialing numbers directly and not charging the bills to their office accounts. Not being able to make or return long-distance calls from the party cloakrooms is a tremendous inconvenience. Hays's decision will outrage my colleagues.

On the floor I stopped to talk to Bella Abzug. She motioned to the gallery and said that some 250 women had come to this opening session to support her resolution censuring Nixon for disregarding an amendment that Congress passed last year calling for all U.S. troops to withdraw from Vietnam subject to the safe return of our POWs. A little while later, after Bella had completed an impassioned speech denouncing the war, the women in the gallery rose and shouted their approval, waving signs and bringing the proceedings to a halt.

Speaker Albert gaveled for order but to no avail. Finally Doc Hall rose on a point of order. "I demand that the gallery be cleared," he thundered. Albert agreed and gave the appropriate orders. Ed Derwinski and I were standing by the back rail on the Republican side of the floor talking about Bella and her noisy supporters. Ed was delighted that Albert had emptied the gallery. I told him that if he really wanted the gallery cleared, *he* should have given a speech—that would have cleared out the place faster than anything else. Derwinski grinned, squinted his eyes and said, "Ya know, Riegle, if you'd cut your hair another half inch, you could join my team."

In the Republican cloakroom, I learned that Bill McCulloch, the ranking minority member of the Judiciary Committee, has decided once and for all to retire at the end of this year. I was thinking how much we'll miss his leadership in the field of civil rights when Ed Hutchinson approached me and offered congratulations on my marriage. Flo Dwyer overheard him and added her own good wishes. She stood at the food counter with me and said quietly that she hoped my divorce wouldn't have a negative political effect. She mentioned that Catherine May, a senior Republican from Washington, was divorced early in 1970 and then was defeated in her bid for re-election.

Meredith got a promotion and a raise in salary today. It has taken me a long time to understand her need and desire to work, to have something apart from us. In the past it's been my tendency to expect to dominate a relationship, to have my job be the center of existence. That won't work with Meredith. There's a battle of wills going on—in a constructive sense. Of course, I want her to do whatever makes her happy. But this has meant that I've had to change some of my attitudes about man-woman relationships. Rationally, I know that true equality is the only thing that can work for us, and this is something she's helping me learn emotionally as well.

Wednesday, January 19. A roll call was under way on the floor this afternoon and we were in the P's when I noticed Bob Price, a Republican from Texas, ready to answer his name. I slipped up behind him just as his name was being called, slid my hand in front of his face and cupped it over his mouth. His "Aye" became a muffled grunt. The reading clerk looked up, called his name again and I pulled my hand away. Bob replied, then turned and punched me on the shoulder. "You sonofabitch," he grinned. "I almost blew that one out the wrong end."

A few minutes later in the hallway of the Capitol, I spotted Chuck Teague approaching me. I spoke first, bowing slightly and addressing him as "Mr. Ambassador." He was obviously surprised but he recovered quickly. "Mr. President," he mumbled and bowed in return.

Thursday, January 20. There was a breakfast for Michigan Republicans at the Capitol Hill Club this morning and it produced a wide-ranging discussion that lasted for more than an hour. Bob Griffin indicated that in the past two months he has received some 48,000 letters opposing school busing and only 238 in favor of it. My mail reflects a similar ratio. Jerry Ford spoke with great feeling about the situation in Grand Rapids and expressed his fear that the courts would order busing there. He said he had decided to sign the discharge petition to let a bill which would amend the Constitution and ban busing come to the floor for a vote. Apparently he's concluded that eighty-three-year-old Manny Celler, chairman of the House Judiciary Committee, has no intention of holding meaningful hearings on the issue. If that's true, I may sign that discharge petition myself.

As the breakfast was ending, State Chairman Bill McLaughlin took me aside and said that the latest congressional redistricting plan under discussion in Lansing would cut my district into four pieces. Setting aside the fact that this would destroy my political base, it's a bad idea. Genesee County is virtually a congressional district by itself. To split it into so many pieces would make it impossible to co-ordinate federal grant applications for the area or deal with community problems in a workable way. Once back in my office, I made some telephone calls to rally opposition to the plan. This could get hairy before it's over.

The President was scheduled to give his State of the Union address to a joint session of Congress at twelve-thirty today. I arrived on the floor just before noon and found a seat next to Flo Dwyer, who was wearing a bright red dress. She smiled and said she felt "in the middle with Barry Goldwater, Jr., sitting on one side of me and Don Riegle on the other." Barry and I reached across, shook hands and welcomed each other to the second session. Senators were filing into the chamber. Senator Goldwater spotted his son and signaled that he wanted to talk. Barry, Jr., got up to leave. I asked him if he was going to get his allowance. He smiled and said that he was.

Ambassadors, associate justices of the Supreme Court and the members of the Cabinet entered the chamber. Then Mrs. Nixon, Julie and Tricia arrived with White House aides John Ehrlichman and Henry Kissinger and sat in the President's box. Finally, in the glare of high-intensity TV lights, Nixon strode into the chamber and—as is the custom—was greeted with a prolonged standing ovation.

The tone of his address was moderate, a sharp contrast to the stridency of 1970. He used the phrase "law, justice and order"; he talked about putting space technology to work solving domestic problems and he ended with an appeal for a political debate that would be spirited but wouldn't cause bitterness or deep division. Clearly, he was trying to move away from his old rhetoric and make a high-road appeal. I mentioned this to Tom Railsback, who was sitting on my right. Tom nodded. "I think he's finally gotten the message," he said.

After the speech I stood near the Capitol door talking to Meredith on the phone. I noticed Martha Mitchell, wife of the Attorney General, walking toward me engrossed in conversation with a friend. As she was about to pass, she smiled and on impulse I said, "Here, you probably want this," and handed her the phone. She stopped, laughed, took it and drawled a loud "Hi" into the receiver. Then she turned to me, shook the receiver and asked, "Who's this?"

"My new wife," I replied.

"Hi, new wife," Martha hollered. Then she laughed again, gave me the phone and went on her way.

Friday, January 21. Early this afternoon Meredith and I were walking along Connecticut Avenue when we passed a stooped old man hobbling across the street. Meredith stopped and for a moment she seemed very depressed. All her life she's had a special feeling for old people. Several years ago, for example, someone called her attention to a newspaper article about an old man in West Virginia who had installed a telephone in his home because he wanted to feel more in touch with the world. He'd waited several months for the phone to ring, but when it finally did it was a wrong number. Meredith brooded about this for a day or two and then called the man long distance from New Mexico.

Seeing the stooped old man today changed her mood completely. She had been laughing a minute earlier; afterward she became quiet and reflective. If the past is any guide, she'll think about that man for the next several days, wondering who's taking care of him.

Monday, January 24. There was a meeting of Michigan Republicans in Cederberg's office at ten o'clock this morning. We're approaching the final nut-cutting in the drawing of new congressional district lines. Cedie said he had been approached last week by Lou Nedzi, a senior Democrat from Detroit. Nedzi suggested that House Democrats be given a free hand in drawing the new districts in the three metropolitan counties of Wayne, Oakland and Macomb. The Republicans could then carve up the rest of the state as they desired. This would be a way not only to protect all incumbent members but also to break the redistricting stalemate in the state legislature. Nedzi had added one further caveat: Genesee County had to remain intact. Presumably the Democrats feel they can win my seat if and when I'm out of the picture.

During this past weekend, Cedie continued, Michigan Republicans had worked to draw new district lines equalizing population and protecting the incumbents as fairly as possible. The plan he unveiled this morning met with general approval.

Wednesday, January 26. Late this afternoon the House assembled for its official photograph. Speaker Albert gaveled for order and asked members to clear the aisles. When the milling around continued, he banged his gavel again and repeated the request. Finally the chamber hushed. "Members will all be seated and look at the camera for the next ten minutes," Albert explained. "Okay, now, look at the birdie," he called out and sat back in his chair, grinning hard at the camera in the gallery.

Thursday, January 27. At ten o'clock this morning I arrived at the Government Operations Committee room in the Rayburn Building for the annual open hearing. During this hearing Administration spokesmen present the President's budget requests to the full Appropriations Committee. After calling the session to order— with TV cameras whirring and flash bulbs popping—Chairman George Mahon welcomed George Shultz, the Office of Management and Budget director, and said that he was very concerned about the size of the federal budget and its ever increasing deficits. Mahon's remarks contained a few barbs, but it was a warm embrace in contrast to the searing partisan attack that a Wayne Hays might have made.

Shultz listened courteously, occasionally interjecting remarks of his own and putting his case on the record just as Mahon was doing. In due course he began his formal presentation, referring at frequent intervals to flip charts covered with hundreds of numbers. His nervous aide kept darting back and forth to turn over the charts on cue. The official stenographer typed frantically in an effort to catch every word. But the discussion wandered. The cross-examination seemed uninspired and soon the spectators and newsmen began drifting from the room.

To relieve the boredom, committee members whispered small talk. Burt Talcott and I exchanged words on the Vietnam war.

"No one's *for* the war," he insisted.

"That's just horse shit," I replied, "when everyone keeps voting money to continue it."

Lou Wyman was sitting next to Talcott and he was doing a slow burn. "This is a lotta crap," he fumed. "It's meaningless." Talcott replied cryptically that he had a plan to force a change in committee procedures. Wyman interpreted his remark as implying that he favored some kind of disruption. As an ex-attorney general of New Hampshire and a "law and order" man, he recoiled immediately. "No siree," he said, "I wouldn't be a party to breaking any of the rules."

Talcott assured him he hadn't meant to suggest anything like that. Wyman began muttering to himself while he shuffled his papers together. Finally, his face a storm cloud of exasperation, he rose and stalked out of the room. After another fifteen minutes of listening to meaningless colloquy, I followed his example. Had I decided to wait another hour or so, I would have received my chance to cross-examine Shultz for a full five minutes. As a practical matter, I had better ways to use my time so I walked back to my office and worked on the mail.

Friday, January 28. On a flight to Oregon this afternoon—where I was scheduled to give a speech in favor of community schools —I sat next to Senator Mark Hatfield. With his handsome features and engaging smile, he appears much younger than forty-eight. We shook hands warmly, then talked about this year's presidential race and our respective relationships with Nixon. Since 1968, Mark said, his contact with the President has been negligible and he has been removed from the White House invitation list. Over the past three years he has disagreed with the Administration fifty-five per cent of the time in votes on the Senate floor. According to an analysis by *Congressional Quarterly,* that was the highest percentage of opposition of any Senate Republican. I remarked that I, along with Brownie Reid, had earned the same dubious distinction as regards votes in the House. Mark grinned. "I always felt we had a lot in common," he said.

In a more serious vein, he noted that Nixon seemed like a computer, "almost a mechanical man," and he was equally concerned about Agnew. He voiced the opinion, shared by others, that Agnew's sudden emergence as a national figure has gone to his head. "He's like a child who's asked by his parents to sing a song for visitors," Mark said. "When they clap after the first verse, he feels he has to go on and sing all the other verses."

At the airport in Portland, I was met and driven fifty miles or so to Whitaker Junior High School in Salem. Some three hundred and fifty people from around the state had gathered in the auditorium to discuss community schools. Ten minutes after my arrival the lights went out and stayed out for the next hour. We ate dinner in the dark.

There was a small candle on the head table and as I used its flickering light to scribble a speech outline, I felt weary and somewhat apprehensive. But just before I was introduced the lights came on again. The speech went better than I had expected. After urging the creation of community schools, I pointed out that the money needed to fund them was going instead to the Indochina war—more than $10 billion in 1972 alone. One year's *interest* on that sum would enable us to start community schools in every neighborhood in the U.S.

During the question-and-answer period an outraged woman—later identified as a member of the John Birch Society—rose and insisted on reading a five-page tract that she had written denouncing community schools. The audience seemed upset by her interruption, but I waited for her to complete her statement. When she finished her monologue, she asked me a question about the financing of these schools. As I started to reply, she cut me off again and began another diatribe.

"Wait just a minute," I said. "I didn't interrupt you when you were making your statement. Now don't interrupt me."

Her voice rising, she continued to speak and it was clear that she was not about to listen to me. Then from the rear of the auditorium came a rhythmic hand clapping which increased very quickly in its intensity and soon drowned out all her remarks. With an angry expression on her face, the woman finally sat down. She didn't speak again. I don't think she realized that her behavior had probably aroused more support for community schools than I had with my speech.

Sunday, January 30. I got back to Washington last night. I had planned to spend today with the children but Nancy called this morning to say that it would be inconvenient. I was really looking forward to seeing the kids today. Next weekend I'm committed to fly to New Hampshire, so I probably won't see them for another two weeks. That really bothers me.

Monday, January 31. On the floor this afternoon I was talking to Bob Mathias, a Republican from California, when I noticed that he was wearing tennis shoes. A two-time Olympic decathlon winner in the 1950s, Bob had been working out in the House gym when the quorum bells rang.

The House gym in the bowels of the Rayburn Building is strictly off limits to the public. That's one place where a member can't take a guest. There is a beautiful swimming pool, a steam room and a rubbing room for massages. There is also an equipment room filled with side horses, punching bags, medicine balls and weights that you pull from the wall. You seldom see members in that room. The most popular activity in the gym is a variation of paddle ball and the courts are usually full. Paddle ball, in fact, is almost sacrosanct here. I didn't discover that until May of 1970.

At the time the House was considering a series of amendments to the Defense procurement bill. Some of those amendments were aimed at ending U.S. military action in Cambodia. House hawks controlled the time and used up most of it themselves to present arguments supporting the war. Although dozens of anti-war members were seeking recognition, they were repeatedly ignored. After about three hours of this, most of the hawks had finally had their say. The late L. Mendel Rivers, the super-hawk chairman of the Armed Services Committee, moved to limit further debate. That would leave only about an hour to be divided among the sixty-five or seventy doves who had been waiting all afternoon for a chance to speak. Rivers' motion was shouted through and it was arranged that each of us would receive a mere forty-five seconds.

The hawks then added insult to injury by deserting the chamber. The gallery was jammed with spectators, many of whom had traveled great distances to hear the debate and watch the vote. That they should have to witness this travesty of the legislative process was more than I could stand. I was boiling mad.

When I was recognized for my forty-five seconds, I grabbed the microphone at the Republican committee table and started to unload. "What a sham!" I cried, speaking directly to the people in the gallery. "I ask you, have you ever seen a worse sight in your life?"

I was dimly aware that Doc Hall from Missouri had jumped to his feet and was angrily shouting, "Point of order! Point of order!" And I could hear the acting Speaker pounding the gavel on his desk. But I ignored them. "For eight years," I continued, "we have fought an undeclared war. What can be more important than fully debating this issue? And where are those members who minutes ago voted to cut off debate? They're down in the House gym playing paddle ball!"

The bedlam in the chamber made it impossible to go on. The gallery spectators were applauding furiously and so were antiwar members. Doc Hall was still shouting, "Point of order," and Dan Rostenkowski from Illinois was sitting in the Speaker's chair, still flailing away with the gavel with all his might. My time had expired so I left the mike.

Not long afterward I learned that by addressing the people in the gallery I had violated the rules of the House. But that wasn't all that had angered my colleagues. My cardinal sin was that I had exposed the members who had gone to the gym to play paddle ball. Cederberg, for one, deeply resented the fact that I had referred to Cambodia and the House gym in the same speech. "You know darn well we need a House gym," he said. "Members just don't get enough exercise!"

In the office this afternoon, Lisa, my legislative assistant, asked me why I'd sponsored a bill to provide federal funds to train firemen without telling her. I replied that I knew nothing about any such bill. Yet somehow a bill bearing my name had been dropped in the hopper. After investigating, Lisa reported that several other members were in the same boat: bills had been filed in their names that they knew nothing about.

The explanation was bizarre. For the past several months Bob Steele, an able Republican from Connecticut, has been drafting a comprehensive fire-fighting bill. Apparently some of his disgruntled former employees split the bill into seven pieces and succeeded in introducing it under bogus sponsorship. Under House rules there's no provision for withdrawing a measure once it has been filed— even if it's fraudulent. I can speak on the floor disavowing "my" bill, but neither I nor anyone else can strike it from the record.

For the past several weeks Clarence Miller, who used to give the House short speeches on U.S. egg production and other matters of similar consequence, has been inserting into the Congressional Record a series of brief tributes to famous Americans on an almost daily basis. I had thought he was about to run out of candidates, but today's two-sentence entry shows I was mistaken. "Mr. Speaker," he wrote, "we should take note of America's pioneers of progress and in so doing renew our faith and confidence in ourselves as individuals and as a nation. American Willis H. Carrier first devised air conditioning in 1911."

XI. FEBRUARY

Tuesday, February 1. Late this afternoon I was working in the office when the bells rang indicating that a recorded teller vote was about to start on the floor. At issue was an amendment that would have cut in half the $320 million authorization bill for the International Development Association. When I reached the floor I spotted Jim Harvey and asked how he was planning to vote. "No," he said. The amendment was irresponsible and might damage the balance of payments situation. As I signed a red card, he indicated that the Administration also opposed the measure. Walking through the well on my way to the "no" box, I caught Jerry Ford's eye. Raising my red card, I asked him if I was right in assuming that a no vote was in support of the Administration. He smiled and said that it was. "Just checking," I explained.

About six-fifteen this evening, sitting in the chamber waiting for the final vote, I struck up a conversation with Peggy Heckler. She said she hoped that McCloskey would do well in New Hampshire. I asked if there wasn't any way that she could help him there. "No," she replied. Maybe afterward, when the challenge was over, she could act as peacemaker. But party regulars, I pointed out, won't forgive Pete. They'll hold him in the same contempt that they hold Charlie Goodell. I told Peg that we needed her voice, her public commitment now. I said I thought she could be a marvelously effective speaker. She listened but didn't respond.

Later this evening Meredith and I—and my friends Mr. and Mrs. George Whyel from Flint—attended the annual reception and dinner hosted by Michigan members of the American Bankers' Association. Jerry Ford was asked to introduce the members of Congress present. Before doing so, he offered a few extemporaneous remarks. Mellowed by a couple of oversized martinis, he started to say, "We're delighted to be here . . ." Somehow it came out, "We're delightful . . ." and laughter rippled through the room. As the dinner ended, Cederberg walked across the room, introduced himself to Meredith and welcomed her to the Michigan delegation. It was a gracious gesture.

Wednesday, February 2. Visitors to the House gallery shortly after noon today heard an interesting mixture of messages during the one-minute speeches. Herman Badillo, a Democrat from New York, spoke with great feeling about the weekend's bloody clash in Northern Ireland. "When," he asked, "will armies and police and government learn that violence begets only violence, that the use of arms is more often the catalyst of violence than a deterrent, that an army of occupation serves only to stiffen the resolve of the citizenry?"

He was followed by Ed Roush, a Democrat from Indiana, who explained with a smile that he had ordered some government furniture for his district office but had received instead "315 pounds of floor sweeping compound, 1625 pounds of paper toilet seat covers and 1950 pounds of toilet tissue. Mr. Speaker," Roush continued, "I don't *need* all of these items."

Thursday, February 3. Because I'll be in New Hampshire on my birthday tomorrow, the staff surprised me with a small party at the office this afternoon. There was ice cream and a rich chocolate cake—compliments of Sears, Roebuck and Company (which provides all members with cakes on their birthdays). The troops had pitched in to buy me the *Jesus Christ Superstar* album. Meredith came by after work to help celebrate, and as I was leaving the office Kathleen gave me a card with my New Hampshire schedule. At its end was this message: "We are advised that presently there is a driving snowstorm in New Hampshire. After much discussion on the part of the McCloskey workers, they have decided to call it 'The Donald W. Riegle, Jr., Memorial Storm.' "

It was raining as I drove to McLean to pick up the kids and take them to dinner at the Evans Farm Inn. After dinner, as we were leaving, we walked through a reception room. Two older women were sitting in front of a roaring blaze in the old stone fireplace. Suddenly one of the logs made a loud popping sound. Donny's voice filled the room. "Daddy," he cried, "did you fart?" The women looked shocked as I hurried the kids out the door.

Friday, February 4. Thirty-four years old today. Meredith and I left National Airport at seven forty-five this morning for Boston, then on to New Hamsphire to campaign for McCloskey. After an airport news conference, an hourlong radio station talk show appearance, and lunch with young McCloskey supporters at Wellesley College, we headed for the North country.

My first speaking engagement in New Hampshire this afternoon was at St. Anselm's College in Manchester. We were ushered into a large room that could seat a hundred and fifty people but only thirty or so were waiting. On the walls hung a dozen old paintings of distinguished-looking men. I pointed to them as I began my talk. "I see you've got pictures of all this year's presidential candidates," I said, and waited for a laugh or two. The silence was deafening. I cut out the attempted jokes and tried to explain the reasons behind McCloskey's challenge, but I felt flat and uninspired. Bill Kovach of the New York *Times* was sitting in the back row staring out the window. Afterward, McCloskey's staffers didn't seem discouraged at all. I asked for their reactions, fearing the worst. "It was great," one enthused. "You outdrew Yorty by three."

Saturday, February 5. Up early this morning for another wild day of campaigning. We drove up the Connecticut River Valley, stopping at small general stores and shopping areas along the way. In Lime we stopped at Nichols Hardware, a combination lunch counter, post office, hardware store and gas station. We were late; some people who had come to see me had already left. Mr.

Nichols was tall, wore glasses and limped, dragging one foot. He had strong feelings about the economy and was disturbed about Nixon's "big spending." I talked about Pete, but mainly I listened. The dissatisfaction is there. The question is how to coalesce it.

On up the valley we'd ride for twenty minutes, then out and into another general store. "Hello, I'm Congressman Riegle from Michigan campaigning for Pete McCloskey. I'd like to give you one of these campaign brochures. We'd like to earn your support." At Pierpoint, we stopped at Gould's Country Store. The butcher was friendly. I talked about McCloskey and bought some cheddar cheese off the wheel. At the check-out counter an older man hearing McCloskey's name asked, "Who is he? I've never heard of him."

"That's why we're here," I replied.

The woman behind the counter chimed in, saying to the man, "You haven't been reading the papers."

At the Grafton County Farm we talked to the nurses and several of the elderly men who live there. Speaking of the old men, the administrator advised me: "Some of them left off with Teddy." She meant Roosevelt.

As I lie in bed I'm trying to sort out all the impressions I gathered. I conclude Pete's vote performance will go one way or the other: either twenty to twenty-five per cent or forty per cent plus. It all depends on whether or not the independents can be persuaded, en masse, to vote in the Republican primary. Pete has to try to build the psychology of winning—actually beating Nixon and forcing policies to change now.

Sunday, February 6. Meredith and I rose at eight o'clock this morning to go skiing on Wildcat Mountain. She's been teaching me how to ski, and this was my third time on the slopes. After an initial spill, everything went fairly smoothly. Following a late lunch, we made a second run. My legs stiffened, I had to stop often to rest, and I had trouble with turns. I fell only once but that was enough. I really crunched my right shoulder. My energy was gone and when I reached the bottom I was tired and sore. My shoulder hurt so much that I couldn't lift my arm. I consoled myself with the thought that at least I had not come down strapped to the rescue sled.

As our driver headed toward Logan Airport in Boston three and a half hours away, I twisted and turned in the back seat of the Volvo trying to get comfortable. It was impossible. My shoulder was throbbing. At the airport we bought a copy of the Boston *Globe*. On its front page were recent New Hampshire poll results. Nixon had 71 per cent, McCloskey had 14 and Ashbrook trailed with 4. We have a long way to go and little more than one month to try to narrow that gap. Shortly after ten o'clock we landed in Washington. I walked through the rain to the congressional parking lot. The damn car wouldn't start. We waited there forty-five minutes before we were finally able to hail a cab.

Monday, February 7. On the Today Show this morning, White House chief of staff H. R. Haldeman bitterly attacked anti-war critics and those who have expressed doubts about Nixon's latest peace plan. In blunt, searing language, he accused these critics of "consciously aiding and abetting the enemy." His comments were unprincipled and indefensible. They gave more evidence of a White House psychology that equates thoughtful dissenters with traitors. Martha Mitchell displayed this same psychology at a White House dinner last week. When a member of the Ray Coniff singers unfurled a hidden anti-war banner and asked the President to stop the killing, Martha became apoplectic. She said the young lady should have been "torn limb from limb." I don't think she was kidding.

Tuesday, February 8. Chairman John McMillan, the aging czar of the House District Committee, is the most heavy-handed and, I think, the least respected autocrat here. An anti-civil rights Democrat from South Carolina, he has used every means at his disposal to keep the District of Columbia pinned under the heel of Congress. In recent years, as pressure has mounted to grant home rule to the District, McMillan's obstructionism has been flushed out more and more into the open. This morning's developments during a home rule debate provided a fine example.

Walter Fauntroy, the District's able non-voting representative in Congress, was slated to be the first witness. But McMillan exercised his prerogatives as chairman and called on John Rarick in Fauntroy's place. Gilbert Gude, a liberal Republican from Maryland, protested immediately. McMillan tried to gavel him down, but Gude wouldn't surrender. "The question is," he continued, "whether the white majority of this country and the Congress has the grace to grant basic rights to the Capitol city which has a black majority."

When order was restored, Rarick began to speak. Predictably, he labeled the District "a sink-hole, rat-infested . . . the laughingstock of the free and Communist world [which lacks] even a proper racial balance." Arguing that home rule would invite a takeover by Black Muslims and labeling the District's citizens "transients and migrants," Rarick suggested that a sensible answer would be to force the relocation of District residents to "areas like Montana, South Dakota, Minnesota or Kansas." If the costs of such a move were prohibitive, then the District should become part of Maryland.

At that suggestion, Charles Diggs exploded. A black member from Detroit, he attacked Rarick bitterly: "The gentleman is pursuing a racist line. . . . He is a leading racist in Congress." McMillan banged his gavel repeatedly, trying to silence Diggs. When Fauntroy said that Rarick's testimony had been laughable, "a waste of time," he, too, was gaveled down. Instead of hearing witnesses who favored home rule, McMillan then called upon Virginia Republican Bill Scott. And Scott also recommended that the District be given to Maryland. As soon as Scott had finished, McMillan moved to adjourn the hearing until February 24.

"What about tomorrow, Mr. Chairman?" Fauntroy appealed.

"I'm going home," McMillan grumped.

That triggered a chorus of objections from other members of the committee. Reluctantly, McMillan agreed to hear witnesses in an afternoon session.

On the floor this afternoon, at least fifty colleagues went out of their way to inquire about the sling the doctor had prescribed for my arm. Men I would normally pass with a nod or a brief hello stopped and were most solicitous about what had happened. Ed Patten rolled his eyes and asked, "What did the other guy look like?"

Thaddeus Dulski, a Democrat from New York who is chairman of the Post Office and Civil Service Committee, looked at me and remarked, "You never should argue with your wife. Take it from me. I've been married thirty years and I haven't won a fight with mine yet." I'd never spoken with Dulski before and his friendliness came as a surprise. I may decide to wear this sling indefinitely.

Wednesday, February 9. This morning I drafted a one-minute speech expressing my opposition to H. R. Haldeman's recent comments on the Today Show. If the Administration people remain true to form, they'll let Haldeman's charges get plenty of circulation, then issue some nice-guy rhetoric explaining that they didn't mean to impugn anyone's patriotism. It's the same old game: use a henchman to label your opponent a traitor, then issue another statement calling for fair play and welcoming open debate on all important issues. What unprincipled sons of bitches. Haldeman should either retract the charges or resign. That's what I planned to say on the floor this afternoon. I wrote four short paragraphs on a legal pad, asked Lisa to rough-type them and walked to the Capitol.

A quorum call was under way on the floor of the House. I sat down to reread my statement. Then I read it aloud softly, timing it with my new watch to make sure that it took no longer than one minute to deliver. Ed Derwinski shouted, "Hey, Riegle," and I looked up. "Oh," he said, "you're timing a speech. I thought you were talking to yourself and I was going to call the guy with the butterfly net."

When Speaker Albert recognized me, I walked to the microphone. There were probably a hundred members on the floor, and when I finished I headed toward the Republican cloakroom. Someone there mentioned that Lou Wyman had just taken the floor and was referring to me. I turned and walked down to the mike at the minority leader's desk to be able to respond to anything Wyman might say.

With some irritation, Wyman noted the remarks of "the gentleman from Michigan, my good friend and colleague," and referred to a statement that Nixon had made this morning calling for open debate. As Wyman left the well I asked, "Will the gentleman yield?" He stepped back to the mike. "Has the President in fact repudiated the remarks made by Mr. Haldeman on national television? Yes or no?"

"As the gentleman knows," Wyman replied, "Mr. [Ron] Ziegler has publicly indicated that what Mr. Haldeman said he said for himself. I would construe the President's remarks this morning as the very antithesis of the implications of the gentleman from Michigan concerning President Nixon's position, which I deeply resent." Time had expired and there was no way to continue our debate. Later, one of the clerks brought me a transcript of our colloquy in order for me to make changes before its publication in the Congressional Record. Wyman had already corrected and initialed his portion. I noticed that he had crossed out the adjective "good" in his reference to me as a friend.

Early this afternoon Joe Skubitz from Kansas sat down beside me to share a joke he had just heard. A small Midwestern town, he said, had a run-down zoo. In that zoo lived an old lion and a bear and a few prairie chickens. The lone monkey had just died. The city fathers bought a young lion and placed him in a cage next to the old lion. Every day the zookeeper threw raw meat to the old lion. He fed the young lion only bananas and nuts. After a week or so of this, the young lion was starving. He asked the old lion why there was such a discrepancy in their daily rations. "This is a small zoo," the old lion replied, "and there's only one lion cage. You're in the cage that says 'monkey' on the front."

Skubitz laughed heartily as he finished the joke, but then he turned serious. There was a moral to the story. He was having great difficulty securing federal grants for his district. Although he's a Republican, the change of Administrations hasn't helped him at all. The Budget Bureau still turns a deaf ear to projects he suggests. "I'm beginning to feel like I'm in the monkey cage," he said.

The 123-day-old dock strike on the West Coast has reopened some old wounds here. For weeks the Education and Labor Committee has tried to report out a bill legislating an end to the strike. It has had no success. As pressure mounted to settle the strike, the Rules Committee began considering whether or not to exercise one of its seldom-used prerogatives and draft a bill of its own. House rules allow the committee to by-pass the Speaker and the various legislative committees and order proposed legislation directly to the floor for a vote. Understandably, the leadership seldom encourages the Rules Committee to follow this route. No committee chairman wants to see Rules usurp his authority.

With pressure building on all sides for a settlement, the Rules Committee let it be known that it intended to offer its own legislation. By an 8 to 7 vote—and amid much bitterness—the Rules Committee shunted Education and Labor aside and reported out its own bill to the floor. As an added indignity, Rules actually forbade any consideration of the Education and Labor proposal as a possible substitute.

Late this afternoon the Rules Committee's bill came to the floor. Ranking members of the committee controlled the time for debate. H. Allen Smith, a stone-faced Republican from California, yielded himself fifteen minutes and began to speak in a dreary monotone. When his time expired he yielded himself another five minutes to defend the committee's intrusion. By the end of that time he still hadn't completed his statement. He gave himself another three minutes. Wayne Hays interrupted and asked him to yield.

"In just one minute, I will," Smith replied.

Hays made a point of order that a quorum wasn't present. This suspended all debate and left Smith standing in the well. The Speaker began to count the members in the chamber. Smith asked, "May I finish my statement?"

"The gentleman has been finishing for twenty minutes," Hays snapped. He repeated his point of order with acid dripping from every word.

The Speaker ordered a quorum call. The clerk began calling the names. It is considered a gross discourtesy to demand a quorum call in the middle of another member's speech. Hays had zapped Smith just as mercilessly as he would have humiliated some helpless newcomer. Worse, Hays had been denied the chance to speak himself and it was obvious that he was raging inside. About an hour later he got the chance to vent his feelings. His eyes narrowed into slits, he waited to be sure he had everyone's attention. Then he ripped into the Rules Committee, castigating "this very arrogant, drastic usurpation of the powers of the leadership." He concluded by saying that he might vote to change the seniority system so "we will get some chairmen who are responsive to the leadership and not a power unto themselves at eighty or ninety years of age."

For a moment the chamber was absolutely still. Hays had skewered Bill Colmer, the eighty-two-year-old chairman of the Rules Committee, and he had done it in public and to his face. Then the buzz began as members reacted to this bitter and almost unprecedented attack. Hays's blast will reverberate around this place for the next several weeks.

We voted on final passage about eight-thirty this evening and the bill was approved by a significant margin.

Thursday, February 10. The House was not in session today because of the Lincoln's Birthday recess. I worked with Lisa this afternoon drafting a response to people who have written me urging that I sign the school busing discharge petition. In the letter I explained that, while I oppose wholesale interdistrict busing, I feel it is wrong to use the constitutional-amendment approach. Lisa will work on the letter this weekend and we will agree on a final draft sometime next week.

Friday, February 11. En route to Michigan this morning, I read in the Washington *Post* that Nixon subordinates are continuing their criticisms of Democratic presidential candidates. Communications Director Herb Klein charged that Muskie has "bolted beyond the bounds of criticism and dissent" and is "toying with the lives of Americans." GOP National Chairman Robert Dole said that Nixon would like Muskie "to accept the responsibilities of a presidential candidate." Attorney General Mitchell used a different ploy, praising Senators Humphrey and Jackson for "not undercutting the President's negotiating position" and "encouraging Hanoi to prolong the war." Meanwhile, Nixon sits above it all giving no public clue that he's the leader of the band.

Late this morning I went to Flint Junior College for a question-and-answer session. "How do you feel about equal rights for women?" I said I'm in favor. "Legalization of marijuana?" Favor doing away with criminal penalties for its use; not yet sure about legalization. "Should women be drafted?" Yes, provided that the draft is reformed and other forms of national service is made available. No woman should enter combat, of course. "Amnesty for draft dodgers?" I said I favor an amnesty program after the Vietnam war requiring a term of service in some non-military role. "Do you favor an all-volunteer army?" No, I prefer an army made up of reluctant citizens over a professional war machine composed of mercenaries. The session ran overtime and I had to leave in a hurry.

My father has spent the last few days at Hurley Hospital being examined for chest pains, and I stopped by to visit him today only to find that his room was empty. I was heading back to the elevator when I saw him walking slowly down the hall near the X-ray room. He looked pensive and seemed worried about the tests he was undergoing. "They were just X-raying my brain," he joked. "I asked them if they found one."

Sitting on the side of his bed in his navy blue pajamas, he told me about his chest pains, then sheepishly reached for a cigarette. "I've got to be careful that Mother doesn't see these," he said. The doctor had ruled out cigarettes too, and I asked Dad if he thought he could quit. "Probably not just now," he said. There was just too much tension.

Jim Sharp of my district office and his wife Tess drove with David Laro, Dave Brunell and me to Lansing this evening for the Lincoln's Birthday Republican dinner. I shook a few hands in the VIP reception line, then listened as a state party functionary stood on a chair and shouted instructions about the order of march for those of us who were to sit at the head tables. The scene was thoroughly depressing. I detest having to serve as a smiling robot fitted somewhere into the backdrop of a party extravaganza. To appear at something like that just for appearance's sake is a real drag and I'm near the end of my rope in terms of my capacity to do it any more.

We filed into the darkened auditorium, were introduced and walked to our seats in a spotlight's glare. Each of us received applause, but as the clapping for me subsided, a group in the corner of the room let loose with a chorus of boos. I gritted my téeth and waited for the invocation to start. The program itself seemed to last for days. Dinner was a fist of cooked ground beef covered with rank black gravy. A high school chorus sang patriotic songs ending with "God Bless America." As they sang I was thinking about Meredith, what she was doing, what she had eaten for dinner, whether she was as lonesome as I was. We were only halfway through the schedule of events when I got up and we left the dinner and headed back to Flint. During the trip Dave remarked that he was very uncomfortable at the banquet tonight. "Just imagine," he said, "what a dinner like that must be like in the Democratic Party. We could laugh and really enjoy ourselves."

Sunday, February 13. This evening Meredith and I drove to the home of her aunt and uncle, Justice Byron "Whizzer" White and his wife, for a buffet dinner. A member of the Supreme Court since 1962, Justice White is a tall, trim man with a strong handshake, an engaging smile and penetrating, gray-blue eyes; he rather resembles movie actor Paul Newman. We talked about the likelihood that Congress would pass some sort of anti-busing legislation. From his comments I sensed that the Court was bracing to deal with lower-court rulings on the busing question.

When we were ready to leave I walked into the bedroom to pick up our coats. On one wall in a simple black frame hung the typewritten statement that President John F. Kennedy had read in announcing Justice White's nomination to the Supreme Court. Kennedy had edited the statement in two or three places; later he inscribed it to Justice White's two children as a remembrance. I stood and looked at those pen strokes for a long time.

Tuesday, February 15. After dinner this evening, I thought about how the ambling pace of the Congress handicaps a diary like this one. Unlike a novel where you structure your own pace, a congressional diary is restricted by the often moribund character of the House itself. The Congress can be sleepy, sluggish and uninspired, and life here for the most part is boring and unexceptional. While there are exciting moments when ideas and personalities clash, moments of high drama are rare. Usually, the unexciting bit-by-bit compromises and adjustments of interests govern developments here. The Congress is ordinary people behaving in ordinary ways. That explains why our work product is so ordinary and poorly suited to extraordinary problems and needs. Congress is a mirror, and as we look into it we see our own reflection. While it is not the worst we have to offer, neither is it the best.

Wednesday, February 16. The House went back into session today and shortly before noon two members of the Flint area electricians' union stopped by the office to toss a problem in my lap. It was typical of the complicated tangle of pluses and minuses that a congressman must constantly try to sort out for his constituents. The union men said they were having trouble trying to comply with the requirements of the Housing and Urban Development Department for increased minority hiring on federally financed building projects. To avoid a cutoff of all federal funds, contractors are being forced to hire less-skilled black electricians and by-pass the hundred and twenty-five presently unemployed white electricians who hold top skill and experience ratings. This is causing enormous resentment within the union, my visitors said. The less-skilled electricians take much longer to finish their job assignments, so it is also resulting in higher construction costs.

Not long ago, my visitors went on, HUD told one local contractor that the government wouldn't pay any of his expenses until he hired more minority electricians. The contractor had already spent $90,000 of his own on a housing project. Unable to locate any minority electricians—and desperately needing the money from HUD—he was forced to fire all but two of his white and one of his black electricians. That way, the ratio of minority workers would meet HUD's guidelines. I asked Lisa and Angie Hogan to sit in on this discussion so we could at least begin to try to solve the dilemma.

At three o'clock this afternoon I began to feel the bottom dropping out of my spirits. I was weary and depressed. I wandered onto the floor. A scant two dozen members were finishing debate on an OEO bill. The actual vote won't take place until sometime tomorrow.

I stopped in the barber shop on the first floor of the Capitol. The shoeshine man began to tell me about his recent operation for bleeding ulcers. I walked across to the Longworth Building and rode the elevator to the fourth floor. Dave Brunell was on the telephone in my office and he had a number of papers spread out over my desk. Our eyes met for a second—no sign from him that we needed to talk—and I drifted out again.

The House had just adjourned so I drove to the apartment to sleep until Meredith came home. I explained my draggy feelings to her and we sorted out my worries together: missing the kids, having to fly to New Hampshire and Michigan this weekend, the approaching election, feeling scheduled and mechanized, cumulative fatigue with no time for a vacation. . . . After getting out of the apartment, and going to dinner, I felt almost human again.

Thursday, February 17. As I approached the elevator just off the Speaker's lobby this afternoon, Fishbait Miller, the assertive House doorkeeper, was pushing the down button. We were exchanging pleasantries when the elevator arrived and a group of members stepped out onto the floor. In the group was Bella Abzug. Our eyes met; we smiled and Bella said, "Hello, dear." Fishbait's mouth dropped open. He looked at me in disbelief and began to shake his head. On the opening day of the 92nd Congress, Fishbait had approached Bella and told her to remove her hat as required by House rules. Bella had looked him in the eye and replied, "Go fuck yourself." She still wears her hat on the floor. I told Fishbait that if he had other matters to discuss with Bella, I would be happy to serve as a liaison man.

Late this afternoon I was talking with Peggy Heckler in the hallway of the Capitol. I remarked that I'm flying to New Hampshire tomorrow to campaign for Pete. She smiled and said she was glad. "Why don't you come with me?" I asked. "You'd be twice as effective." She smiled again, then said the White House had asked her to fly to New Hampshire on March 3 with a group of congressmen who are going to plug for Nixon. She had declined the invitation. Both of us knew that saying no to White House staffers would mark her in their eyes as a member of the enemy camp. Hers was an act of courage. Obviously, she's more troubled about the President than she was several months ago.

Friday, February 18. A McCloskey volunteer met me at Logan Airport in Boston this morning and drove me to Derry, New Hampshire, where I was just on time for an assembly of two hundred high school seniors. Many speeches you give are variations of things you've said dozens of times before. This was a new, young audience and needed a special message. I talked about the inequities of campaign financing and said that, while Pete had to run without much money, the Nixon people could rely on the funds they'd received from the dairy interests. Then, too, former Secretary of Commerce Maurice Stans was busy raising money from the same corporations that he had just recently administered. In this primary, I went on, we had an opportunity to defeat the special interests—and that could alter American politics for a long time to come. It was one of those times when everything you want to say comes together in your head and flows out of your mouth the way you want it to.

During lunch today I was told about an incident that took place last Tuesday when Pete addressed the Dover Kiwanis Club. An elderly man challenged him on the war, saying he felt that any young American who wasn't proud to fight and die in Vietnam was a disgrace to his country. Pete answered him bluntly: "That's easy for an old man to say." His reply wasn't calculated to win votes and the Kiwanians seemed shocked. Later, however, the restaurant's waitresses came forward as a group to request McCloskey buttons. The snow was coming down hard as we drove over slippery roads to several radio stations for brief interviews, then to the town meeting in Durham. Pete spoke without notes. Standing flat-footed, legs about a yard apart, he faced the crowd without a microphone or lectern. He was steady, low-key and persuasive and he didn't seem distracted at all by a noisy young child in the front row. He received enthusiastic applause and I was really proud of him. No matter what the outcome, I'll never regret having been a part of this fight.

Saturday, February 19. In Concord today, we drove to the home of Bill Reno, McCloskey's New Hampshire state chairman. A tall, lean attorney with an engaging smile, he welcomed us inside. Over coffee he described the campaign's experience to date and focused on one revealing incident. Several months ago he invited a number of prominent Republicans to meet McCloskey at an informal gathering. As the date of the meeting approached, he was asked through an intermediary if one more name could be added to the list of guests. This prospective guest, he learned, wanted to attend as a sub rosa White House observer. His assignment, Reno was told, was not to research McCloskey's statements or positions. Rather, it was to compile a list of all Republicans present for future blacklisting and retribution. Reno was infuriated and didn't invite the man.

As the meeting broke up, Pete approached me with a tight smile and gave me a light punch in the mid-section—his way of expressing his appreciation. I drove off into one hell of a snowstorm. The weather seemed to worsen as our car approached Boston. Logan Airport was closed. Luckily, the airport in Providence, Rhode Island, was open and I managed to get a seat on a plane headed for Washington.

Tuesday, February 22. After a busy two-day trip to Flint, I returned to Washington. At two o'clock this afternoon the Foreign Operations Subcommittee met behind closed doors to discuss last-minute developments before going on to the long-awaited Senate-House conference on the foreign aid appropriation bill. Otto Passman was talking excitedly, shuffling his papers and exhorting us to support all of his recommendations. Conscious of his own fidgeting, he muttered, "I feel as nervous as a reformed whore the first time in church."

Frowning and waving his arms, Otto warned that the Senate conferees wanted to "roll us" in the conference. They wanted to cut out military assistance programs and would seek an agreement that the House would have to reject. Otto lamented the fact that he had been forced to become "a defender of foreign aid." But he was only against "these irresponsible reductions, ya understand?" Sweeping his arms, blinking his eyes and looking over the rims of his glasses, he urged us to concentrate on his words. "As Governor Long used to say, 'Listen good.' Now Senator Fulbright . . ."

"You mean Senator Half-Bright," John Rooney interrupted.

". . . Senator Fulbright," Otto went on, "has kept this bill bottled up for nearly eight months. Obviously, those people want to embarrass the President while he's in China. I'm not gonna let them do it." Otto ran through the list of items to be considered in the conference: Alliance for Progress, international organizations, population control programs, American schools abroad.

"What's the money for in this population control program?" Doc Long asked in a nasal voice.

Otto ignored him, but Long persisted. "The population control money—what's it being spent on?"

"Rubbers!" Otto thundered, and the subcommittee roared.

Later we walked as a group to the Senate-House conference—five Republicans and five Democrats—with Otto setting a brisk pace. It was clear he took a dim view of Wisconsin Senator William Proxmire, the chairman of the Senate conferees, who was thought to oppose many of his favorite projects.

"This man Proxmire," Otto said, grabbing my arm, "he doesn't know sheep shit from cotton seed."

Bill Hathaway, a Democrat from Maine, overheard his remark. "Is this the Agriculture Committee?" he asked with a smile.

The conference itself lasted two and a half hours but turned out to be no contest. Proxmire seemed preoccupied. In a gesture of seeming good will and flexibility, Otto conceded several minor points to the Senate conferees. But when it came time to discuss the major items his graciousness turned to granite. He had his facts and figures in order and used his expertise to bulldoze the conference. Everything considered, Otto won the day. Had this been a football game, the score would have been something like 52 to 6. As one of the conferees remarked to me when we left the room, "Otto sure took Proxmire's pants down this afternoon."

Wednesday, February 23. The Republican cloakroom was crowded at noon today. Sober-faced H. R. Gross was standing at the food counter holding a cup of coffee; seven or eight other members were sitting in their leather chairs eating lunch or waiting to be served. Sam Steiger from Arizona was wearing his cowboy boots. With something of a beer gut hanging over his belt, he remarked that he had just talked to a lobbyist who was complaining that he had 162 fund-raising cocktail parties to attend between now and April 7. The new campaign financing disclosure bill takes effect on that date and contributions after that will have to be recorded publicly. Understandably, the lobbyists and large contributors are scrambling to disburse their 1972 gifts while they can still do so anonymously.

Les Arends from Illinois began telling us about his opponent in the Republican primary. "Twenty-three years without opposition [in the party] and now this," he said, shaking his head resignedly. He had just booked forty-two billboards at a cost of $4500. Don Clancy, a smoothly conservative Republican from Cincinnati, said he was in the same boat. He's being challenged by a twenty-six-year-old woman. Arends and Clancy aren't used to such challenges. While they pretend to kid about them, they're nervous.

Later this afternoon I stopped by the news ticker in the Speaker's lobby and read that John Dowdy from Texas had just been fined $25,000 and sentenced to eighteen months in prison. He has said he will appeal and won't seek re-election to Congress this November. His wife, J.D., has announced that she will run in his place. Another story on the wire reported that Senator Proxmire had appeared on the floor with his head swathed in bandages. Several days ago, he showed up with a pair of unexplained black eyes and it was generally acknowledged that he had undergone surgery to have the bags removed from under his eyes. Now it appears that he's getting a hair transplant as well. In a statement today, he noted that the treatments would continue for several months and that his hair wouldn't grow out fully for another year and a half. "Even then," he said, "I will still be a semi-baldy, but a little more semi and a little less baldy. I expect humorous, critical, outraged or even ridiculing reactions, but I will acknowledge none of them. I consider the hair transplant to have no public significance." Now I know what was on Proxmire's mind when Otto Passman was working him over the other day.

Thursday, February 24. Early this afternoon, rushing to the floor for a quorum call, I found myself wedged into an elevator with about ten other members. Ed Derwinski towered above us. Spotting Leonor Sullivan in the rear of the car, he drowned out all other conversations by saying, "If you weren't here, Mrs. Sullivan . . ."

"I'm closing my ears," she said.

"Then I'd tell the joke about the Polish grandmother who began taking birth control pills . . . because she didn't want any more grandchildren." Noticing a member of Polish descent in the elevator, Derwinski grinned sheepishly. "Oh, I shouldn't have said that," he continued. "Our colleague here doesn't like these Polish jokes."

The Detroit *Free Press* this morning carried a column by Saul Friedman on the busing dilemma. It excoriated white liberals—especially Democrats—who have jumped on the anti-busing bandwagon. He criticized "the knee-jerk panic and the unstatesman-like stampede that swept through the House when the entire Michigan delegation save the two blacks voted for a barrage of anti-busing legislation, even including one measure to deprive Federal funds for busing from those districts complying with court orders."

Friedman went on to portray a black-white split on the issue. The truth of the matter is that on the occasion in question Charlie Diggs, a black from Detroit, was absent from the chamber and didn't vote at all. The other black in the state delegation, John Conyers from Detroit, did vote against several amendments including the one Friedman specifically mentioned. But then so did I. It really hurts to be carelessly reported on. This struck me as the sort of journalism that deepens divisions on this explosive issue.

Friday, February 25. When I arrived at my district office in Flint today eight young black mothers were waiting to urge a continuation of federal financing for the Follow-Through Program, an effort to help inner-city youngsters break out of the depressing cycle of poor education, poor self-development, poor achievement and lifetime potential. They were concerned because they'd heard that funds for the program might be cut. We agreed to seek ways to keep the program alive.

Then I asked their views on school busing programs to achieve racial balance. If given the choice of equal resources for neighborhood schools in all black areas—or integrated schools with busing

—they indicated by a vote of 7 to 1 they would prefer the up-graded neighborhood school. Only one mother said she would prefer to bus her children—arguing that, for blacks, racially unmixed education could not really be equal. Ola Mae Young, a former schoolmate of mine, was adamant the other way. "No busing for my kids," she said.

There was a reception at the Durant Hotel this evening before the start of the fund-raising program that featured Jerry Ford. Jerry urged my re-election and appealed for a party broad enough to accomodate different views. He went so far as to say that he him-self couldn't be elected in this district, "but Don can and with over-whelming majorities." Considering that he's the Republican's top man in the House, it took some courage and largeness of spirit for him to openly endorse a maverick like me. Not only that, but Jerry an-nounced that he would co-sponsor my community schools bill next week.

Saturday, February 26. As Jim Sharp and I were driving to the air-port in Detroit this morning, I noticed that he had a slight chest wheeze that made him cough periodically. I've had the same affliction on and off for the past six years. It comes from driving yourself beyond your physical limits. During election campaigns, Dave Brunell and I have always kidded each other about our respective wheezes and concluded that anyone who didn't wheeze was loafing, holding back. No sooner had I mentioned this to Jim than both of us began to cough. "I guess that means," I said, "that you've really proven yourself."

Sunday, February 27. Donny clomp-clomped out to my car in McLean this morning wearing an oversized pair of boots and carry-ing a note that said he had to be back at four o'clock. Cathy and Laurie, the note continued, weren't feeling well and wouldn't be able to see me today. After stops at National Airport and the play-ground at Haines Point, we returned to my apartment. I don't know which one of us had the idea first, but we decided to take a shower and spent the next half hour splashing around together. We dried each other with a towel, then stood in front of the bathroom mirror.

Our smiles are similar, we agreed. Donny's eyes are shinier than mine, but I have a bigger nose and am hairier.

Donny was interested in having me brush his hair just right and I finally parted and styled it in the manner he preferred. He checked it from two or three angles before deciding it looked okay. Unconsciously, as we dressed to leave, we started to slow down to prolong our time together. Later, at a candy store, I filled three bags with an identical mixture of sweets and wrote notes to Cathy and Laurie on the sides of the bags. By the time we pulled up in front of the house in McLean, Donny and I had pretty well sealed off our emotions. Both of us have learned that we have to express our strongest love feelings in the middle of our times together. We're just too vulnerable when the moment comes for us to say good-by. We glanced at each other and exchanged a kiss. I watched him walk up the hill and enter the front door before I turned the car around and returned to Washington.

Monday, February 28. At ten-thirty this morning I attended a meeting of our Foreign Operations Subcommittee. The Export-Import Bank—Eximbank, as it's called—is seeking financing authority in the amount of $7.3 billion to stimulate world trade—particularly the export of American products. Bank president Henry Kearns, a rotund, florid-faced man, was a non-stop talker. On the surface he seemed to be agreeable enough; friendly, open and obliging. Yet under cross-examination he turned out to be just another slippery bureaucrat.

U.S. trade problems, he told me, stem primarily from poor American selling efforts abroad. More aggressive marketing would solve the problem, he said. I pursued the point, using an old cross-examination ploy. "Am I right, then, Mr. Kearns, in assuming that I can tell the workers and business firms in my area not to worry about the trade differentials because more aggressive marketing of our products is all that's required to solve the problem?"

To my surprise and disappointment, he said that I could do just that. I'm certain he's wrong. The reasons behind our trade problems are surely more complex and I think he's damaged his credibility with the members of this subcommittee. His statement was overdrawn and deceptive. Sometimes you can learn a lot about a witness in a very short time.

Tuesday, February 29. Early this afternoon I was walking to a meeting of the Foreign Operations Subcommittee when I overtook Andy Jacobs from Indiana and Ken Hechler from West Virginia. We exchanged hellos and I remarked that it was encouraging for me to see "two of the good guys" walking together. They are so few in number that two constitutes a group. Pretending that we made too tempting a target, Jacobs chuckled and replied, "Yeah, don't bunch up."

In the subcommittee room I began reading the prepared statement of the witness testifying on behalf of the Inter-American Development Bank. It was a standard pitch. Glancing around the room, I noticed Doc Long sucking on his finger, seemingly lost in his own thoughts. Otto Passman was fondling an antique pocket watch. Bill Hathaway was poring over background information on the bank. Bob McEwen from New York was sitting on my right. We whispered briefly about the ITT case and the apparent involvement of Attorney General-designate Richard Kleindienst. Referring to back-room wheeling and dealing, McEwen deadpanned that his seventeen years in politics had taught him a valuable lesson: "Honesty is no substitute for experience."

After answering a quorum call I walked into the Republican cloakroom and bumped into Ed Derwinski. "Did you just get married?" he asked.

"Yes," I replied, "over a month ago."

"I guess that's why you haven't found time to get your hair cut," he said.

"Are you kidding? I married my barber."

Some of the members in the cloakroom were talking about the recent flock of retirement announcements by our senior colleagues. It's without precedent for nine ranking minority members to call it quits voluntarily over the span of several months. In a sense it's a McCloskey challenge in another form. Both Pete and the senior members see that the party is wrecking its own future. While Pete expresses his concern by making a challenge within the party, the senior members are expressing theirs by throwing in the towel and leaving. Included in this group are the ranking Republicans on the Appropriations, Ways and Means and Judiciary Committees as well as the senior Republicans on Rules, Interstate and Foreign Commerce and Merchant Marine and Fisheries. This exodus surely reflects a collective belief that the party has no chance to capture control of the Congress in the foreseeable future. Otherwise, these men would be determined to hang on until they received the chance to serve as chairmen of their respective committees. It reflects other factors as well: the pressures of redistricting, the higher pension benefits available for retiring members—it's possible now for some of them to draw as much as $34,000 per year; the frequency with which senior members are being stricken fatally while in office here; the longer sessions of Congress and the growing assertiveness of the newer members.

In recent years a congressman's job has changed dramatically and this has imposed a new set of pressures on the old soldiers of both parties. Fifteen years ago the House was largely an island unto itself. Few Americans knew or seemed to care very much about what happened here. That's not true any longer. Today the country is peering directly over our shoulder. It's Ralph Nader who is watching us, and Common Cause and the League of Women Voters. It's newly politicized groups of blacks, women, young people and chicanos. It's such groups as SOS, NAG and Vietnam Veterans against the War. They've learned that Congress determines our national priorities; that we provide the men and money to fight undeclared wars; that we have the power to clean up the environment, restore the cities and help old people. They're letting us know their demands and lobbying aggressively to make sure we act. The pressures on members, already intense, are multiplying rapidly. As Cederberg said to me, "It's just not as much fun to be here any more."

After dinner this evening Meredith and I took a long walk on the Capitol grounds. Heavy police security makes it relatively safe to walk there at night. The moon was full, and it was a pleasant evening with the temperature in the sixties. Spring was arriving tonight. I could feel it in the soft ground under my feet, new smells in the air and an almost indescribable sense of anticipation in my own body. I felt caught up in the rebirth process myself. I feel as if I'm coming out of a long winter, moving toward a newness that I can't fully define yet. But it's a young feeling—of exciting possibilities, of hope. It's elusive but it's there.

I'm still the captive of my schedule cards and the bells that ring on the floor. Yet during the last few months I've learned that I must begin to strike a better balance between my work in the House and my personal life. My existing job responsibilities and financial obligations make any thought of a new career pretty academic now. Yet for the first time in my life I'm beginning to learn the value of slowing down, trying to relax. Meredith has helped me enormously in this respect. I want to rearrange my priorities so I can have more time to share with the people I love.

The next two weeks, of course, will be impossible. I'll have to fly to Flint once and to New Hampshire twice. Then I'll journey west—first to Albuquerque and then to Aspen, Colorado, for a seminar on contemporary issues and values. All of this will involve precise plane connections—and too many days on the road.

Yet during our walk this evening the whole world seemed to be at peace. It was easy to believe that this spring would be the best one yet.

XII. MARCH

Wednesday, March 1. During this afternoon's first quorum call Cederberg walked by wearing a pair of bell-bottom trousers. I couldn't believe my eyes and made a mental note to give him the business later. Then Wayne Hays walked past and stopped and looked at me. "When are you going to run?" he asked. His meaning was obvious, so I asked if he would be willing to run as my Vice President in order to balance the ticket. "I can't," he said. "I've already promised Shirley Chisholm that I'd run with her. That's a ticket with perfect balance. She's black, female and women's lib. I'm white, male and a chauvinist pig."

After a quick dinner at the apartment I packed my suitcase hurriedly and Meredith drove me to the airport to catch the seven-thirty flight to Detroit. Jim and Tess Sharp met me at the airport and drove me through fog and freezing rain over the icy roads to Flint. The promise of spring that I detected just twenty-four hours ago seemed unreal tonight, a distant memory.

Thursday, March 2. At seven forty-five this morning I had breakfast with Harding Mott, a solidly built, rather handsome man with bushy eyebrows who is heading the Mott Foundation. We spent about an hour exchanging ideas on the proposed downtown college in Flint, the future of the Republican Party and my involvement in the McCloskey campaign. I was frank to say that my efforts to help revive the party—and the two-party system—were as frustrating to me as they were to him. The McCloskey challenge, I conceded, was not the perfect vehicle. Still it seemed the best way to try to force the issue. Harding listened carefully and offered some thoughts of his own.

After breakfast he and I drove to a meeting of community leaders convened to consider the relocation of the Flint College of the University of Michigan in the downtown riverfront area. Shortly before I was scheduled to drive back to the airport, Mel Brannon, a black community leader, stopped me to say that several blacks in the community were upset with my statements on busing. I had "lost some votes," he said. "They feel you're straddling the issue, that you haven't taken a clear-cut stand."

"Are people aware how I voted on the busing amendments? My public statements on the issue?"

Mel wasn't sure but he said again with a shake of his head that I had "lost some votes."

On my way to the airport I stopped at my district office and asked Nancy West to put a list of all my votes and all my statements on busing in one package and get that information out into the district without delay.

The grilled and unheated building that serves as McCloskey headquarters in Concord, New Hampshire, looks like something that barely survived the worst air raids of World War II. The windows are bare, the pipes exposed, the walls dingy and peeling. Yet on the third floor I found a smoothly functioning operation. Pete's aide, Janet Brume, had tied an open umbrella to the back of her chair to prevent falling plaster from landing on her head. Behind her desk sat three cases of throat lozengers donated by a woman who said she worried about Pete's cough.

Dressed in a faded sweatshirt and tan corduroy pants, Al Toffel briefed me on the latest developments. Yesterday he made a full public disclosure of Pete's financial contributors. Dave Brunell is devoting part of his vacation time to the campaign. He has been placed in charge of the eastern part of the state. A planeload of Pete's California supporters will arrive sometime tomorrow. Celebrities Paul Newman and Bob Cousy will be campaigning with Pete.

Toffel managed to find $15,000 for television, half of it coming from Newman personally. Toffel went on to say that he's trying to raise the $1000 filing fee for McCloskey in the North Carolina primary. Pete could win committed delegates there if he could garner fifteen per cent of the vote. "He wants some delegates," Toffel explained, "so he can raise hell at the convention. We don't care if they're from Guam—just as long as we have some."

Friday, March 3. Up at seven-thirty and on the road at eight for a full day of speeches, handshakes and harrowing rides on icy highways.

One stop was at an asbestos factory in the town of Meredith. Meeting workers on the job in a place named *Meredith* had to be a good omen, I thought. On the way there, I noticed that my feet were wet and that the headache that had begun in the morning had now moved to the back of my head. Inside the plant I took off my suit coat, rolled up my sleeves and moved quickly among the machines—introducing myself, offering McCloskey brochures, saying to each person that I hoped we could earn his support.

Afterward we drove to the McCloskey headquarters in Concord. As I stepped from the stairway into the second floor of the headquarters I couldn't believe my eyes. There was Jeff Flynn, one of my interns from Flint. I rushed over and pumped his hand. He explained that he had just driven in from Michigan with five other college volunteers. God, I was really tickled to see them—it was the highpoint of the day. I showed them through the headquarters. They laughed at its squalor, happy to be there. Kids are beautiful; if there's cause for hope, they're it. We may not win, but there's no way we can lose. Our day is coming.

Chris Finch, my young driver, and I pulled out of Concord at four-fifteen and, through a heavy snowstorm, headed for the Nashua shopping center to meet Pete and Paul Newman. We finally arrived, behind schedule, and I followed two shrieking teenage girls who were running to the center of the shopping mall where Newman was standing on a folding chair speaking into a microphone. I shouldered my way through the crowd and into the small open space in front of Newman. Looking at him, I was stunned by the incredible blueness of his eyes. He was wearing a navy knit pullover shirt and slacks and he seemed smaller and more lightly built than I had imagined him. If anything he is better-looking in the flesh than in the movies.

Concluding that Pete is the best man running, Newman asked the crowd to support him. And then he stepped down, handing the mike to Pete. Amnesty, the POWs, defense spending, why-are-you-a-Republican—in his intense but low-key way, Pete answered the questions one by one. After ten or twelve minutes he thanked the crowd and then introduced me, citing our earlier efforts together in opposition to the war.

As he handed me the mike he whispered: "Give them a three minute wrap-up." I said we have a chance on March 7 to give politics back to the people with a McCloskey win—that we can set America on a new course—and that we need their help. When I finished and stepped down, several young people came up to volunteer. I quickly introduced them to the McCloskey staff man, who signed them up.

I gave Pete a punch on the arm as he stood encircled, autographing paperback copies of his book—and told him I'd see him election day. We looked at each other for a moment.

"Hang tough, Peter," I said.

"Thanks, Donald," he replied with a smile.

I piled into the back seat of the car at five-fifteen. The storm had worsened and rush-hour traffic was beginning to clog roads. I had to take a leak badly, but we just didn't have time to stop. When we hit Route 128 around Boston we found bumper-to-bumper traffic crawling through the slush. We kept checking our watches; we knew it would take a minor miracle to make the six-thirty plane to Albuquerque. From time to time Chris would slam the steering wheel with his hand in frustration. But he got me there. It was six thirty-three and the attendant had just sealed the plane door shut. "Wait!" I yelled. He paused, turned around, and then opened the door for me.

I arrived very late in Albuquerque. Meredith met me at the airport and we drove to the home of her parents, Dr. and Mrs.

White. After thirty minutes of talk over a Coors beer, I headed for bed.

Saturday, March 4. I awoke after a good night's sleep and looked around at the bright bedroom that had been Meredith's when she was a girl. The sunshine poured through the window and I lay there a long time enjoying the quiet and the sense of calm. I thought how different it was from where I grew up—on the industrial east side of Flint, where you wake to the sound of factory whistles.

Breakfast was hot ranch sausage and scrambled eggs with green chilies, English muffins and hot coffee, with the Sandia Mountains in the distance through the picture window.

At one point in in the early afternoon, I flopped down on the back lawn and lay facing the sun. The temperature was in the seventies and the blazing sun felt hot and good. It seemed unreal that I had been fighting a blizzard just eighteen hours earlier. After a while I trotted across the road in front of the house, jumped a two-strand barbed wire fence and began running across an open mesa covered with sagebrush and tumbleweed. I ran and jumped until I was winded and sweaty. It didn't take long in the mile-high altitude. Meredith joined me, and we took a long walk together.

Sunday, March 5. Today I had to fly to Aspen, Colorado, to participate in an executive seminar program on human values at the Aspen Institute for Humanistic Studies. I had committed myself to this program six months ago, after canceling another invitation a year earlier. Despite the unfortunate timing of this year's program, I felt I had to keep my commitment. About forty people from business, medicine, journalism, education and other fields had gathered to share ideas on the nature of man and our possible future on this planet. I appreciated being asked. It's not often that one gets a chance to step back from it all and consider the deeper questions of human nature and the pressures working on mankind.

Monday, March 6. The opening seminar session today concerned a comparative analysis of Socrates, King Oedipus and B. F. Skinner's

Beyond Freedom and Dignity. In a circular conference room fourteen people spent three hours discussing human behavior and the implications of social values in an increasingly complex world. On my left sat a senior IBM executive. On my right was a young Mexican-American woman activist. It was a fascinating discussion, one that triggered several new ideas in my mind.

At the end of the day I was flying east against the clock, headed for New Hampshire and tomorrow's primary election. On page one of the New York *Times* I picked up in the airport, I was surprised to read that eighty-two-year-old House Rules Committee Chairman Bill Colmer had announced his retirement. At the end of this term, he will close out forty consecutive years in the House. Not surprisingly, the next man in line for the chairmanship is an eighty-year-old, followed next by a seventy-one-year-old.

I also read that the New York State legislature had just announced its congressional redistricting plan. The carving district turned out to be Bella Abzug's, which was cut into four different pieces, thus destroying her political base. Predictably, Bella charged that it was an obvious anti-feminist move by the male-dominated legislature. She's probably right. My hunch is that she'll find a way to beat them at their own game and win re-election. I hope so.

A close shave at the Boston airport. As my plane landed it blew three of its four tires, finally bumping to a hair-raising stop at the far end of the runway.

Tuesday, March 7. Election day dawned gray and overcast—plenty of snow on the ground but none in the air to keep voters away from the polls.

The tattered McCloskey campaign headquarters in Concord hummed with excitement and hope—volunteers manned phones and prepared for the vote returns that would come this evening. Al Toffel said he felt that everything had been done that was humanly possible. Now, like everyone else, he was waiting for the hours to pass. Election days always seem impossibly long. Pete was on hand, weary from months of campaigning and lack of sleep, with dark bags under his eyes. Occasionally he would slur his words in fatigue. But he seemed at peace with himself, ready for the verdict.

The first bit of data was sour. All seventeen eligible voters in Dixville Notch, near the Canadian border, voted early in the morning. Eleven of them cast Republican ballots, all for Nixon. McCloskey grumbled that he should have been scheduled into Dixville Notch for a personal appearance. "We blew that one," he muttered, shaking his head.

For months Pete has said publicly that he will withdraw from the race if he failed to win twenty per cent or more of the New Hampshire vote. In a TV interview this morning with Ike Pappas of CBS, he made twenty per cent the absolute cutoff figure. "Nineteen-point-nine per cent and I drop out," he said. "Twenty per cent plus and we continue to make the fight." To the bone-weary volunteers who have been trudging through the New Hampshire snow for months, Pete's statement was very distressing. "What the hell difference does one tenth of a per cent mean?" Chris Finch said.

As the hours ticked by, spot checks at precincts across the state indicated that the Republican turnout was lighter than anticipated. That suggested there was no great upheaval occurring—not encouraging from our point of view.

In the early evening, with the polls closing around the state, Pete's oldest and best friends began congregating at the Concord home of Pete's New Hampshire chairman Bob Reno—for fellowship, drinks and buffet supper. Pete and Cubby stood in the foyer and greeted people as they arrived. A radio was propped on a chair in the dining room, and everybody crowded around to hear the early returns. With a thousand votes counted from scattered precincts, Pete had thirty-four per cent of the vote—that set off a chorus of shouts. We struggled to fight back euphoria.

At one point I left the crowd and stepped into the kitchen to call Meredith. I found Pete there alone, pacing the floor with his head down and his jaw set, a bloody mary in his right hand. "I'd like to go on," he said quietly, shaking his head. "I want to make this fight."

We didn't pursue the matter just then. The campaign is $55,000 in debt. Unless a miracle happened, there would be no practical way to continue the presidential challenge. The Nixon people can fly in the hundred beautiful young pom-pom girls anywhere, any time, as often as necessary. The President can go on free national television at a moment's notice. The available financial resources for his campaign are unlimited. For Pete it's probably the end of a direct presidential battle, despite his will to go forward and the strength of his positions and his quality as a candidate. No matter what the final vote total, there just isn't the money needed to go forward.

Pete's friends Audrey and Harlan Logan took me aside and told me they had written my name in for Vice President when they voted today. So had two of their neighbors, Harlan explained. "You got four write-in vice presidential votes in Meriden," he said proudly. I laughed and thanked him and his wife, but I was deeply touched by that. The faith represented by those four votes means as much to me as if they were four hundred thousand.

At one point I was talking with Bob Reno, who introduced me to a young campaign worker as "the congressman from Alaska who runs on the Farmer/Labor ticket."

"Don't laugh," I said, "it may come to that."

The returns were beginning to pile up. The early thirty-four per cent figure had been a fluke. With seven per cent of the statewide vote counted, Pete was receiving twenty-three per cent of the Republican ballots. It was a solid total—above his twenty per cent cutoff but nothing approaching the McCarthy upset figures of 1968. An hour later Pete stabilized at exactly twenty per cent. At the same time our conservative House colleague John Ashbrook was drawing ten per cent of the vote.

Later, in the hallway, Bob Reno reflected on the fact that Nixon was losing three of every ten Republican votes and said that the insurgents might have to leave the country to escape Nixon's wrath. "How about Yemen?" he asked me. "Maybe you could run for sultan." Just then, twelve-year-old Cathy McCloskey ran by announcing excitedly, "Daddy's in second place! Daddy's in second place!"

I decided to go over to the New Hampshire Highway Hotel, where more than five hundred volunteers had gathered in a large ballroom which served as "election central" for the McCloskey campaign. Ironically, the Nixon victory party was being held in the same building, and hotel waiters kept walking past carrying huge platters of sumptuous hors d'oeuvres. There was no free food in the McCloskey ballroom, and Pete's young volunteers, who had been living on just a dollar a day, looked at the passing Nixon food with large longing eyes.

I saw Al and Jenny Lowenstein in the ballroom and we exchanged warm greetings. Within minutes, McCloskey arrived and was immediately surrounded by a swarm of cheering supporters. In his measured way, he thanked everyone for their help and faith.

"We haven't exactly overwhelmed the President with our twenty per cent," he said, "but we've just begun to fight." Applause and cheers rocked the room. "We have run an issues campaign," he went on, "and I will continue to debate them.

"I don't know now whether it will be as a candidate or as a citizen," he said as the hushed crowd listened. "I just don't know what the future will bring."

The rest of the evening was a high-speed blur. Pete and I walked to John Ashbrook's campaign suite in the same building to congratulate him for a tough, hard, clean campaign. Ashbrook and Pete agreed that their combined thirty per cent total showed serious Nixon erosion among Republicans. As we were walking back, a serious young man caught up with Pete and asked his position on legalizing gold.

"Gold?" McCloskey asked in amazement. "I've had people ask about legalizing abortion, marijuana and homosexuality, but never gold. Hell," he confessed, "I don't even know what the issue is." He accepted a brochure from the young man, promising to read it.

Word reached us that the crowd in the ballroom was again clamoring for Pete. This time Pete talked for nearly a half hour. Obviously moved, he wanted to give his troops all the encouragement possible. When one young volunteer yelled from the back of the room, "Where do we go from here?" Pete answered without hesitation, "Down to Massachusetts."

Interpreting this as a commitment by Pete to press on with the campaign, the crowd went wild. I looked at Chuck Daly, who grimaced and shook his head in disbelief. He obviously wanted to snatch those words out of the air and shove them back down Pete's throat. Then Pete introduced Bob Reno, Al Lowenstein and me to make brief remarks. When my turn came I pointed out that the real significance of the election results was the fact that Nixon could not be re-elected President unless he could win back the support of the twenty per cent of Republicans who voted for Pete. "We've proven our point, I think, under almost impossible handicaps." There is a mandate, I said, from a significant number of Republicans to end the war and change the national direction. If those votes go to support a moderate Democrat in November, Nixon is finished. For all practical purposes, so is the Republican Party.

Milling in the crowd afterward, I bumped into Jeff Flynn, my intern from Flint. We hugged each other. He told me that coming to campaign for Pete, despite the hardships, was the greatest thing he'd ever done.

Lowenstein has worked in front of a precinct all day long. He said an old woman had also campaigned there the whole day, holding a sign for one of the Democratic candidates, Senator Hartke. "She looked exactly like Hartke," he continued, "so much so that I began to think that it might be Hartke in drag."

About twelve-thirty it was time to close ourselves off from the world and try to make some critical judgments. We knew now that Pete had gotten twenty per cent of the vote—enough to make our point but not enough for a breakthrough into a full-fledged presidential candidacy. Toffel, Reno, Brunell, McCloskey and I and several others positioned ourselves around Pete's hotel room. For the next hour and a half we tried to define Pete's options. The filing deadline for the congressional race in California is March 10, three short days away. It seemed clear to all of us that Pete should file for re-election to Congress. No matter what, Pete said, he was going to continue the debate. "I'm going to keep pressing these issues in every way I can," he said.

Someone pointed out that Pete had given the impression in the ballroom earlier that the presidential campaign was continuing, moving on to Massachusetts, then to other states. Realizing he had been carried away, Pete asked rather sheepishly, "What exactly *did* I say?" Everyone laughed at that.

There was a knock on the door. Cubby McCloskey stepped in, and she asked with a hopeful smile: "Are you fellows ready for bed?"

There was a momentary pause. "That's an awfully nice suggestion," Pete answered with a devilish grin.

In the hallway, Dave Brunell and I bumped into Lowenstein, and the three of us went to my room where we talked until nearly four o'clock in the morning—about Pete's future, Al's plans and my own situation. We concluded that it's almost impossible to see very far down the road just now. Things are in flux—in politics, in the country and for each of the three of us. I sat on the edge of my bed, clipping my toenails as we talked. I felt physically wiped out, more like a mechanical man than a human being. We finally shook hands and they left.

For the first time in twenty-one hours I was alone. I went into the bathroom to wash up and to brush my teeth. Then I crawled into bed, fluffed the pillow under my head, shut my eyes and thought about the special quality of the people packed into that ballroom four hours ago, and I wondered if we'd ever put it together again.